# Applied Computing

## Springer

*London*
*Berlin*
*Heidelberg*
*New York*
*Barcelona*
*Budapest*
*Hong Kong*
*Milan*
*Paris*
*Santa Clara*
*Singapore*
*Tokyo*

T0223177

The Springer-Verlag Series on Applied Computing is an advanced series of innovative textbooks that span the full range of topics in applied computing technology.

Books in the series provide a grounding in theoretical concepts in computer science alongside real-world examples of how those concepts can be applied in the development of effective computer systems.

The series should be essential reading for advanced undergraduate and postgraduate students in computing and information systems.

Books in this series are contributed by international specialist researchers and educators in applied computing who draw together the full range of issues in their specialist area into one concise authoritative textbook.

*Titles already available:*

Deryn Graham and Anthony Barrett
*Knowledge-Based Image Processing Systems*

Linda Macaulay
*Requirements Engineering*

Derrick Morris, Gareth Evans, Peter Green, Colin Theaker
*Object Orientated Computer Systems Engineering*

John Hunt
*Java and Object Orientation: An Introduction*

*Forthcoming titles include:*

Jan Noyes and Chris Baber
*Designing Systems*

Derek Wills and Rob Macredie
*Applied Computer Graphics*

David Gray
*Real Time Systems Design*

*Available in the Advanced Perspectives in Applied Computing series:*

Sarah Douglas and Anant Mithal
*The Ergonomics of Computer Pointing Devices*

Mike Holcombe and Florentin Ipate

# Correct Systems:

## Building a Business Process Solution

Springer

Mike Holcombe, BSc, MSc, PhD, CEng, MBCS
Department of Computer Science, University of Sheffield,
Sheffield, S1 4DP, UK

Florentin Ipate, BSc, MSc, PhD
Computer Science Department, Romanian-American University, Bucharest,
Romania

*Series Editors*

Professor Peter J. Thomas, BA (Hons), PhD, AIMgt, FRSA, FVRS
Centre for Personal Information Management, University of the West of
England, Coldharbour Lane, Bristol, BS16 1QY, UK

Professor Ray J. Paul, BSc, MSc, PhD
Department of Computer Science, and Information Systems at St. John's,
Brunel University, Kingston Lane, Uxbridge, Middlesex, UB8, 3PH, UK

ISBN-13: 978-3-540-76246-1        e-ISBN-13: 978-1-4471-3435-0
DOI: 10.1007/978-1-4471-3435-0

British Library Cataloguing in Publication Data
Holcombe, Mike
  Correct systems : building a business process solution. -
  (Applied computing)
  1.Computers 2.Computer software 3.Business - Data processing
  I.Title II.Ipate, Florentin
  004'.024658


Library of Congress Cataloging-in-Publication Data
Holcombe, W. M. L. (Williams Michael Lloyd), 1944-
    Correct systems : building a business process solution / Mike
  Holcombe and Florentin Ipate.
        p.    cm. -- (Applied computing)
    Includes bibliographical references.
    1. Production management--Computer simulation.    2. System
  analysis.    I. Ipate, Florentin, 1967-    . II. Title. III. Series.
  TS155.H637    1998
  658.5'0285--dc1                                        98-24072

Typesetting: Gray Publishing, Tunbridge Wells, Kent
Printed and bound at the Athenaeum press Ltd., Gateshead, Tyne and Wear
34/3830-543210 Printed on acid-free paper

# Contents

# Preface

A correct system is one that works, one that I understand how to use, one that does not keep going wrong and one that solves the problems that *I* face.

(a user)

A correct system is one that has been formally proven to satisfy the mathematical formula that defines it.

(an academic computer scientist)

Are these two statements talking about the same thing? The first statement is a perfectly reasonable desire. Does the second statement offer anything relevant to this desire? In order to try to bridge what seems to be an enormous gap – a chasm, in fact – that exists between the two points of view, we need to consider further the fundamental issues involved.

We will ask the following questions:

- What do we mean by a *correct* system?
- What do we mean by a *system*?
- How can we build correct systems?
- What has software engineering to offer in our endeavours to do this?

These and other questions will form the focus of this book. We will also try to look at some of the wider issues involved in building systems that work, examine a number of myths about the subject and look a little into the future. Some of the emphasis on the development of correct systems is oriented around the use of mathematical techniques, notations and proofs. Although mathematics is an important facet of the process of creating a correct system we will not let ourselves become too obsessed with it! It will be necessary from time to time but we hope to emphasise the use of simple, *user-friendly* mathematical methods rather than the usual battery of high powered techniques.

We have endeavoured to make Part One accessible to anyone with a computer science background and have tried to motivate the work with some simple, practical examples. Hopefully this is enough to provide some insight into the overall method. Part Two focuses on the mathematical theory underpinning the approach. We believe that it is important to provide the details to those who wish to study them. This book is different, in this respect from many others in the field. Usually, books either ignore the foundations of their subject – if any exist – or treat them in great detail at the expense of providing an understandable and practical introduction to the techniques.

We begin by considering a number of fundamental questions.

# 1. What is a System?

Computers and software are affecting our lives in more and more ways. Society is becoming very dependent upon them and we expect this trend to continue. One might ask whether this is a desirable trend – the answer is, *probably – yes and no*, but the fact remains it is happening and so we must try to address the consequences for systems and software engineers. Without computers, many things that improve the quality of life – even save and preserve life – would not be available; for example, medical treatment systems, smart environmental protection systems, transport systems, and many, many more. There are also computer systems that might threaten our quality of life, either directly – such as systems for controlling information about people and observing their activities in totalitarian states – or indirectly, through the computer system being badly designed, such as faults in the software that controls, nuclear power stations, aircraft or radiation treatment.

In many situations the computer is used as part of a solution to some problem. This problem can manifest itself in many different contexts – in business, in engineering, in education, in the home. We need to examine the problem carefully. Once this has been done we may be able to devise a solution involving the use of computers in some way.

> The first step in solving a problem is understanding it. However, we often propose solutions to problems that we do not understand and then are surprised when the solutions fail to have the anticipated effect. [1]

This "problem of understanding the problem" is crucial. If we want to build computer systems to solve problems we need to be able to understand what the system has to do in order for it to be a solution.

This raises the task of being able to reason about a problem in a coherent, consistent, complete and meaningful way. This subject could be called Systems Modelling. We need to be able to model systems, so what is a system? It is not just the computer, the hardware, the software – it includes these but also a number of other aspects, including:

- the operators, if any,
- the communication links between different components,
- the interfaces between the system and its environment,
- the documentation,
- the data upon which it depends,
- its economic, legal, human and social context.

Without taking into consideration all of these things we may not understand the system and the way it operates sufficiently well to be able to build and operate it properly – and thus solve the problem.

In principle, we need to be able to model all these aspects of a system, its environment and its behaviour in some detail – before we can understand the problem and its potential solutions. How is this modelling achieved? A number of approaches to modelling are available.

## 2. Modelling Systems

Informal descriptions, usually in natural language, are used to describe some of the aspects of the model, and informal "common-sense" reasoning is then applied to explore the consequences of the model. This approach may be adequate if the situation is fairly simple and the consequences of getting the solution wrong are unimportant. Despite these qualifications, this is the main method used over the years and we haven't done too badly, so far, have we? However, increasing demands for quality, safety and economy, and the increasing complexity of both the problems and the solutions, are creating requirements that this approach may not be able to satisfy.

Problems include:

- ambiguity inherent in the method and its languages;
- inadequate methods of analysis;
- difficulty in using computers to help with the analysis;
- the problems caused by the management of the analysis of these large-scale problems.

Another approach is to use what are often referred to as *structured analysis* techniques [2], or what we would call *semi-formal* approaches. These are a blend of diagrams and text, usually satisfying a standard format.

They can be very effective and the majority of systems modelling and development is carried out using them, but they still have problems with:

- ambiguity;
- incompleteness;
- lack of rigorous analysis – it is difficult to reason in a precise way with inherently imprecise concepts.

This approach is nevertheless commonly used in software engineering-oriented industries and is fairly well supported by tools.

A further approach is through the use of *formal notations*. These are essentially mathematical and often involve unfamiliar and abstract symbolism. They are:

- not usually very easy to use without extensive training;
- not well supported by tools;
- easily affected by problems of scale.

They have do, however, benefits:

- they can be used for rigorous analysis,
- they are unambiguous;
- they have a strong theoretical foundation (sometimes).

There has been much emphasis, particularly among the academic community, an the use of these abstract methods, formal notations and mathematical processes as the means for achieving the goals of creating robust, correct and usable systems in an efficient and cost-effective way. There has been little real evidence, however, either that the industrial take-up of these ideas has occurred to any significant extent, even in highly specialist niche application areas, or that they deliver what is claimed of them.

There are a number of possible reasons for this, including:

- The unfriendly nature of many of the notations used, particularly those based on symbolic mathematical notations. Away from the rarefied atmosphere of the mathematically-oriented research laboratory, these notations appear to be obscure, artificial and unusable. The use of the phrase "formal methods" is also misleading since few of the notations actually involve any sort of mature and explicit *methodological* framework – formal specifications can be understood with suitable training in the language but the construction of correct specifications is a problem which is several orders of magnitude greater.
- The basis of many of the notations is not adequate for the sorts of applications that need this approach most. For example, traditional formal methods are capable of describing simple information systems applications where time, dynamic event handling and concurrent processes are not major issues. Process algebra approaches can handle concurrency but the modelling of time or of complex data structures as well is very difficult and rarely practicable.
- The essence of constructing a "correct" system is to identify the needs of the client or user requirements accurately and completely. Currently this is an area where formal notations have proved inadequate. Numerous prototypes are built and evaluated in an incremental way and this is costly and error prone.
- The building of a working implementation is generally regarded as a separate process which should be isolated from the specification process. This philosophy seems to result in the erection of barriers between the specification and the implementation which reification and refinement have great difficulty in overcoming in a practical context.
- Formal methods rarely consider the fact that the system will be tested, and the testing of an implementation is usually relegated to the last phase of a project. This results in ineffective test management and poor quality products. Testing must be considered at all stages of the product life cycle and in particular a "design for test" philosophy must pertain throughout – it is possible to take design decisions that make future testing of components and the complete system difficult or, indeed, impossible.

Another approach is the use of *simulation*. Essentially, this involves the construction of a software program that will behave like a particular part of the system being modelled. This is then investigated to study its properties. Simulation requires the repeated use of representative input values to animate the program and demonstrate what part of the system might do or how several simulated parts might interact together. *Prototypes* are often used as simulations; the lessons learned help to guide the production of the final product. This approach suffers from many of the problems of the semi-formal approach.

In many problems there are opportunities to use all of these approaches, using the more intensive and difficult methods for the more critical and sensitive areas of the problem. This may create difficulties, however, if parts of the system cannot be depended upon because of poor understanding of some aspects of the problem. We may not understand the problem sufficiently well to be able to identify the less critical parts. If we are to use this approach and to economise on using formal methods we must be aware of the dangers. There is a belief that we will eventually be able to use formal methods as part of a software engineering approach to model any problem and develop an effective solution. We will examine this belief later.

# 3. The Empirical Gap

In Software Engineering there is little empirical evidence of the superiority of one method over another in large-scale projects. There is a crisis of intellectual respectability in the subject. Not only is the evaluation of the methods used weak, the selection of the types of system and problem to focus on is very restrictive. In order to convince, in a scientific manner, that method A is better than method B in large design projects (and that is where the problems are), we must present rigorous evidence drawn from carefully controlled experiments of suitable complexity. This is, more or less, impossible in practical terms. Is there an alternative approach? The use of theoretical models of computing systems can provide some alternative approaches, and this is the fundamental philosophy underlying this work.

We will develop our ideas around the concept of a *computational model*. This is a class of mathematical theories which are thought to encapsulate the essence of the sort of systems that can be built with computer technology. There are a number of such theories, all of which have been shown to be equivalent. These include Turing machines [3], Markov algorithms [4], recursive functions [5] etc. Our approach is closest to the Turing model but it possesses a rather more practical flavour and, at the same time, the overt mathematical nature is modified and made more appealing by the judicious use of diagrams.

In the absence of a realistic empirical method for evaluating a design method by the use of large-scale and repeatable scientific experiments, we will focus on building a complete method for the identification, design and testing of systems based on our theoretical foundation and framework. The full benefits of this will become more apparent later but it is possible, at this stage, to get some insight into what we hope to show.

Suppose that we have an easy to use modelling language that is based on a computational model paradigm. The first stage of solution building is to develop a model of the proposed system in its environment and to analyse the behaviour of this model. In order to discuss the model with the domain experts (the clients) we need to be able to represent it in a way that is understandable to them. The analysis should lead through a number of steps – we will call them *refinement steps* – to more complete models and, ultimately, to models that can be implemented in a more or less automatic form. Now we are in a position to examine what we have built and to try to establish if the behaviour of the executable/code/fabrication (in the case of a hardware design) matches up with the detailed behavioural model we have built up during the requirements and specification stage. Because we are using computational models we know that both the specification and the implementation are just computational systems and thus expressible in our modelling language. So we can now use the theory of our computational models to develop powerful methods for comparing them; in other words, testing the functionality of the implementation to see if it agrees with the specification. It is important to note that we must carry out some testing process since the implementation will have been generated by software tools, such as compilers, synthesisers, etc. which are always going to contain faults. We cannot assume that they always operate 100% correctly. Going one stage further, the operating environment, the operating system, the fabrication process etc. are also going to be subject to faults. Hence, the final working system may be faulty because of all sorts of problems. We need to carry out functional tests to try to establish whether the system is working properly. Formal verification cannot guarantee this since it will be based on a highly simplified model of the system generation process and its working environment. If we are going to have a powerful testing method, we will need to integrate this into the design process, introduce concepts such as *design for test* to make best use of our testing methods and look at the way in which test refinement can progress alongside design refinement in a practical way.

To be convincing, the approach should address as many types of system as is possible, although allowing for the fact that certain types of system will require certain types of specialised design.

Consider a list of types of systems which we might like to use as representatives of the sort of challenges faced by computer scientists and software engineers:

- an automatic bank machine;
- a confidential database/management information system;
- an airline flight control system;
- a speech recogniser;
- an automatic reasoning device (theorem prover);
- a natural language processing system.

These systems/problem domains pose many different issues for the software engineer. We will try to explore some of them.

# 4. Correctness: What Does This Mean?

We now turn to the question of trying to understand what it means for a system to be correct. The simple answer is that the system is correct if it can be shown to satisfy the requirements.

Two issues arise:

- what is a requirement?
- how do we demonstrate that the system satisfies a set of requirements.

What is a *requirement*? This, and the process of *requirements engineering*, is the subject of considerable current research. Capturing the requirements from a client is difficult. It is also an ongoing process, since requirements can change with time. It requires that both client and software engineer can articulate clearly and communicate effectively. Both must have a consistent understanding of the problem, the environment and the solution constraints. Ideally, they should also share some similar social, cultural and political attitudes, otherwise they may have rather different objectives when making judgements about unwritten aspects of the requirements.

Consider some alternative social paradigms (Table 1):

So, the underlying attitudes might be somewhat in tension – a client might think that safety means doing the minimum required, whereas a designer might regard safety as being much more than that, perhaps the best that current knowledge can provide (we have to accept that no safety-critical system is likely to be totally safe).

In a perfect world the entire set of requirements should be expressible in a precise, unambiguous language so that there can be no misunderstanding. However, the requirements must not only describe the functional behaviour that is required but many other issues: the cost of production, operation, change and maintenance, the needs of operators, customers, regulators and government authorities, and the general public.

**Table 1.** Social paradigms.

|  | Technocratic paradigm | Environmental paradigm |
|---|---|---|
| Core values | Economic growth, nature is a resource, controlling nature | Self-sustaining, nature respected, harmony with nature |
| Economy | Market forces, risk + reward, individual perspective | Public interest, safety, social perspective |
| Society | Centralised, large-scale, ordered | Decentralised, small scale, flexible |
| Knowledge | confidence in technology, rationality of means | Concern about technology, rationality of ends |

Source: Adapted from Cotgrove, "Risk, value conflict and political legitimacy" in [6].

Solutions must be *legal*. They must not expose users or developers to breaking the law, perhaps through the unauthorised use of someone else's property, ideas, designs, etc. or through some other aspect of the system.

Solutions must be *clearly definable*. For example, saying that the solution system has to be "easy to use" is not very helpful if the phrase is not defined in a way that enables potential solutions to be judged properly. Thus, if the delivered product is found wanting under this category a messy court case is avoided. Ease of use can conflict with other issues such as safety – asking operators to confirm critical input values by repeating them conflicts with ease of use as commonly perceived but might be important to safeguard safety.

Thus, even if the requirements could be expressed very precisely, we have to resolve conflicts between many different aspects. In academic software engineering the common belief is that the requirements must be identified precisely. A formal specification can then be built so as to be a technical reference point for subsequent design and implementation activity and quality control. This might be valid if the detailed requirements statements could always be used as a basis for system understanding and design.

This is not the case. In "straightforward" situations – perhaps well-understood information systems, databases and in real-time control systems – formal languages have been developed which allow for the construction of a formal specification of aspects of the required system. Much current thinking is based around the belief that a formal specification will prevent problems with the design and implementation of the system since it will act as a clear, unambiguous definition of the required solution. However, creating a formal specification is hard. In most cases only the functional behaviour of the system is considered. The more qualitative attributes such as user friendliness rarely feature. In many applications even the construction of a functional specification is far from straightforward. Even experts in formal methods rarely use their methods in the development of their tools. This is something of a sham but there are good reasons for it. For example, how can the functional specification of an automatic theorem prover be made explicit? Here is an example where a very general, and thus vague, statement can be made about a system, but it is very difficult to turn it into a precise, formal specification. This, despite the fact that formal logic and the definition of what a theorem is have been extensively studied by logicians for centuries.

Artificial Intelligence (AI) systems are also often like this. A speech recogniser is very difficult to specify except in general terms: "a system that will recognise speech utterances in (British) English to an accuracy of 99% using a dictionary containing 10,000 words." How can that be made more explicit in such a way that it could then be used as a basis for design refinement, implementation and correctness proving?

A similar problem exists for natural language processing systems, where the sort of sentences that might need to be analysed or translated might never have been written before.

Software engineering does not seem to be addressing these issues very successfully.

Thus, there are problems deciding what the requirements should be. Not only are the non-functional requirements difficult to express in precise terms but also the functional requirements for many types of systems are hard to describe. If an attempt is made we still face the problem of validating them with the client or user. The communication gap between client and engineer will pose a considerable obstacle here.

Many alternative approaches exist to try to deal with these problems. Gilb [7] describes ways in which metrics can be used to define and measure almost any type of non-functional requirement, then the process of establishing whether a solution meets that requirement can be attempted. The problem of functional requirements for AI are addressed in many ways. Test corpora might be available which will be the basis for seeing if the system behaves in an appropriate way. The problem here is that one might tune the system to fit the test sets but these may not be typical. Similar problems occur with neural net solutions. Requirements might be expressed in the form of examples – essentially, representative sets of test sets – which, hopefully, create enough cases to test a system effectively.

In all of these approaches the question of *validating* the system – establishing that it is correct – or in accordance with the requirements for a solution – will depend on the methods used to define the required system. The requirements may include the need for the system to be safe. Note that ensuring that a system is safe is not the same as ensuring that the system is correct – unless safety is a specific issue identified in the requirements and being correct can guarantee safety.

Correctness, then, is concerned with the requirements. It should include more than functional correctness: things like reliability, safety, usability etc. are all aspects that must be verified if they feature in the requirements. But we must also recognise that we may have a complete set of requirements but they may be for the wrong system; in other words; *the requirements are not correct*. This will always be a risk, and whatever techniques we use to represent our requirements must be understandable to the clients. This may then help to overcome the requirements capture problem to some extent.

# 5. Designing for Correctness

Transforming the requirements into a working system is the next issue. Consider a number of different contexts and possibilities. Firstly, there is the formally specified system, with a precise mathematical definition and a formal reasoning process that provides correctness by means of mathematical proofs that the implementation must satisfy the requirements. This is a dream of many in the formal methods community. It is probably unrealistic. A proof of correctness may be necessary but cannot be sufficient –we cannot model precisely the operating environment, including the users, the hardware and the communication channels, which are all vital aspects of the system. Correctness proofs can offer some assurance but not *total* assurance.

No system will be released without extensive testing. Testing is a major activity of system development – up to 90% of project effort is involved in testing in some highly critical systems, and even ordinary solutions may consume 50% of the project in testing. Techniques for designing testing strategies are mostly based on experience and "ad hoc" approaches. Myers [8] states that testing is much harder than design. It is also often less rewarding: no one loves the test engineer.

Most approaches to testing systems depend on the existence of some detailed starting information – generally the code (in the absence of a formal specification) – from which test sets can be constructed systematically. A functional testing method requires some functional specification as a starting point, and effective techniques for constructing efficient and revealing test sets are not available. Methods such as category-partition and boundary value testing, for example, are highly dependent on random effects.

Any methods must be well-founded and capable of robust analysis – it is particularly important to be quite clear about the foundations of any approach when the evaluation of any design method cannot sensibly be carried out on the basis of industrially sized case studies.

At the end of any testing process a decision has to be taken as to the likelihood of serious faults remaining in the implementation. This decision, up to now, has had to be taken on the basis of economic and marketing considerations, rather than on the basis of scientific analysis.

Little underlying theory exists; the evaluation of the effectiveness of testing methods is based on small case studies. Convincing empirical results on test effectiveness from large-scale projects is lacking. Some attempts at utilising a formal specification as a basis for generating test sets have been made, with limited success. A new technique for building test sets, based on a proper theory and which relates to an overall design method, isdescribed in this book.

Turning to less formally defined requirements, how do we achieve correctness in such contexts? Here some comments by Wilks and Partridge [9] are relevant. They conclude that software engineering has little to offer AI. Rarely are the methods of software engineering appropriate. This is because the problem domain is very often poorly defined; the systems are not closed and easily formalised. One needs to use an experimental approach in an attempt to understand the problem domain better, let alone the problem itself. Often a series of computational models (programs) are built which are then iterated until some reasonable approximation to the ill-defined system is available. This can then be tested at some considerable length and cost, if usually randomly. The *run–understand–debug–edit* approach seems to be popular in this domain.

If a precise definition of the requirements is not available, what does correctness mean? It is probably best approached from another direction. Wilks and Partridge talk of a system being "adequate" rather than correct. So perhaps a system is adequate if it is not inadequate. If we can say more about what we don't want, rather than what we do want, this might be a productive approach. This is not entirely crazy! Safety analysis in safety-critical systems is based on identifying unsafe states and removing them.

So safe = not unsafe, and correct = not incorrect.

Thus we enter a philosophy of verification that is fault based. We wish to demonstrate that undesirable behaviour is absent and to do this we will use formal proofs, where possible, but always rigorous testing. Looking at other things from this angle might be valuable. In other words, the requirements document should also include what is *not* required.

There is a tendency to overkill in software design, to add to overspecify, too many features, offering more than is really required rather than what is essential. Kletz [10] said "We spend money on complexity but not on simplicity." How many of the features in an everyday word processor are used by the vast majority of people? Just because we can do it does not mean we should do it. We should concentrate on what is adequate, not what is possible. However, there are compelling practical reasons for making systems as powerful as possible. We may need some of the extra features soon. It is very hard to adapt and extend existing systems when we need to. Part of the problem is that we rarely have enough detailed information about the existing system; developing new modules and bolting them on is a complex and error prone activity.

Possible solutions include a more modular or component-based software industry, reusing as much as possible. Reuse is one of the motivating pressures on object-oriented design. But it raises as many problems as it solves. Reusing objects and classes that have been developed successfully in other contexts is a plausible strategy. However, there are problems. One is finding the right things to reuse. The problems of classifying, cataloging and retrieving suitable objects and classes are very hard. The context in which they are used might be very different. The modern air traffic control system is a case in point. With the greatly increased level of traffic expected should we adapt the present systems and reuse what we can or do the new demands on the system require us to completely redesign the system from scratch? Wiener considers this and other issues in [11].

Object-oriented systems [12] and, in particular, object-oriented programming languages such as C++ [13] and lately Java [14] have become extremely popular and widely used. Testing object-oriented systems, however, is not well understood [15]. Assuming that an object that has been well tested in another system/context can be used without repeating much of the testing in the new context is erroneous. A common place for programming errors to occur is at interfaces in software. Object-oriented systems have many more interfaces than traditional systems.

Therefore the testing problem and the demonstration of correctness or adequacy appear to be much harder. So we are coming to the conclusion that correctness or adequacy will be dependent on testing and, where possible, formal proofs, assuming that we can identify what the solution is supposed to be like; that is, that the requirements can be identified.

In summary:

- defining systems and understanding their properties is difficult;
- engineering requirements is not well understood;

- identifying the functional requirements of AI systems may be difficult or even impossible;
- software engineering has focused on a very restrictive class of problems;
- correctness has many facets – adequacy is another view of it;
- we may wish to have correct systems but this may not be achievable, adequate; systems are a possible substitute;
- testing is and will remain a vital part of software engineering;
- more research on the relationships between testing and design is required.

# 6. An Outline of the Book

## Part 1. Building Correct Systems

### Chapter 1. Models of Computer-Based Systems

The book begins with an introduction to the modelling of types of computer-based systems. The most well-known method is the state machine model, an integral component of most university computing courses and a widely used method in parts of industry, notably in hardware systems design and real-time systems design. The model is very restricted, however, and we examine some more general approaches. Statecharts are an attempt to use finite state machines in the context of industrial reactive systems. This model enables a complex state machine to be divided into manageable "chunks" and consequently more complex systems can be examined. We note some limitations with this model and introduce our main idea, a very general, powerful but intuitive model called the X-machine. We conclude with some simple examples.

### Chapter 2. Business Processes, Problems and Solutions

What is a business process? What is an enterprise model? These issues are both key and universal. By constructing precise models of business processes and the way they interact with each other – the enterprise model – we can better understand the context and the problem. Identifying the requirements using a formal business process model is then possible. We look at this process and show how the X-machine can be used to think about the system from the user's perspective. Examples of X-machine specifications of a simple business process are examined. A business process that involves time is also considered and this, together with a microprocessor example, demonstrates the generality of the approach.

### Chapter 3. Testing, Testing, Testing!

A review of the practice of testing begins a more detailed look at an important method of functional testing, namely state machine based testing. The limitations of the finite state machine model described in the previous chapter restrict the applicability of this type of testing. The complete testing method derived from the stream X-machine theory is then described in the context of a simple example. An important aspect of the approach is the clear and unambiguous identification of design for test conditions that must be satisfied by a specification if the full power of the testing method is to be exploited. The design philosophy is one of defining a model and a system in terms of the integration of its lower lever components. If these are tried and trusted then the testing method will find *all* faults in the system. This then gives us a way of reasoning about the faults that remain in a system when testing has been completed.

## Chapter 4. Building Correct Systems

Refinement is a key concept in our approach to software and systems engineering. It is unlikely that a complete model can be built in one go. The need to explore, understand and confirm the functional requirements of a system necessitates an incremental approach. The application of the refinement principle to the generation of a test set is a major advantage in terms of the time and cost of creating test sets and carrying out testing. The development of incremental models and test sets can be linked naturally with the idea of a component. We consider a precise definition of a component which can be related fully to the refinement design and testing strategy outlined.

## Chapter 5. A Case Study

This chapter is an account of applying the approach to a real problem and the client's reaction. We describe the client's business processes and build a complete enterprise model. This leads to a formal specification of the proposed solution. Extracts from this model are given. The specification was implemented incrementally using a widely used 4GL (Visual Basic) and this enabled the client to comment on and confirm the requirements. Such changes must be addressed by any specification method and were dealt with comfortably in this case. The complete system was tested using the method explained above; it has since been in use for many months with no faults of any kind. The case study demonstrates that the methods outlined constitute a simple and effective procedure for building a correct system.

## Part 2. Theoretical Foundations

## Chapter 6. The Theory of X-Machines

The basic theory of X-machines is introduced in this chapter. A particular class of X-machines, called stream X-machines, is investigated in depth. The theory of stream X-machine refinement, a key concept in the desire to model and analyse systems incrementally, is examined in detail.

## Chapter 7. Complete Functional Testing

This chapter begins with the background necessary to understand the testing method. Thus, state machine morphisms, state machine minimality and state equivalence are discussed. The basic results of state machine testing theory, test set construction, transition cover, characterisation set and the complexity of this method are examined. The stream X-machine testing theory is now studied and this leads to a consideration of the design for test conditions, the fundamental test function and the fundamental theorem of complete functional testing. We conclude with a discussion of the complexity of this type of testing.

## Chapter 8. Refinement Testing

The theory of refinement testing is introduced and described in detail. The testing of refinements is studied and is followed by the details of how the refinement testing method can be used in the context of a component-based design process. This is illustrated by a simple example.

## Acknowledgements

We would like to thank the members of the Verification and Testing Research Group in the Department of Computer Science, University of Sheffield. In particular, Kirill Bogdanov has read much of the manuscript and contributed in many ways to the development of the testing method and its associated tools; Sarah Chambers, Tony Simons, Camilla Jordan and Matt Fairtlough have all read parts of the work and provided many helpful comments. Thanks also to Klaus Grimm, Heiko Doer and Harbarjhan Singh of Daimler-Benz Research Laboratories, Berlin, who have funded work on the method and supported the research in many ways. We would also like to thank Mohamedd Al-Qaed, who took the ideas and applied them to a real development project. Much of the detail in Chapter 5 is due to him. Both Gilbert Laycock and Andreas Grondoudis have made important contributions to the X-machine testing method. A number of our senior students have also contributed to the greater understanding of X-machines in the design and testing of specific systems and have acted as "guinea-pigs" in trying out these ideas in their projects and assignments.

# Part 1
# Building Correct Systems

# 1  Models of Computer-Based Systems

*Summary. Modelling systems, finite state machines, statecharts, X-machines.*

The fundamental desire of all those involved in the development of new computer systems, whether business software solutions, real-time control systems or hardware devices, is that the final product behaves correctly. In traditional computer science research this means that some formal mathematical proof must exist that establishes the logical equivalence of the implementation with some mathematical definition or specification of what the system should be like. This has always been a very difficult task that is rarely achieved except with very small systems and under very restricted conditions. Practising software and hardware designers rarely consider even attempting to do this – even supposing that they knew how to. The existence of such a formal verification is insufficient to guarantee that the system is correct, anyway.

We take a different approach. Our starting point, as we will see in Chapter 2, is the client and the client's needs. A problem exists; this problem needs expressing and analysing. Possible solutions can then be investigated. At this stage it is vital that we do not lose contact with the client's perspective, otherwise we might find that our potential or actual "solution" is a *solution to the wrong problem*! No matter how much mathematical analysis and formal verification has been carried out on the system, if it is the wrong system *it cannot be correct*!

So, our interpretation of a correct system is one that can demonstrably solve the required problem within the constraints agreed with the client. In order to do this we will be investigating ways in which we can communicate with the client using a mixture of easily understood diagrams and carefully worded text which contains a fully formal and precise model of the system and a potential solution. This formal structure can be analysed by an engineer in a number of ways. It is possible to "check" the model by establishing that certain necessary properties are satisfied by it. It is possible to use such a model to generate, automatically or semi-automatically, an implementation (either software or a hardware design in a suitable technology) and also to develop a powerful complete functional testing method that will provide a rigorous and searching examination of any final system in its operating environment.

If the system that we finally construct is such that:

1. the initial model of the requirements has the required functionality in the opinion of the client;
2. the model can be shown to satisfy any necessary properties;
3. the implementation is generated directly from the model using reliable techniques and tools;
4. the implementation passes *all* the tests constructed using the complete functional test generation model

then we may be justified in calling the system a *correct system*.

In the preceding discussion we used the word *model* in several places. The process of designing correct systems depends on building accurate and useful models of the processes that are being investigated, and eventually of the proposed solution. There are, however, many types of models that are proposed in computer science. Some of these are useful for specific types of application; many of them are either too restrictive in their scope or very difficult to use. We have to be realistic. If we wish to encourage engineers to use a formal model in a coherent and productive way we must ensure that it is usable and sufficiently powerful for the job in hand. In the first section we will be looking at the sort of models that might be useful and, eventually, concluding that one particular model is the most appropriate. This model is a full computational model, something that we believe is vital if a complete model of a system is to be built. It is also a new type of model and the claim that we make is that it is the first truly integrated and general modelling language that has been developed which is usable by any proficient engineer.

We begin by reviewing some of the previous attempts to construct formal modelling languages for the specification of computing systems.

## 1.1   INTRODUCTION TO MODELLING SYSTEMS

A major thrust of software system specification, in recent years, has centred around the use of *models of data types,* either functional or relational models such as Z [16] or VDM [17] or axiomatic ones such as OBJ [18]. This identification of data types and the definition of algorithms as functions or relations on these mathematical entities has led to some considerable advances in software design, and has even given rise to attempts to specify the human–computer interface of an interactive system using these ideas [19]. However, one basic problem with these abstract specification methodologies, whether Z, VDM, OBJ or whatever, is that they lack the ability to express the dynamics of the system in an amenable manner. It is, for example, very hard to describe the menu structure of a user interface in an intuitive way using Z or VDM. They are also quite difficult to use and have failed to penetrate the industry to any significant extent, despite the fact that many computing undergraduates have attended courses in them during their degrees.

Generally, all that these specification methods can describe is what the system does rather than how it does it. In fact, part of the culture of these languages is to avoid any tarnishing of the specification with information that relate to the way the system might be implemented. If the system has to perform many "basic" operations in order to attain the final configuration, it is usually quite hard to describe the system evolution in an intuitive way using such a specification method. From a theoretical point of view one can argue that at the specification phase all we need to know is what the system is supposed to do, and that the algorithm to be used is left to the implementation. This is obviously true when the task in hand is quite simple and there is no doubt as to how it will be implemented. If the system to be specified is, for example, a simple program that finds the maximum of two numbers it is very unlikely that anyone will require the corresponding algorithm. However, if the program is more complex it sorts the elements of an array, for example – the declarative specification might not be considered to be sufficient and the algorithm might also be needed. In this case the choice of algorithm can affect the effectiveness of the program, for example. In some instances, the choice of algorithm may even effect the final result – if the program to be specified solved a polynomial equation then the results would depend on the method used to approximate the solutions.

As we have noted, there is a tradition within the formal methods community for trying to avoid any consideration of the way in which a program is to be implemented. This encourages implicit styles of specification. The problem with this approach is that it succeeds in erecting barriers between the formal specification – the *what* question – and the possible implementations – the *how* questions. Overcoming these barriers is not always straightforward and, despite the achievements of modern theories of refinement, the practical obstacles to transforming an implicit formal description into an effective working system seem to be huge. Furthermore, we can use Z or similar methods to specify something that cannot be implemented on a computer system, i.e. there is no algorithm that produces the result given in the specification. This is due to the fact that Z is not based on a *computational model* and so non-computable functions can be specified within the language.

Another issue that needs to be addressed is that of the scope of a formal specification language in describing dynamic aspects of a system. The user interface, for example, is a vital and complex part of most of today's software systems. Trying to specify this in an intelligible and useful way with a language like Z is very difficult. In safety-critical systems the software is usually an example of a *reactive system* [20], where both the dynamics and the timing of events and computations are of vital importance. It is, again, difficult to use a language such as Z to deal with these dimensions.

Although it might appear that we are belittling the effectiveness of these abstract specification methodologies, this is not the intention. Clearly, the use of these methods has resulted in an important advance in the specification of systems, especially for safety-critical applications. However, we believe that there is a need for a unified specification methodology (or a meta-method) that can be used to describe both the data processing and the dynamic information of the system. Such a methodology would have to provide means for specifying what the system does as well as how it does it. Here, when we say "how it does it" we refer to an algorithm that can run on a computer system and which produces the desired result. If we describe the dependency between the inputs and the outputs of the system as a function, then we say that the function is *computable by an algorithm* or simply *computable* [21].

What we are advocating here is the idea that the process of software design, including within that activity all phases of requirements capture, specification, design, prototyping, analysis, implementation, validation, verification and maintenance, is one that should be oriented around the construction of *computational* solutions to specific problems. When we are constructing a software system (this also applies to hardware) we are attempting to construct something that will, when operating, carry out some computable function. On the other hand, computable functions have been identified as functions computed by some algebraic models called machines, Turing machines or similar alternative models [22]. Generally, the Turing machine is accepted as the main model of computation. However, although the Turing machine has received much study in a variety of theoretical areas, it is not used by software engineers for the specification and design of systems, the principle reason being that it is based at a very low level of abstraction and is not very amenable to analysis and/or system development. Less general models, such as finite state machines [23] and Petri nets [24], however, are the basis of many system specification and development methodologies. We will consider finite state machines in the next section. Petri nets have a substantial literature and have evolved a number of different variations and generalisations to try to make them more expressible. Although they have a role in system design and the modelling of concurrent systems they are not easy to analyse in a general way. We will not focus on them here.

## 1.2  FINITE STATE MACHINES

In this section we will consider ways of modelling a variety of systems using the ideas of *machine theory*. Basically, a machine is a system that interacts in some way with its environment. There are many areas of applications for these ideas, ranging from mathematical models of computer hardware systems to models of power station generators, from the biochemical activity of a living cell to the definition of a compiler for a programming language.

The purposes of studying these machines range from attempts to simulate the behaviour of a complex system to the specification in a formal way of some system by modelling it with a suitable machine in order to analyse it and then to use this model to develop an implementation of the system. These two applications of *simulation* and *design* are of great importance in many practical areas and we shall look at some examples soon. There are also good reasons for studying the mathematical and philosophical basis for computation using the models of machine theory.

There are two fundamental concepts associated with any *dynamic* or *reactive* system that is situated in and reacting with some environment:

1. The environment itself must be defined in some precise, mathematical way. This will usually involve identifying the important aspects of the environment and the way in which they may change in accordance with the activities of the system.
2. The system will be responding to environmental changes by changing its basic parameters and possibly affecting the environment as well. Thus there are two possible ways in which the system reacts:

   i. it undergoes internal changes;
   ii. it produces outputs that affect the environment.

We can display the situation shown in Figure 1.1.

The finite state machine is a mathematical model of a system with discrete inputs and outputs. The system can be in any of a *finite* number of internal states. The state of the system summarises the information concerning past inputs that is needed to determine the behaviour of the system on subsequent inputs. To describe these ideas mathematically we introduce suitable sets and functions that will form the basis of a machine description of the system and its environment.

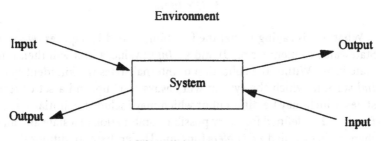

**FIG. 1.1.** A dynamic system.

We will describe the environment first. The important aspect is the elements of the environment that directly affect the system. These elements will be collected together to form an *input* set, which we will denote by the symbol *In*, with *in* representing a typical input element. It is important that we keep an open mind about the sort of candidates that exist for the input set, and to emphasise this we will examine a few widely different examples, showing that machines can arise naturally in many situations. In many situations there will also be an output generated by the system and this will affect its environment. Initially, however, we will only consider systems which react to inputs and do not generate outputs.

It is thus emerging that, for some dynamic systems, there are three essential factors to consider:

1. set of appropriate environmental stimuli or *inputs*;
2. a set of suitable internal *states* of the system;
3. a *rule* of some sort that relates the two and tells us what the system state will change to if a particular input arrives while the system is in a particular state.

There are many different types of models of systems based on these considerations, some more sophisticated than others. We will consider a variety of these. They all have their uses and often the secret of good design and systems analysis is the correct choice of the type of model for the problem in hand.

For the moment we will look at the basic ideas presented here in more detail. Note that we have described some of the essential features in terms of two sets, the input set and the state set. For much of what we will be doing it is sensible to assume that both these sets are finite. The essential feature that we are trying to capture is *change*. How do changes in the environment affect the system's internal state?

Consider a system with state set Q existing in an environment with input set *Input*. Let the system be in state $q$ and receive input *input* at time $t_0$. The next state which the system "jumps" to at time $t_{0+1}$ will be determined by a function (or partial function) which describes the behaviour of the system as the environment changes, that is, as inputs occur. The form of this function, called the *next state function*, is:

$$F: Q \times Input \to Q$$

What this is saying is that the function, named **F**, requires two values, a State value (a member of Q) and an *Input* value, and it will then return a State value. Within the collection of internal states we will identify an *initial* state, in which the system will always start up, and a set of *terminal* states, which may be different or which may include the initial state. If the function **F** is defined for every possible combination of a state and an input then it will be called a *complete* function. Under these conditions the behaviour of the system is fully determined. If there are situations where the function is not defined when in a specific state and receiving a specific input then the system will simply halt and no further behaviour is possible, unless the system is reset in some way.

We now proceed to the formal definition.

### Definition 1.2.1

Let *Input* be a finite alphabet. A *finite state machine* (or *finite automaton*) over *Input* consists of the following components (see [25]):

1. A finite set $Q$ of elements called *states*.
2. A subset $I$ of $Q$ containing the *initial states*.
3. A subset $T$ of $Q$ containing the *terminal states*.
4. A finite set of *transitions* that give, for each state and for each letter of the input alphabet, which state (or states), if any, to go to next. This can be represented as a, possibly partial, function:

$$F: Q \times Input \to \mathcal{P}Q,$$

where $F(q, input)$ contains the states the machine is allowed to go to from state $q$ when it receives the input *input* (recall that $\mathcal{P}Q$ denotes the set of all subsets of the set $Q$, usually referred to as the *power set of Q*).

The set *Input* can involve many different things. It could be specific user keyboard actions or commands, perhaps mouse clicks or movements or the receipt of a signal from a sensor or other monitoring device.

The set of states, $Q$, could be indicated by the values of certain important system variables, by the mode of behaviour of the system and so on. In a user interface the sort of screen that is visible could be a state; in a control application the state might indicate whether some device is active or not.

The transitions could be such that in a given state and under the influence of a particular *Input* value the system could respond with several possible operations; in other words, the next state could be a set of possible states and there is no information as to which one it might be. This is described by the term *nondeterminism*.

Each triple $(q, input, q') \in Q \times Input \times Q$, where $q' \in F(input, q)$, is called an *arc* of the automaton.

We frequently use the notations:

$$q \xrightarrow{\ input\ } q'$$

and

$$input: q \to q'$$

to indicate the edge. If F($input$, $q$) is a set of values, say $\{q_1, q_2, ..., q_n\}$ then the picture could be:

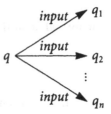

A sequence of arcs is called a *path*.

$$q \xrightarrow{input_1} q_1 \xrightarrow{input_2} q_2 \xrightarrow{input_3} q_3 \xrightarrow{input_n} q_n...$$

Here a path starting from state $q$ is labelled by the inputs: $input_1$, $input_2$, $input_3$,..., $input_n$,... and passes through the states $q_1$, $q_2$, $q_3$,..., $q_n$ and so on.

The automaton, or machine, is presented with an input string of letters (or characters) representing the abstraction of the set of actual inputs that it reads letter by letter starting at the leftmost letter. Beginning at one of the initial states, the letters determine a sequence of states along a path. The sequence may be interrupted when there is no edge corresponding to the letter read and, in this case, the input string is rejected. Otherwise, the sequence ends when the last input letter has been read. If the last state of the sequence is a terminal one, the input string is accepted, otherwise it is rejected. A sequence of inputs may determine a *set* of paths if there are situations where several transitions with the same label leave a particular state.

The set $L \subseteq Input^*$ of all the strings accepted is called the *language accepted* (or *recognised*) by the automaton.

*Note:* $Input^* = Input^+ \cup \{< >\}$, where $Input^+$ is the set of all finite sequences of characters from $Input$ and $< >$ is the empty sequence. In some cases we also refer to $Input^*$ by the formula seq($Input$) and the empty sequence is sometimes denoted in some works by the symbol 1, $\lambda$ or $\varepsilon$.

If $input_1$, $input_2$, $input_3$,..., $input_n \in Input$ then the sequence consisting of these elements assembled in this order will be written as:

$$input_1 :: input_2 :: input_3 ::.... :: input_n$$

which is an element of seq($Input$).

The automaton is called *deterministic* if there is only one initial state (i.e. $I = \{q_0\}$ ) and for each state and each letter there is at most one single next state (i.e. F can be regarded as a partial function F: $Q \times Input \rightarrow Q$). Thus, all the arcs leaving a given state must have different input labels. Otherwise, the automaton is called *nondeterministic*. Obviously, the path through a deterministic automaton is fully determined by the input string, whereas for the nondeterministic case, the choices of the initial state and the next state selected for each letter and current state are made randomly from a set of possible options. In this latter case, a string is accepted if at least one path determined by it through the machine ends in a final state. Although nondeterministic automata appear to have extra power over the deterministic ones, it has been proved that any language accepted by a non-deterministic automaton can also be accepted by a deterministic one [22].

The transition diagram of such a machine is described using circles to indicate the states, arrows to indicate the transitions and labels on the arrows to indicate the transition labels.

In the example in Figure 1.2 there are three states, called $a$, $b$ and $c$. There are two possible inputs, namely $0$ and $1$. The diagram describes the function F: $Q \times Input \rightarrow \mathscr{P}Q$, which in this case can be replaced by a function F: $Q \times Input \rightarrow Q$, which is partial since F($b$, $0$) is undefined.

In Figure 1.2 we have a deterministic machine with three states, $Q = \{a, b, c\}$ and two possible inputs, $Input = \{0, 1\}$, with the function being indicated by a set of labelled arrows. Let us make $a$ the initial state and $\{b\}$ the set of terminal states. If the system is in state $a$ and an input $1$ is received then the next state is $c$; if the input had been $0$, however, the next state would have been $b$. When in state $b$ an input $0$ sends the system to state $b$ (no change in state) whereas an input of $1$ would cause the system to change to state $c$, and so on.

So F($a$, $0$) = $b$; F($a$, $1$) = $c$; F($c$, $0$) = $\{a, b\}$ ; etc. Also, ($a$, $0$, $b$) and ($a$, $1$, $c$) are arcs.

Now we see that the following strings of inputs will be recognised by the machine since there is a path leading from state $a$ to state $b$ labelled by the input sequence: $0$; $0::1::0$; $0::1::0::0$; etc. (there are many more). Note that $0::1::0$ defines two paths, one through $a$, $b$, $c$, $b$ and the other through $a$, $b$, $c$, $a$. Only the former leads to the terminal state. The sequence $0::1::0::0$ defines a path through the states: $a$, $b$, $c$, $a$, $b$ and a path through $a$, $b$, $c$, $b$, ?, which halts before the last input is read.

However the strings $1::1::0::1$; $1::0::1$ are not recognised, the first because it cannot complete the process and the second because it ends in a state which is not a terminal state.

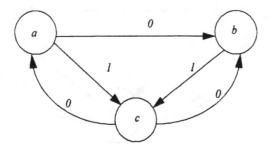

**FIG. 1.2.** A simple finite state machine.

The machines considered above simply react to the environmental inputs by changing state. Some machines, however, do more than this; they generate some message, command or other *output*. These will be called *finite state machines with output*.

### Definition 1.2.2

A *finite state machine with output* consists of the following components (see [25]):

1. A finite set $Q$ of elements called *states*.
2. A subset $I$ of $Q$ containing the *initial states*.
3. A set *Output* of possible outputs.
4. A finite set of *transitions* that give, for each state and for each letter of the input alphabet *Input*, which state (or states), if any, to go to next. This can be represented as a partial function

$$\mathbf{F}: Q \times Input \rightarrow \mathcal{P}Q,$$

5. A function $\mathbf{G}: Q \times Input \rightarrow Output$ which determines for each state and input received the output delivered. Note that **F** or **G** could be partial functions.

We will refer to the machine by its tuple ($Q$, $I$, *Input*, *Output*, **F**, **G** ).

### Example 1.2.1

Consider the following machine, illustrated in Figure 1.3, where:

$Q = \{a, b, c\}$ is the set of states, there are two possible inputs, *Input* = $\{0, 1\}$, and two possible outputs, *Output* = $\{x, y\}$. The function **F** is given in Figure 1.3, as is the function **G**, which is defined by:

$$G(a,0) = x; \; G(a,1) = x, \, G(b,1) = y; \text{ etc.}$$

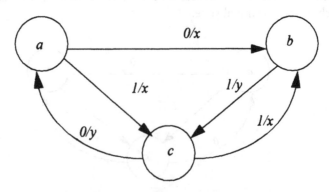

**FIG. 1.3.** A simple finite state machine with output.

An arc of the form:

$$q \xrightarrow{in/out} q'$$

means that $F(q, in) = q'$ and $G(q, in) = out$.

Now consider that the machine is started in state $a$ and receives the input sequence $0::1::0$. The sequence of state is $a, b, c, b$ and as it traverses this path the outputs $x, y$ and $x$ are produced in this order. Thus the input sequence $0::1::0$ produces a corresponding output sequence $x::y::x$, which is an element of seq($Output$). If we were to start the machine off in a different state it would, in general, produce a different output sequence. If we use another input sequence then another output sequence will be generated.

Given a particular finite state machine with outputs, assuming that we always start off the machine in the same initial state, then each input sequence will generate an output sequence or it will halt immediately because the state transition function is not fully defined for the first input. So the machine will act as a translation function from input sequences to output sequences.

The usage of finite state machines is a widely followed practice, particularly in sequential hardware design [26]. In some types of software system design, they are also used, for example in user interface design [27]. To adequately design and test user interfaces we need a sort of formalism for modelling both the computer system and the user. Since many models of human behaviour involve the concept of state, it is natural to try to represent the interaction between the system and its users in this way. Let us illustrate the use of finite state machines for modelling user interfaces with the following example.

*Example 1.2.2*

The system specified here is a very simple word processor that allows the following operations:

- *type* a character;
- insert a mathematical symbol (we call this operation *insert_symbol*);
- insert a drawing (we call this operation *insert_drawing*);
- *delete* a character, a drawing or a symbol;
- move the cursor to the right or to the left using the left and right arrows (we call the operations *move_right* and *move_left*);
- select (highlight) a part of the document. This can be done as follows:

  - the word processor starts selecting a part of the document when a certain input is received – let us call this operation *activate_select*;
  - characters, drawings or mathematical symbols in the document are selected by moving the cursor to the right or to the left (we call these operations *move_right* and *move_left* respectively);

– the action ends when a certain input is received (we call this operation *deactivate_select*) when a character is inserted (*type*), when a character, symbol or drawing are deleted (*delete*) or when the main menu of the processor is selected (*select_menu*);

- *cut* a character, a drawing or a symbol;
- *copy* a character, a drawing or a symbol;
- *paste* a character, a drawing or a symbol.

We assume that the word processor has a menu with the following options: *drawing, symbol, cut, copy* and *paste*. The first two options, if selected, allow the insertion of drawings or mathematical symbols, respectively, into the document.

We can represent the machine in a simple diagram (Figure 1.4) which shows how these different functions are interrelated. So while typing it is possible to select the menu which provides access to the functions for drawing diagrams, typing formulae, cutting and pasting etc. The diagram helps us to organise these functions in a sensible way, to restrict access to some functions when it is inappropriate to use them and to *control* the entire program.

It is quite natural to model a user interface in this way; quite complex user interfaces can be modelled similarly. The state transition diagram gives a clear and intuitive description of the evolution of the system and the operations that are allowed in any state. The current state of the system can be very easily traced using the sequence of operations that the system has

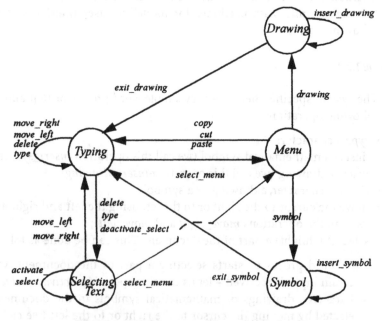

**FIG. 1.4.** A simple finite state machine model of an interface.

already performed. Important properties of the model can be deduced from the diagram, for example if there are states that cannot be reached, or states from which there is no exit. Such information is very important in the analysis of user interfaces. The main drawback is that the modelling of large and complex machines is difficult; in other words, the technique does not scale very well without introducing a more structured model, such as the statechart (see Section 1.3).

It is relatively easy to create an implementation once a state machine description is available, or, at least, in software terms the outline control structure of the software can be generated. State machines do not provide a sensible model of the data and the detailed processing so there are limitations to how far this can be taken. In hardware design, simple sequential systems are often implemented directly from state diagrams and software is available to do this. The solutions may not be optimal but, again, optimising software can be used to overcome this.

The state machine model can be enhanced, thus giving rise to more complex, but similar, models that can be used to reduce the number of states of a state diagram or when the standard finite state machine is too limited to cope with the required application. These have been extensively studied and include pushdown machines, stack machines, tree automata and many more [22, 28]. Rather than cover them all, we will briefly look at another extended state machine. Later on we will introduce our main model, which will be seen to be a generalisation of all of these types of machine. Such a model is, for example, the *traceable finite state machine* (or *traceable automaton*); here we have an additional stack that keeps a record of the states the system has visited up to the current moment.

### Definition 1.2.3

More precisely, a *deterministic traceable automaton* [29] over a finite alphabet *Input* consists of the following components:

1. A finite set of states $Q$.
2. An initial state $q_0 \in Q$.
3. A set of terminal states $T \subseteq Q$.
4. A *state stack* $S \subseteq Q^*$.
5. A partial function $F_t: Q \times Input \to Q \cup \{Trace\}$.

The state stack is a simple memory device that keeps a record of what the last state was in case it is needed. It is represented by a sequence of values from the set of states, $Q$. We can only access the stack through the topmost value. Under certain conditions, when the *Trace* operation is called, the top of the stack is read and the system returns to the state named there.

Initially, then, the automaton is in one of its initial states and the state stack is empty. The function $F_t$ determines the next state according to the current state $q$ and the input symbol in, read by the automaton.

1. if $F_t(q, in) = q'$, then $q$ is pushed to the top of the stack, the control goes to the state $q'$.
2. if $F_t(q, in) = Trace$ and the stack is not empty then the control goes to $p$, which is the state on top of the stack, and $p$ is popped from the stack. If the stack is empty then the machine stops and the input string is rejected.

Using this device we can produce a simpler and more powerful model of the word processor, illustrated in Figure 1.5.

Traceable automata are more powerful than standard finite state machines (see [30]); they can be used to describe user interfaces – especially their menus – that cannot be handled by standard finite state machines. For example, let us consider that the word processor has an *undo* option that cancels the last operation performed and takes the system back to the previous state. If this is to be described in the specification we have to keep track of the operations performed by the word processor up to the current moment and there is no way we can do that using a standard finite state machine. However, a traceable automaton can describe this extra feature very easily – the *Trace* transitions are added to the initial model.

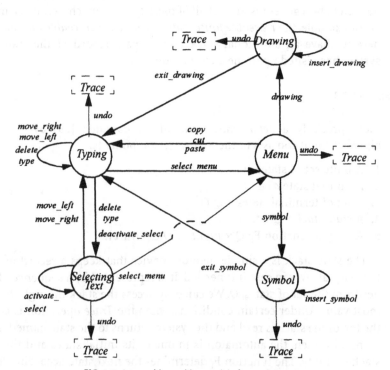

**FIG. 1.5.** A traceable machine model of a word processor.

However, finite state machines alone – standard, traceable or other variants – cannot describe a system completely, since there is no reference to the internal data of the system (i.e. a document in the above example or the records in a database) and how this data is affected by each operation in the state transition diagram. Thus, other specification methods such as Z or VDM have to be used for modelling the data aspects of the system. Furthermore, there needs to be a mechanism (or a meta-model) that unifies the two views of the specification. Without such a mechanism, the two models of the system – one representing the system control and the other the system data – may be inaccurate since there is no way of capturing the dependency between the two models: a transition in the control structure of a problem may affect the program data and vice versa. For example, the *copy* and *cut* transitions from the *Menu* state in the example above will only be enabled if part of the document has already been selected. It is possible to describe the state transitions in a language like Z but it is a clumsy and unsatisfactory way to do it.

## 1.3 STATECHARTS

Finite state machines with output are also the basis of more complex specification languages. *Statecharts* [31], for example, adapt the state machine formalism by allowing nested states, i.e. a state of a chart can be represented itself as a chart at a lower level. In this way the complexities of a large state diagram can be managed. The formalism introduces a structuring facility and a refinement process. When building state machine models we can identify a type of state (called a *superstate*) from which a lot of information is abstracted out and this can be replaced at a later stage by a more detailed part of the model. Thus a superstate can be replaced later with a submachine or a collection of submachines either running in parallel or which allow a degree of choice.

Thus, there are several types of states in statecharts:

1. OR states. If a system is in this state it can only be in one of its substates. Therefore the substates of an OR state behave like a finite state machine.
2. AND states. When a machine is in this state, it is in all of its substates, which are "running concurrently".
3. BASIC states. This is a state with no substates.

If a statechart is in an OR state, some state of the chart within it has to be active. Conversely, if a chart is in some state, the "parent" OR state has to be active. For an AND state, all of its substates have to be active. Such restrictions select sets of states called configurations from all possible sets of states a chart can be in.

A general label of a transition in a statechart specification has the form $e[c]/a$, where $e$ is the event expression (conjunction of events or negated

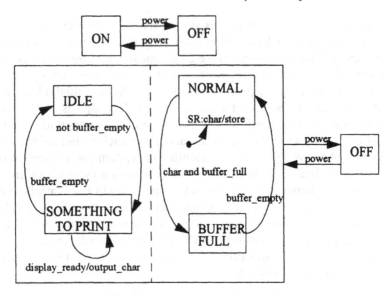

**FIG. 1.6.** A simple statechart model of a buffer.

events) that triggers the transition, *c* is a condition (boolean expression) that has to be satisfied for the transition to fire and *a* is the resulting action. All of the transition label components are optional (e.g. no transitions in Figure 1.6 contain the [*c*] component and only two have the *a* component). Besides allowing actions to appear along transitions, they can also appear associated with the entrance to or exit from a state. There are several models of a *step*, the process by which a computation in a statechart proceeds. They have widely differing consequences. One popular semantics is as follows: actions associated with the entrance to a state *q* are executed in the step in which *q* is entered as if they appear on the transitions leading into *q*. Similarly, actions associated with the exit from *q* are executed in the step in which *q* is exited, as if they appear on the transition exiting *q*. In addition, each state can be associated with *static reactions* (SRs) that are to be carried out as long as the system is in (and not exiting) the state in question.

### Example 1.3.1

An example of a print buffer between a network link and the actual printer is presented in Figure 1.6. The initial specification is a two-state model (shown on top); the *power* button selects between the two states. In turn *On* is an AND state that contain two sub-states – these are separated by a dashed line and run concurrently, the one on the right filling a buffer with data from the network and the other printing. These are both OR states and contain two BASIC states to represent normal operation and no operation when the buffer is full or empty, respectively.

Thus, the process of constructing a statecharts specification is gradual; a hierarchy of specifications can be built and this results in an increase in the clarity and efficiency of the specification and provides a means for avoiding the state explosion problem. As the use of statecharts has developed, a number of special features and customs have evolved. This may have been convenient for design engineers since it enabled them to model certain specific aspects of systems more easily. The consequence of this, however, has been a loss of clarity and consensus concerning the semantics of a statechart. This has been compounded by the widespread use of a tool, STATEMATE [32], which supports the use of statecharts. For example, it has been possible to design models where transitions traverse directly across many levels of superstate boundaries, and to build models where it is unclear what the system should do. There could be several transitions enabled at the same time which could carry out contradictory actions. A number of attempts have been made to describe the semantics of statecharts and of the STATEMATE versions of statecharts. These have partially clarified the situation but there is still much confusion about the true meaning of the differing dialects of statecharts [33].

## 1.4   A GENERAL COMPUTATIONAL MODEL: THE X-MACHINES

Generally, finite state machines and their relatives are very good at expressing the dynamics of a system. The use of graphical elements in a specification methodology is attractive from the point of view of user understanding, conveying dynamic information concisely and intuitively. Thus, control aspects of software programs are very often described as finite state machines. However, all of these state transition models lack the ability to represent complex data structures. In fact, it is difficult to model any non-trivial data structure using finite state machines. Also, other, more complex, machine models such as the Pushdown Automata and Turing machines are too low level and hence of little use for specification and design of real systems.

However, there is a generalisation of all these machines that can, when combined with suitable data processing methods, provide us with an appropriate environment for the description and analysis of arbitrary systems. The *X-machine* integrates the two aspects of a software system specification – the control and the data processing – while allowing them to be described separately. A finite-state-machine-like diagram is used to model the system control while the data processing can be represented using methods such as Z or VDM or any appropriate formal notation. The method can combine the dynamic features of graphical methods with suitable data representations, thus sharing the benefits of both these worlds.

Introduced by Eilenberg in 1974 [28], X-machines have received little further study. Holcombe [34] proposed the model as a basis for a possible specification language and since then a number of further investigations have demonstrated that this idea is of great potential value for software engineers. In its essence, an X-machine is like a finite state machine with a set of states, $Q$, but with one important difference. A *basic data set*, $X$, is identified together with a set of *basic processing functions*, $\Phi$, which operate on $X$; $\Phi$ is called the *type* of the machine.

So we identify a set of basic processing functions and a set $X$ of data that these functions can process. These functions are controlled by way of a state diagram like the finite state machine model.

Each arrow in the finite state machine diagram is then labelled by a function from $\Phi$, thus the *next state (partial) function* will be of the form:

$$F: Q \times \Phi \rightarrow Q$$

Then the sequences of state transitions in the machine determine the processing of the data set and thus the function computed. The data set $X$ can contain information about the internal memory of a system as well as different sorts of output behaviour, so it is possible to model very general systems in a transparent way.

This method allows the control state of the system to be easily separated from the data set. The set $X$ is often an array consisting of fields that define internal structures such as registers, stacks, database filestores, input information from various devices, models of screen displays and other output mechanisms.

Consider a simple, abstract example, illustrated in Figure 1.7.

We have not specified $X$ or the functions $\phi_i$ that belong to the set $\Phi$ but this is sufficient to provide a basic idea of the machine. It starts in a given initial state (control state) and a given state of the system's basic data set $X$ (the data state); there are a number of paths that can be traced out from that initial state, which are labelled by functions $\phi_1$, $\phi_2$ etc. Sequences of functions from this space are thus derived from paths in the state space and these may be composed to produce a function that may be defined on the data state. This is then applied to the value $x$, providing that the composed function is defined on $X$. This then gives a new value, $x' \in X$, for the data state and a new control state. Usually, the machine is *deterministic* so that

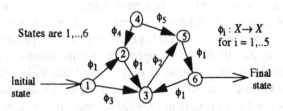

**FIG. 1.7.** A simple X-machine.

at any moment there is only one possible function defined (that is, the domains of the functions emerging from a given state are mutually disjoint).

From the diagram we note that there is a possible sequence of functions from state 1 to state 6, here a specified terminal state, labelled by the functions $\phi_1, \phi_1, \phi_2, \phi_1$. Assuming that each value is defined, this path then transforms an initial value $x \in X$ into the value $\phi_1(\phi_2(\phi_1(\phi_1(x)))) \in X$. So we are assuming that $x \in$ domain $\phi_1$; $\phi_1(x) \in$ domain $\phi_1$; $\phi_1(\phi_1(x)) \in$ domain $\phi_2$; and $\phi_2(\phi_1(\phi_1(x))) \in$ domain $\phi_1$. The computation carried out by this path is thus a transformation of the data space as well as a transformation of the control space.

Clearly we need to specify some relationship between the input and output information of the overall system and the data set $X$, especially when $X$ contains information that is not directly involved with the system input and output. This is done by specifying two sets $Y$ and $Z$, to represent the *input* and *output information*, respectively.

Two *coding functions*:

$$\alpha: Y \to X$$

and

$$\beta: X \to Z$$

describe how the input is coded up prior to processing by the machine and how the subsequently processed data is then prepared (or decoded) into suitable output format.

In many cases the inputs and outputs of the machine will behave as orderly streams of symbols, i.e.:

$$Y = Input ^* \text{ and } Z = Output ^*$$

where *Input* will be called the *input alphabet* and *Output* the *output alphabet*. Then the set $X$ will often have the form:

$$X = Output ^* \times Mem \times Input ^*$$

where *Mem* is a (possibly infinite) set called *Memory*.

In this case the input code will define the *initial memory value* $m_0 \in Mem$, i.e. $\forall\ in^* \in Input\ ^*$, an input sequence:

$$\alpha(in^*) = (<>, m_0, in^* )$$

and the output code will extract the output sequence of any data value $(out^*, m, in^*)$ if the machine has read the whole input sequence (i.e. $s = <>$), i.e. $\forall\ out^* \in Output^*, m \in Mem, in^* \in Input^*$:

$$\beta(out^*, m, in^*) = \begin{cases} out^*, \text{if } in^* = <> \\ \\ \varnothing, \text{otherwise} \end{cases}$$

The basic idea is that the machine has some internal memory, *Mem*, and the stream of inputs determines, depending on the current state of control and the current state of the memory, the next control state, the next memory state and any output value.

Of special interest for specifying user interfaces are those X-machines in which each processing (partial) function $\phi \in \Phi$:

$$\phi: Output^* \times Mem \times Input^* \rightarrow Output^* \times Mem \times Input^*$$

is of the form whereby, given a value of the memory and an input value, $\phi$ can change the memory value and produce an output value; the input value is then discarded.

More formally:

$$\phi(out^*, m, <>) \text{ is undefined } \forall \; out^* \in Output^*, m \in Mem$$

and

$$\forall \; m \in Mem, in \in Input \text{ either}$$
$$\phi(out^*, m, in :: in^*) \text{ is undefined } \forall \; out^* \in Output^*, in^* \in Input^* \text{ or}$$
$$\exists \; m' \in Mem, out' \in Output \text{ (that depend on } m \text{ and } in) \text{ such that}$$
$$\phi(out^*, m, in :: in^*) = (out^* :: out, m', in^*), \forall \; out^* \in Output^*, in^* \in Input^*$$

where *a::b* is the concatenation of two strings or sequences, *a* and *b*.

Machines satisfying these properties are called *stream X-machines* [35].

Clearly any processing function $\phi$ of a stream X-machine is completely determined by the values of *out* and *m'* as a function of *m* and *in*. Thus, we can simplify the notation by referring to such a processing function as $\phi: Mem \times Input \rightarrow Output \times Mem$. That is, instead of saying:

$$\phi(out^*, m, in :: in^*) = (out^* :: out, m', in^*)$$

with $m, m' \in Mem, out \in Output, in \in Input, \forall \; out^* \in Output^*, in^* \in Input^*$, we say:

$$\phi(m, in) = (out, m')$$

the rest being understood implicitly.

Thus we will often describe the functions $\phi$ in the form:

$$\phi: (m, in) \;\; \rightarrow (out, m')$$
$$\phi: (m_1, in_1) \rightarrow (out_1, m'_1)$$
$$\phi: (m_2, in_2) \rightarrow (out_2, m'_2)$$

and so on.

This is the notation we shall be using in the rest of this book.

## 1.5 AN X-MACHINE EXAMPLE

The word processor described in Example 1.2.2 can easily be specified as a stream X-machine. Here, the operations of the processor will become (partial) functions that operate on the Cartesian product of the input sequence, internal data structure (memory) and the output sequence – the set of all these partial functions will make up the type of the machine, $\Phi$. Thus suitable data types must be defined and the input, output and memory set will consist of a Cartesian product or a disjoint union of these types.

Let *CHARACTERS*, *SYMBOLS* and *DRAWINGS* be the set of characters, mathematical symbols and drawings that the system can process (for now we will not make any assumptions about the shape and size of these drawings) and let:

$$ELEMENTS = CHARACTERS \cup SYMBOLS \cup DRAWINGS$$

Let also *STRINGS* be the set of all sequences of *ELEMENTS*, i.e.:

$$STRINGS = ELEMENTS^* = \text{seq}(ELEMENTS)$$

Then the document the word processor operates on can be described as a tuple $(x, z, y, p)$, with $x, z, y \in STRINGS$, and $p$ takes two values, either $p = right$ or $p = left$. Here x is the first non-highlighted part of the document and the reverse of the sequence $y$, $rev(y)$, is the other non-highlighted part of the document. If $p = right$, then the selected text is $z$ and the cursor is on its right-hand side. If $p = left$, then the highlighted text is $rev(z)$ and the cursor is on its left-hand side.

For example, if the document is

"abcdef g"<br>↑

where ↑ marks the position of the cursor and the highlighted section is in bold, then $x =$ "ab", $y =$ "g f", $z =$ "cde" and $p =$ right.

If the document is:

"abcdef g"<br>↑

then $x =$ "ab", $y =$ "g f", $z =$ "edc" and $p = left$.

If no part of the document is selected (i.e. $z = <\ >$), then the value of $p$ is not relevant.

Thus, the set of documents the word processor operates on is defined as:

$$DOCUMENTS = STRINGS \times STRINGS \times STRINGS \times POSITIONS$$

where:

$$POSITIONS = \{left, right\}$$

The internal memory of an X-machine specification of the word processor will consist of suitable representations for the document and for the text selected in the clipboard – this is a sequence of *ELEMENTS*. Thus:

$$M = DOCUMENTS \times STRINGS$$

The current memory value will be denoted by $((x, y, z, p), c)$, where $(x, y, z, p)$ represents the current document and $c$ is the part of the document copied into the clipboard.
The initial memory value is:

$$m_0 = ((\varepsilon, \varepsilon, \varepsilon, left), < >).$$

The input alphabet *Input* will consist of the inputs required for the successful execution of all operations. These inputs are normally defined in some specification document but for now we will make some obvious assumptions about them. Also, the names we will be using are self-explanatory.

We shall assume that, with the exception of *type*, *insert_symbol* and *insert_drawing*, all the commands of the processor are triggered by a single input each (e.g. *back_space* triggers *delete*, *left_arrow* triggers *move_left*, *cut_option* triggers *cut*, etc.). Thus, if we denote by $Input_0$ the enumeration of these inputs, i.e.:

$$Input_0 = \{back\_space, left\_arrow, right\_arrow, cut\_option,...\}$$

then *Input* can be written as:

$$Input = Input_0 \cup ELEMENTS$$

(Obviously *type* is triggered by *CHARACTERS*, *insert_symbol* is triggered by *SYMBOLS* and *insert_drawing* is triggered by *DRAWINGS*.)

For the sake of simplicity, we will consider that a system output will consist of the current document, i.e.:

$$Output = DOCUMENTS$$

Since our specification is a stream X-machine the definitions of all processing functions will be of the form:

$$\phi(((x, y, z, p), c), in) = (out, ((x', y', z', p'), c'))$$

where $out \in Output$, $in \in Input$ and $((x, y, z, p), c), ((x', y', z', p'), c') \in M$. Some samples of processing functions are given next.

If $in \in CHARACTERS$ then **type**$(((x, z, y, p), c), in) = (out, ((x', z', y, p), c))$, where:

$$out = (x', z', y, p)$$
$$x' = x :: in$$
$$z' = <>$$

i.e. **type** removes the selected part of the document – if any – and inserts a character on the left of the cursor.

If $in \in DRAWINGS$ then **insert_drawing**$(((x, z, y, p), c), in) = (out, ((x', z', y, p), c))$, where:

$$out = (x', z', y, p)$$
$$x' = x :: in$$
$$z' = <>$$

i.e. this is similar to **type**.

**delete**$(((x, z, y, p), c), back\_space) = (out, ((x', z', y, p), c))$, where:

$$out = (x', z', y, p)$$

$$x' = \begin{cases} x, \text{if } z \in STRINGS - \{<>\} \\ front(x), \text{if } z = <> \end{cases}$$

$$z' = <>$$

i.e. it deletes the selected part of the document if this is not empty and removes the first character on the left of the cursor otherwise.

*Note:* For an alphabet $A$, **front**: $seq(A) \rightarrow seq(A)$ is a function that removes the last character of a non-empty sequence of elements in $A$ and leaves the empty sequence unchanged, i.e.:

$$\textbf{front}(<>) \ = <> \text{ and}$$
$$\textbf{front}(x :: a) = a \text{ for all } x \in seq(A), a \in A$$

Refinement is quite straightforward in the context of X-machines: a processing function can itself be described – maybe at a lower level – as an X-machine, thus the refinement process is achieved by replacing certain arcs in the original machine with suitable X-machines. For example, we can describe in more detail the process of inserting a drawing by the above word processor. For the sake of simplicity, we shall assume that only lines and rectangles can be inserted and that the insertion process consists of the following sequence of steps:

- select shape (line or rectangle);
- select the first point (this is a corner in the case of rectangles);
- select the second point (this is the opposite corner in the case of rectangles).

Let *POINTS* be the set of points that can be selected and:

$$SHAPES = \{line, rectangle\}$$

and let:

$$DRAWINGS_R = SHAPES \times POINTS \times POINTS$$

i.e. a drawing is considered to be defined by shape and positions of two points.

Let also:

$$
\begin{aligned}
ELEMENTS_R &= CHARACTERS \cup SYMBOLS \cup DRAWINGS_R \\
STRINGS_R &= ELEMENTS_R{}^* \\
DOCUMENTS_R &= STRINGS_R \times STRINGS_R \times STRINGS_R \times POSITIONS
\end{aligned}
$$

and:

$$M_R = DOCUMENTS_R \times STRINGS_R$$

(More generally, for any of the sets, $A$ above, $A_R$ denotes the set obtained by substituting *DRAWINGS* with $DRAWINGS_R$ in the definition of $A$.)

Then the memory, input and output sets of the refined X-machine are:

$$
\begin{aligned}
M_{Ref} &= M_R \times (SHAPES \times POINTS) \\
Input_{Ref} &= (Input - DRAWINGS) \cup SHAPES \cup POINTS
\end{aligned}
$$

where *Input* is the input alphabet of the original X-machine specification.

$$Output_{Ref} = DOCUMENTS_R$$

With the exception of *insert_drawing* no processing function of the original machine was triggered by inputs in the *DRAWINGS* set, so any such:

$$\phi: M \times (Input - DRAWINGS) \rightarrow Output \times M$$

can be transformed into a processing functions of the refined machine:

$$\phi_{Ref}: M_{Ref} \times Input_{Ref} \rightarrow Output_{Ref} \times M_{Ref}$$

in a straightforward manner. Indeed, let:

$$
\begin{aligned}
gamma{:}\quad & M \times (Input - DRAWINGS) \rightarrow Output \\
memory{:}\quad & M \times (Input - DRAWINGS) \rightarrow M
\end{aligned}
$$

be the projections of $\phi$ onto *Output* and *M*, respectively, i.e. for any $m \in M$, $in \in Input$:

$$\phi(m, in) = (gamma(m, in), memory(m, in))$$

Then for any $m_R \in M_R$, $m_1 \in SHAPES \times POINTS$ and $in \in Input - DRAWINGS$:

$$\phi_{Ref}((m_R, m_1), in) = (gamma_R(m_R, in), ((memory_R(m_R, in), m_1)), \text{ where}$$
$$gamma_R: M_R \times (Input - DRAWINGS) \to Output_R \text{ and}$$
$$memory_R: M_R \times (Input - DRAWINGS) \to M_R$$

are obtained by substituting *DRAWINGS* with $DRAWINGS_R$ in the definitions of *gamma* and *memory*, respectively.

For example, **type** becomes **type$_R$** defined by:

if $in \in CHARACTERS$ then
**type$_R$**$(((x, z, y, p), c), (u, v)), in) = (out, (((x', z', y, p), c), (u, v)))$, where
$out = (x', z', y, p)$,
$x' = x :: in$,
$z' = < >$

**Note:** $((x, z, y, p), c) \in M$, $u \in SHAPES$, $v \in POINTS$, $out \in Output_{Ref}$.

The core of the refinement process is achieved by substituting the arc labelled **insert_drawing** with a stream X-machine that decomposes the insertion of a line or rectangle in the three steps described above (see Figure 1.8). Some sample definitions of the new processing functions are given next.

**select_line**$((((x, z, y, p), c), (u, v)), line) = (out, (((x, z, y, p), c), (u', v)))$, where:
$out = (x, z, y, p)$
$u' = line$

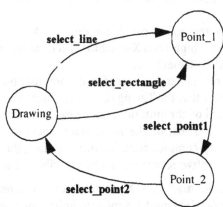

**FIG. 1.8.** A simple stream X-machine example.

If $in \in POINTS$ then:

**select_point1**$((((x, z, y, p), c), (u, v)), in) = (out, (((x, z, y, p), c), (u, v')))$,
where:

$$out = (x, z, y, p)$$
$$u' \ \ = in$$

If $in \in POINTS$ then:

**select_point2**$((((x, z, y, p), c), (u, v)), in) = (out, (((x', z', y, p), c), (u, v)))$,
where:

$$out = (x', z', y, p)$$
$$x' \ \ = x \, (u, v, in)$$
$$z' \ \ = <\,>$$

Obviously, any such refinement process has to be supported by a series of theorems that ensure that the transformations preserve, in some sense, the functionality of the original X-machine. This more theoretical point of view will be discussed in Part 2. In many practical situations though, as illustrated by the above example, the refinement techniques – such as the extension of the state space, the fundamental type X and the set of processing functions – can be appreciated easily from an intuitive point of view. This feature is one of the attractions of X-machines.

The advantages of the X-machine model include:

- It is intuitive and a number of trial evaluations have indicated that it is easy to use.
- It is built on current knowledge and does not involve any revolutionary concept. Indeed, the model is a blend of state diagrams and formal descriptions of data types and functions that can be expressed easily in a language such as Z or as functions in ML or a similar functional language or using traditional mathematical notations.
- It allows for the capture of the dynamic system information in a very intuitive manner. The use of state diagrams helps a great deal in this sense.
- It allows a system to be specified at different levels. Indeed, a processing function from a high-level X-machine specification can be expressed itself as a lower level X-machine.
- It is sufficiently general to cater for all computational problems. Indeed, it is fairly clear that the Turing machine, which is accepted as the mathematical model of computation, can be easily described as an X-machine (see [28, 36]). Thus, unlike finite state machines, the X-machine can cope with very complex functionality – in fact, the functionality of any hardware or software system can be described as an X-machine.

Like finite state machines, X-machines can be extended by adding new features to the original model. Similar to finite state machines, we can define a traceable X-machine by adding a stack $S = Q^*$ that keeps a history of state changes and extending the state transition function $F: Q \times \Phi \to Q$ to $F_t: Q \times \Phi \to Q \cup \{trace\}$; obviously, the semantics of $F_t$ is identical to that defined for traceable automata. For example, the *undo* operation can be added very easily to our X-machine specification of the word processor in this way. Traceable X-machines can be more suitable for describing certain types of user interfaces than standard X-machines. Unlike finite state machines though, this expansion does not extend the computation ability of the model (i.e. it can be shown easily that a traceable X-machine with basic data set X and type $\Phi$ can be simulated by an X-machine with basic type $X' = X \times S$ and type $\Phi'$ obtained by extending the processing functions in $\Phi$ with "push" and "pop" operations performed on the $S$ component of $X'$; another proof of this fact is given in [37]). Thus the theoretical results developed for X-machines that will be presented in the next chapters can also be applied to traceable X-machines after suitable transformations.

One final issue worth discussing is the ability of the X-machine model to deal with real-time behaviour. The main formal specification methods (Z, VDM, OBJ, etc.) do not, in their original form, address the problem of modelling time in real-time systems; coping with time has usually required the augmentation of the language with special constructors and operations, which have often caused a significant increase in the complexity of the notation and method and the consequent reduction in its attractiveness as a useful tool in industry. The same is also true of the process calculi such as CCS [38], which are good at modelling the communication in a concurrent system but need complex augmentation to handle data and time. Unlike these, X-machines allow the integration of time into the model in a very simple manner; for example, the clock can be represented as the set of natural numbers, starting from some arbitrary point and advancing by one for a small enough time interval. The clock can then be easily incorporated into the machine memory and a special input (let us call this *tick*) will be used to increment the time by one unit; thus any "time" transition will be triggered by the last tick that brought the clock to the appropriate value (see [39] for more detail).

Another approach is the extension of the X-machine model so that it can cope with hybrid or continuous behaviour. There are a number of formalisms that incorporate continuous transitions into finite state machines (e.g. phase transition systems [40], hybrid automata [41], hybrid state charts [42]). Their common idea is to use arcs for representing discrete transitions and to associate each continuous transition with a state. This idea has also been used in the context of X-machines, thus giving rise to hybrid machines or hybrid X-machines (see [43]). However, these hybrid X-machines require further study and we will not focus on them here.

# 2 Business Processes, Problems and Solutions

*Summary. Problems and solutions, design methods, business process models, information systems, requirements capture, system specification, dynamic models, the problem of real time, examples of X-machine specifications, microprocessors, implementation.*

With the ever expanding areas of applications of computers today it is often easy to lose sight of the essential similarities that exist between all of these systems. The common theme in many endeavours is one of a problem with a number of important and critical features, and a proposed solution constructed on the basis of a computer program or suite of programs with the desired behaviour. The critical issue, as we have mentioned in the Preface, is the relationship between the proposed solution and the understanding of the "problem's originator" as to whether the proposed solution does, in fact, provide the desired answer.

We will refer to the person with the problem as the *client*. He or she has a problem to be solved, and the solution provider, the *designer*, must endeavour to achieve an *acceptable* solution. What exactly these terms mean will be the subject of much of what will follow. In the course of examining these issues we will explore some of the myths, beliefs and established wisdom about the design of software systems that percolate through the subject.

## 2.1 Problems and Solutions

Our starting point is the following: the clients (and the prospective users of any solution) are the *most important individuals* in the exercise. It is only by understanding *their needs* and *their objectives* that the designers can achieve their aims – which should be client satisfaction and high user productivity.

In order to support this we must ensure that the communication between clients, users and designers is such that all can contribute to the construction of an appropriate solution in a cost effective way. It has been widely commented that one of the key causes of the failure of a software design project is lack of understanding by the designers of the clients' requirements. It could also be mentioned that the clients may not be fully appreciative of their problem, let alone a possible solution. We are thus brought to the position where we must find some effective mechanism to enable us to describe and understand the clients' problem before we can even contemplate the construction of a solution. Our first starting point is to examine the context of the clients' problem area and to build a *simple business process model*. In our main example it is clearly oriented towards a common type of business application that may be solved by constructing a suitable information system of the type commonly encountered in almost every office. Later in the chapter we will use similar techniques to look at a different type of problem domain where *time* is a much more critical aspect of the situation and there is a less obvious business dimension.

## 2.2   Design Methods: Old and New

Much has been written about business processes and business process models. Various notations, languages and tools have been proposed to try to capture the essence of the business process and these have often been related to design methodologies and analysis techniques to better enable software systems to be built for business applications. Many of these techniques and notations have their origin in software engineering; they are the attempts of computer professionals to try to describe the essentials of a business process in their own terms and notations. The supposed benefit of this approach is that the information so gleaned is then suitable for use in the "traditional" software design approaches (e.g.[2]), including, in recent years the object-oriented approach to software production ([12]).

There is a continuing problem with building software systems that provide what the client wants. A great deal of effort has been expended on developing requirements capture notations, methods and tools without much impact on the problem as a whole, which is primarily one of communication between the client and his or her business and the designer and implementer. There are a number of reasons for this. One is the conceptual gap that develops not only between the client and the designer but also between the designer and the developer and the tester or quality assurance process. Many of the design methods that are used reinforce this latter gap in unnecessary ways. For example, the common design methods and tools focus on data and processes in a loose way and ignore the issue of the algorithm. Thus, the opportunity for automatic generation of code for a thoroughly analysed design is limited. To overcome this problem some tools, for example CASE tools [2, 44], allow the designer to annotate processes with code to represent the algorithm, which seems to defeat the object since full analysis is then still not possible with our current techniques. Furthermore, without the algorithm being made specific, the opportunities to carry out detailed and well-founded testing are reduced.

Even attempts to improve the matter through the use of formal methods and notations [16–18] often suffer from similar problems. These focus on notations and concepts that could provide a vehicle for describing and analysing systems mathematically and thus rigorously. It is a commonly expressed philosophy among formal methods practitioners that one should not consider any implementation issues and that implicit specification is preferred to an explicit algorithm. An algorithm does not mean an implementation or a piece of code; it is a mathematical formula which describes in terms of the declared data types the outcome of the process in terms of its inputs. This is something that can be used for analysis, automatic test generation and code construction.

All computer software systems are examples of computational models. If the design languages do not create such models as a by-product of their use then there will be left a significant barrier that needs to be negotiated before the successful construction of a working system. In its simplest form this barrier is represented by the need to construct an algorithm that will implement the function defined during the data analysis and functional decomposition stages of the analysis and design process. Most object-oriented design methods also meet with this obstacle. What this means is that the construction of the algorithms has been separated from the rest of the design process and left to programmers who may not fully understand the problem. The programmers will have to develop code that seems to implement the informal description that they have been given but this is a weak link in the chain, as well as being unnecessary. As part of our integrated approach to design and testing we will be putting the algorithm back into the heart of the activity. Before we do, however, we will consider some of the approaches currently favoured for software engineering.

## Traditional Design Approaches

Many traditional design methods are based on data analysis. This involves identifying the way that data flows through the system, which process needs which data and how the data needs to be organised to enable efficient access and query systems. The methodologies have involved diagramming techniques such as data flow diagrams; entity relationship diagrams, which try to describe the interactions between different types of data; entity life histories, which show how data elements are created and destroyed during the operation of the system; and finite state machines. In none of these is it possible to construct a coherent, integrated model of the system that could be analysed and used as a basis for full code generation or functional test set construction. The structured analysis and design approach – in its many variants and embedded into many different software life cycle models, ranging from the waterfall, through incremental delivery [7] to Rapid Application Development [45] – has failed to deliver the quality of solution that is required. The costs of developing systems using these methods has become uneconomic, especially now that the amount of effort needed for testing has escalated to between 50% and 90% of many projects. Couple this with the observation that even if the systems more or less work they may not be the solution to the problem – which may have changed during the long, slow process of construction anyway.

The classical approach of *relational data analysis* [46], while serving an important purpose in the days where all applications were extending the capabilities of slow computers with small areas of storage, is probably no longer necessary. For many applications nowadays the capabilities of the modern microprocessor and the availability of cheap and fast storage result in there being much less of a speed or memory problem. It is possible to organise the data as a flat or linear file, nowadays, without any serious loss of performance in searching and querying operations. It is the limitations of the human operator in terms of speed of reaction in carrying out these operations that we are now reaching. There are also considerable benefits in relaxing the *relational tyranny* in the design of databases when it comes to one of the major challenges of software engineering – the easy maintenance and redevelopment of systems that may have been solutions of problems that time has rendered obsolete.

How can businesses keep paying for their databases to be redesigned whenever their business environment changes? One solution may be to empower business people so that they can configure and reconfigure their system to their needs without having to explain their requirements to a software analyst. But how could this be done? We cannot expect them to learn how to program; they must be given sensible metaphors, notations and tools that will help them to model their business processes in a convenient way and which will generate correct implementations, painlessly. This is an important issue, which we will return to.

Another possible approach, related to the philosophy outlined later in relation to software systems in general, is that of components. Why cannot we have modular database systems where new standard database components can be bolted on in a robust way when the need arises without having to go through an expensive re-analysis and design process?

## Object-oriented Design

Object-oriented programming languages [13, 14] were invented by programmers who were looking for a mechanism that saved them from having to keep writing very similar code for different applications. This concept has caught the imagination of many and has led to the introduction of a number of design methodologies to support it. One of the driving forces behind it is the idea of *software reuse*. Sadly, this is a poorly understood phenomenon. The principal is that the generic framework of commonly used software segments can be identified as a system of classes that collaborate to provide some generic system architecture. A *class*, on the other hand, is a description of a collection of specific *objects* that carry out some coherent software function. These objects are convenient packages of data and process (methods) that provide a controlled mechanism for communicating and manipulating the data. Further, these classes can be placed in libraries and reused for similar purposes in different applications. The ideas have been taken further with the concept of *inheritance*, whereby some of the features that belong to one class can be used to define other classes, and in *polymorphism*, which involves the generalisation of some functions to apply to many different types of data. The object metaphor enables the programmer to collect together into convenient bundles the data and its related processing functions (algorithms) in such a way that prevents the programmer from interfering with the internal workings of the object. This is seen as a good thing since one of the big problems with programming – this distinguishes software engineering from all other types of engineering[1] – is the ability the programmer has to change any part of the program at any time prior to delivery, thus creating the potential for disaster. Unfortunately, the unstated implication of the reuse of classes was that this would reduce the amount of testing needed, for, after all, if the classes had been used previously with success in some other system then they would be successful in other applications. This is a very dangerous myth, which we will come back to. Suffice it to say that many experts, for example [15], comment that testing object-oriented systems is considerably harder and more time consuming than testing traditional systems.

With the development of object-oriented languages came a plethora of object-oriented design methodologies [47, 48]. Here the claim was that the use of objects was a natural human process and this could be utilised when it came to the design of systems and in the description of requirements. The client and the designer would find that they shared a common language which would assist in the understanding of the problem. In fact, this is probably a case of *after the event justification* because the origins of the object are to be found in the theoretical work on abstract data types [49], an attempt to bring some mathematical order to the programming chaos of the 1970s, and in a more cognitive analysis of the ways humans approach the understanding of a problem using object-like metaphors such as an icon, window, stream etc. [50]. Over the subsequent years these ideas have crystallised into the object-oriented paradigms of today. At no stage was there any emphasis on the development of models of business processes and problems. Because of its origins in programming rather than in applications we are in danger of recycling object-oriented solutions to the wrong problems. In [51] Sommerville and Sawyer remark on the use of object models in requirements capture and system modelling: "...because they [object models] are based on independent objects, the models do not give a clear

---

[1] In other types of engineering there is a fabrication phase, where the designer hands over the design to the technicians, who then build the artefact. This does not happen in software, where the engineer can be involved all the way from initial concept to the installation of the final product.

picture of end-to-end processing in the system." They go on: "...if you do not develop object-oriented programs, we do not recommend the use of object models. Making the transition from an object-oriented model to a system based on functions is not easy."

With so many different approaches to design notations, there has been an attempt to integrate some of the more popular techniques into a Unified Modelling Language [52] but the result looks more like a classic committee compromise solution than a coherent and usable mechanism for building a bridge between the problem and a solution. It is not a methodology as such, and much remains to be done before something emerges that can satisfy all the challenges that we are faced with. Existing attempts at constructing design methods still suffer from the problems of *algorithm neglect*, although things are beginning to change, and the work of Selic and colleagues [53] does address the issue of algorithm description through the use of state machines within objects.

## Formal methods

The issues of quality and correctness have also been approached through the use of *formal methods*. Here the solution is to develop rigorous techniques based on mathematical notations and to use these to specify the required system in a precise way which could then be analysed formally. It had a lot of good things going for it but has rarely delivered in practice. The problems arise in a number of ways. The notations were often outside the experience of many programmers and engineers, who may not have studied discrete mathematics. There was something unfriendly about the languages that was to prove an enormous obstacle to their use in industry. The notations were just that – notations. They were not explicit methods and many engineers who managed to learn the notations could not build specifications using the languages successfully because they did not know how to organise the task effectively. The notations were supported by some of the poorest software tools one is likely to meet – tools which were built by formal methods practitioners who did not practise what they preached. The user interfaces, in almost all cases[2], were and are appalling. There was also the belief that formally specifying the system and transforming this specification, using some mathematically-based transformation mechanisms, into code would result in a correct system. This is, of course, nonsense; it is impossible to formalise *fully* all the aspects of the operating environment of the system, the operating system functions, the hardware etc. so as to ensure that it functions correctly. *Testing still has to be carried out,* an important factor at the heart of our approach.

---

[2]The next generation of tools may be better; for example the VisualZ concept of an icon-based Z specification environment inspired by some of the visual programming languages has demonstrated that it is possible [54].

One of the unfortunate developments in the subject is the philosophy that the specification must not be influenced by the likely implementation. The reason given is that this would become a distraction from the purity of thought required to construct a correct specification. So the style tends to be one of defining, in an implicit way, the properties of what a function should do rather than trying to construct a definition of the function. This has a number of consequences. Firstly, it is erecting another barrier between the specification and the implementation that has to be overcome, possibly with difficulty, and secondly there may be important limitations that the implementation environment may impose on the solution, limitations that are not recognised in the specification. An example of this will be seen later.

The most positive aspect of the use of formal methods is that a specification, if correctly captured from the requirements, does offer a formal basis for analysing and understanding the proposed system better. It can be the basis for the construction of test sets but this can still be a problem, as we will see later. The most damning indictment of formal methods is the difficulty of applying them to industrial sized projects despite the fact that during the past 10 years almost all of the country's computing graduates have been taught formal methods and large amounts of research money have been spent on "industrial demonstrator projects". There have been some successes but there must still be something wrong with the approach if it has had such a small impact.

We will now turn to trying to overcome some of these problems and describe how it is possible to put the client and his/her problem (including the users) at the centre of the stage and introduce a formal mechanism for the capturing of the problem, the analysis of the problem, the construction and delivery of a *correct* solution. We will also lay the foundations for a genuine component-based approach, which does not suffer from the excessive testing demands of object oriented approaches, is firmly based on formal computational modelling and is yet practical and effective.

There are a number of important criteria that need to be considered when thinking about requirements modelling, analysis and design, in order to ensure that we develop correct systems – systems which work and solve the right problem. We will approach these criteria from the point of view of what sort of product a problem and system modelling method must produce.

## Principles for Correct Systems Design

The full model of the system or subsystem must be:

- sufficiently close to the client's/user's view of the business process that misunderstandings can be avoided;
- easily modified and developed in the light of changing requirements;
- amenable to mathematical analysis;
- suitable for the automatic generation of code;
- suitable for automatic functional test set generation.

Finally, we should ask ourselves whether a fully computerised solution is actually needed. For example, in one problem brought to us by a client who owned a chain of retail shops the most obvious solution was not necessarily the best. The issue was concerned with keeping a record of the hours worked by a large number of part-time sales assistants. Many of these were of a mature age and were not familiar with computers. There was also a very high staff turnover. The initial solution of a program which all assistants were to use to log their hours worked relied on the assumption that they could be trained to use the system. Subsequent analysis rejected a computerised interface in favour of one involving a pencil and paper and the use of computer readable cards for the key data entry.

## 2.3  BUSINESS PROCESS MODELS

There are many ways in which a business may be modelled, some of which have been made into methods supported by tools of various types, e.g. [55]. There is, however, a lack of precision about these techniques which makes them unsuitable for the sort of analysis that we wish to carry out. We will introduce an alternative and simple method which can be used to derive detailed models of the systems that we wish to build to support the business process. Many processes share the following common features (Figure 2.1):

- there is some *receipt* of information or data necessary for the process to operate;
- there are some aspects of the context of the business, internal knowledge of some sort;
- the process then *evaluates* the received data in the light of this context and produces or *generates* some resulting observable output, information or other product;
- the context is *revised* or updated ready for the next time that the process operates.

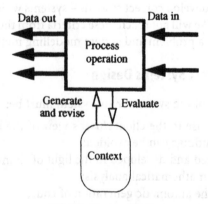

**FIG. 2.1.** A business process.

Examples of this might include the process of updating a customer's records, whereby the new information about the customer is fed into the process, the database provides the context and the output is the confirmation through printout or screen display that the record has been updated. The database updating is the context being revised in the light of the process operating. Another, higher level, example might be a factory receiving orders and raw materials, producing some artefact and delivering this to a customer together with an invoice. The context will include information about the way the factory operates and all the planning, management and production control systems that are involved.

If we can identify a set *Input* of data that it is possible to supply the process, a set *Output* of possible output data and a set *Memory* consisting of the internal context or data associated with the process, then we can model the business process as a *partial* function of the form:

$$\textbf{process: } Memory \times Input \rightarrow Output \times Memory$$

In the cases we consider here the sets *Memory, Input* and *Output* are all discrete, and with the possible exception of *Memory*, are finite.

*Definition 2.3.1*

A **business process** is a partial function of the form:

$$\textbf{process: } Memory \times Input \rightarrow Output \times Memory$$

where the sets *Memory, Input, Output* are defined for that specific process.

## Integrating Business Processes

A complete business will be made up of many interacting business processes and so we have to construct a more general model that will integrate all of these functions. The organisation will be such that at any one time there will be some, many or no processes operating. In some cases one par ticular process must be completed before another may begin and so the complete model must reflect this. The way to do this is to arrange the processes into a dynamic network where the interrelationships between them can be described. Before we can do this, however, we need to normalise the processes into a more uniform structure.

Suppose that there are a number of processes:

$$\textbf{process}_i\textbf{: } Memory_i \times Input_i \rightarrow Output_i \times Memory_i \text{ for } i = 1,...,n$$

We first consider the memory sets and orthogonalise them by forming the union of any two that overlap until we have a collection $\{Memory'_j\}$ for

$j = 1,...,m$ satisfying the property that the intersection of $Memory'_j$ and $Memory'_k$ is empty for $j \neq k$. Such a collection is called an *orthogonal memory set*.

Now we form the set $Memory' = Memory'_1 \times Memory'_2 \times... \times Memory'_m$. We also construct the sets $Input' = Input_1 \cup Input_2 \cup... \cup Input_n$ and $Output' = Output_1 \cup Output_2 \cup... \cup Output_n$.

Each process function **process**$_i$ can be transformed into a function:

$$\textbf{process}'_i: Memory' \times Input' \rightarrow Output' \times Memory'$$

by extending the definition to be:

$$\textbf{process}'_i((m'_1,...m'_i,...m'_n), input_i) =$$
$$(\textbf{proj}_1(\textbf{process}_i((m_i), input_i))), (m'_1,...$$
$$\textbf{proj}_2(\textbf{process}_i((m_i), input_i),...m'_n))$$

where **proj**$_1$ and **proj**$_2$ are the projection functions.

We can attempt to integrate all these process functions into an X-machine. This is dependent on the degree of parallelism and synchronisation that there is among the business processes. In the simplest case the functions become the basic functions of an X-machine model. We will call this an enterprise model.

*Definition 2.3.2*

An **enterprise model** is an X-machine whose basic functions are business processes. Clearly in this situation we require the *Memory, Input* and *Output* sets to be defined for the complete enterprise, which will be achieved, in many cases, by forming a global product from among the individual business process sets.

It is not always a simple task to put together a collection of business process functions into a coherent and coordinated enterprise machine model. In some complex cases it is better to construct a collection of enterprise models of subsystems of the complete organisation and then to construct a network of collaborating X-machine models. These may or may not synchronise easily with one another. This analysis may identify problems with the way the organisation operates and could suggest a mechanism for improving matters. The communication and synchronisation models built may be analysed to solve some of these problems. It might, for example, be necessary to restrict when some process can operate. Perhaps they should be shared by several enterprise machines, to ensure that the overall enterprise is working effectively. There are many complex issues in this area and it is not the focus for this particular investigation. We will assume that we are dealing with a coherent enterprise model; that is, one which can be represented as an X-machine.

Note that a business process can itself be representing an X-machine so we have a hierarchical situation which allows us to consider an enterprise as a collection of component business processes which are, in turn, enterprises and so on. This allows us to move between the macroscopic and the microscopic views of organisations, thus providing us with a coherent and flexible mechanism for modelling almost any organisation and its behaviour. So, we are contemplating the main ingredients of a business model from the perspective of computational processes and a potential computer-based solution. The use of computational models is crucial: if we cannot model some business process or enterprise as a computational model we will not be able to implement any solution relevant to the enterprise *faithfully*.

There are many aspects of any organisation or application that can be addressed in this way. In *all* cases there is data associated with the situation, and this can take many forms. This data is being processed in some way; *when* and *how*, is dependent on a number of environmental and other considerations, which can change over time. It is important that we recognise this as far as possible. Many of the processes will involve and depend on the activities of people in the business. We must think about the people who might be using the system. They will need to understand what is going on and what they are expected to do.

It may come as a surprise that this approach might also be applicable to applications in, for example, process and control engineering and in the design of microprocessors, but there are enough similarities to enable a common approach to work. We will call the modelling of the requirements and the environment of all these applications *business process modelling* (control engineering applications are as much a part of business as the banking and insurance industry!) and use the metaphors that we defined above in all of them. The next task is to try to see how the business processes and enterprise models might be constructed for a specific application.

One approach to identifying the business process is to try to identify scenarios of activities that take place during the operation of the business or application. For example, the creation of a new customer account in a sales office, the setting of an alarm clock as part of setting up a hi-fi system, the loading of a 32-bit data value in the register of a microprocessor all involve the creation and manipulation of data that can be done at certain moments and contexts within the system. We will look at some simple examples of these to see how they might be dealt with.

## 2.4 A SIMPLE BUSINESS PROCESS CASE STUDY

We will consider the development of a solution to the following problem, which is a simplification of a real business application that we managed.

The client has a business selling boxes and other products manufactured from metal. Customers supply a blueprint or detailed design drawings of the required items and the company then builds them to this specification. The problem that the client identified was the estimation of the cost of the customer's job. This was done by hand and involved the client's manager studying the blueprints, and working out the amount and type of sheet metal and other components required, together with the time and labour needed for the different types of manufacturing process – metal cutting, welding, polishing, painting etc. The estimate was achieved by looking up various tables containing the prices of the raw materials and the labour costs of the processes involved and formulating a total price for the job. The problems with the system was that it was very time consuming if the customer wanted any changes – for example, modifications to reduce the cost – then the process had to start again. Also, there was no connection with the production line management system or the stock control system – in both cases, the data for an estimate that had been accepted (and an order placed) had to be typed in by hand. The objective of the project was to build a simple to use system that would automate this process as far as possible and act as a database that could be connected to other systems, specifically the accounts, production management and stock control systems.

There were a number of non-functional requirements that had also to be considered, one being that the company had a PC network running Windows NT and the software needed to be compatible with this. This immediately restricted the implementation language options – as did the time available for building the solution. We will see later the effect that this had. Suffice it to say that it is another indication that the purist approach to formal specification – which demands that all implementation issues must be ignored during specification – is untenable in the real world for many applications. Other requirements were concerned with the user friendliness and efficiency of the tool. These sorts of requirements are often difficult to incorporate into the software development process and yet without achieving them the solution will be flawed: it cannot be correct if it fails to satisfy, for example, the criterion of user friendliness! However, we must consider how we might define these requirements in a precise way. This we will do shortly.

To make further progress we need to consider some of the typical scenarios that the estimator will be involved in. The following represent a number of business processes. Note that they are identified, initially, by the business person's view of the data, in general the equivalent of the sort of forms that may need to be filled in or changed, and the type of processing that these forms undergo.

2.4.1 New customers arrive with orders to estimate. A record therefore needs to be made of who the customer is, their address, phone numbers etc. and, usually, a unique customer reference number will be generated. Old customers may change their address, etc. and this also needs to be recorded.

2.4.2 The prices of sheet metal and other components as well as the cost of different production processes have to be recorded and updated from time to time, with a record kept of past prices.

2.4.3 The estimates for possible new jobs need to be created and, from time to time, updated.

2.4.4 A comprehensive help facility is also desired. This corresponds to the process of seeking assistance concerning the other processes.

So let us try to identify the sorts of data and processes that might be involved here. Traditional structured systems analysis and design methods tend to start with an analysis of the data using techniques such as data flow diagrams, which model process communication, and entity relationship diagrams, which describe the relationships between different types of data. In both cases the choice of which processes and data are regarded as the important aspects is a key one, and it is this that can introduce problems in the communication with the client. The client may not look at the business in the same way. In early object-oriented analysis the designer might start with a class of objects called **customers**, a class called **suppliers** and a class called **estimates**. These would then be defined with respect to the types of data and the methods that they might contain as a separate activity. By doing this we have already lost sight of the person at the heart of the process, the intended user of the system, something we want to avoid. We have also started looking at the system from a disembodied form as a collection of parts rather than as a coherent whole. The dynamic aspects of the system are missing and users will usually see their interaction with the business as being involved in tasks of a particular type at an appropriate time. In other words, we have sunk to too low a level too early in the game.

Modern object-oriented design techniques attempt to overcome these problems by introducing diagrams to help relate the class structures and through the use of use-case descriptions, which are like scenarios. This is an improvement but there are problems due to the nature of objects and how we tend to think about them. If really we want to reuse components we need to get the component idea well defined. A component must be fully specified and tested if it is going to be useful. This is rarely the case with classes and frameworks at present, and the embedding of a specific object from one application or library into another application is fraught and full of difficulties. The integration of the objects into the system is only loosely specified through the use-case information, and it is exactly this integration that needs to be precisely described at an early stage.

We want to emphasise the integrated nature of the system, the control structure of it, and approach it from the perspective of the user at all times. This will assist us in extracting and confirming the requirements of the system. The enterprise model of the system will thus emphasise the business processes we have identified together with their relationships. In a first model we would expect each business process to be carried out separately and be integrated through a single access process. We will try to look at these processes and their possible implementation through the eyes of the client or user. We are thus interested in what will be appearing on the screen during the operation. We will, first, design the screens to provide the client with a clear and concrete understanding of what is going on in the system. These screens will give us a "handle" on the processes that the client wishes to support with the solution. If we build the interface screens and produce a prototype of how the screens might appear and how the different parts of the system relate to one another we are more likely to be able to communicate effectively with the client and understand the business process better.

For the Estimator system this will entail developing the welcome screen to provide access to the different parts of the business processes. These have been identified from the scenarios as being the *creation and updating of the customer records,* the *creation and updating of the prices of the raw material and labour* and the *creation and updating of the individual orders.* There is also the need to introduce a *help system* at the beginning. We will restrict the help system to providing help for the customer records updating area only; it is easy enough to extend this to other parts of the system. Each of these models of the system will be accessed from the welcome screen by clicking on a suitably labelled button and this will determine the layout of the initial screen display and its role in the control of the process model and the system. This is illustrated in Figure 2.2.

Once a particular form (screen) has been accessed there will be specific types of processing applicable to each form. The more detailed models will reflect this. Thus, the enterprise X-machine model might be represented by the "state diagram" illustrated in Figure 2.3, where the circles indicate states and "superstates", which will be refined to a more detailed model later. Thus the **edit_cust, edit_order, edit_price** and **help_cust** operations represent business processes which will be refined into subsidiary models (X-machines) involving more detailed screens at a later stage. The diagram

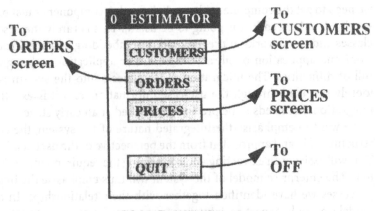

**FIG. 2.2.** The MAIN-MENU screen.

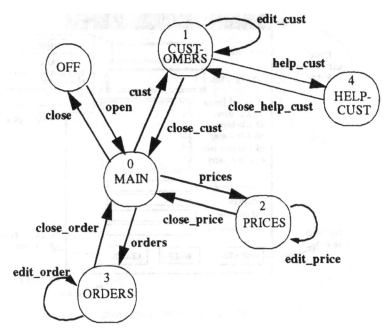

**FIG. 2.3.** The Estimator: top-level system design.

in Figure 2.3 is not yet a fully defined X-machine but it is part of the process of developing a model of the business process as interpreted through a computer-oriented context.

The interpretation of this diagram is that when in a given state, for example MAIN, the operation of the function **cust** will cause a state change to occur, resulting in a new screen which will provide the (business) processing required to deal with the creation or updating of the customer records. Initially this screen may contain blank entries coupled with a question as to whether the user wishes to open an existing customer record or create a new one. Perhaps something like Figure 2.4, where there is a "pop-up" menu under the name field to enable the user to choose between a new entry or the revision of a previous entry, would be appropriate.

The numbers in the angle brackets are data labels used in the specification and do not appear on the screen displays. Thus labels of the form <1.n>, <1.n.m> indicate data values that are provided in screen 1 at level n and sublevel m, respectively. This enables us to keep track of where data comes from during the design and analysis. Some of this data will be displayed on other screens; for example, <1.0> will appear on screen 3 also during the compilation of an order (see Figure 2.5). The critical point to remember is that each screen will have a set of data fields of given types associated with it.

The information contained in these fields will be part of the internal memory that the system in this superstate can have access to. While that

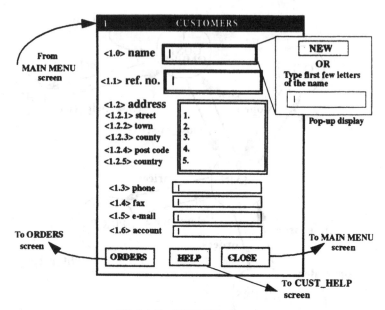

**FIG. 2.4.** The CUSTOMERS edit screen.

screen is active this information can be changed or enhanced using the appropriate functions defined by the X-machine that is representing this superstate.

This screen now identifies the type of data that is required for a customer entry. Each data entry field will have a type associated with it the complete set of data entry fields will form the structure of part of the internal memory of the system.

Note that the input required of the user is of two main types, the input of information to be stored or used in the processing and the input used for navigating through the system, so that pressing the button marked *CUSTOMERS* in Figure 2.1 is a navigation (or control) input entry whereas the entry of "J. Smith (Containers)" is a data entry for placing a specific type value in the <1> field of the customer records. Nearly all applications will involve these two different types of input. Such inputs require the existence of trustworthy low-level functions that can read suitable input events a button click, mouse movement, typed string of keyboard characters or a value supplied by an external device such as a sensor – and either use this event to generate a state transition or insert the information reliably into part of the internal memory. Since most programming languages offer well tested and used functions, procedures or objects to do this we will not concern ourselves with this level of detail in future. However, it is possible to build much lower level models to describe these operations using the methodology if one so desires. In a highly critical application this may be necessary.

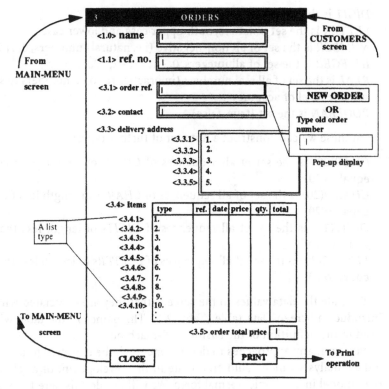

**FIG. 2.5.** The ORDERS edit screen.

The output from the system also needs some explanation. In many cases the outputs will be conveyed to the user by means of a screen display. The structure of this can be defined abstractly using a suitable convention which defines the required graphical elements of the display. In some applications the outputs will be commands or messages which are used to control other devices, for example in process control applications. Thus there are two types of common outputs – informational screen displays and control commands.

Figure 2.4 illustrates a possible first draft of a screen display for the customer edit screen. It is meant to be as similar as possible to the "paper" version that the client might be used to.

The types of data that might be entered in the slots provided need to be defined and named. This will help us to define the structure of our internal memory and thus the underlying database. The types of the various data entry values can be defined once we have introduced some standard notation, which we will keep as simple as possible. We need some basic types to start with:

*CHAR* is the set of all alphanumeric keyboard characters.
*CHAR@* is the set *CHAR* together with the symbol "@".

*DIGIT* is the finite set {0, 1, 2,3, 4, 5, 6, 7, 8, 9}.

*LETTER* is the set of letters, both upper case and lower case.

*NUMBER* is the set of all non-negative (i.e. natural) numbers, 0, 1, 2,.....

*INTEGER* is the set of all integers, 0, +1, −1, +2, −2,....

*REAL* is the set of all real numbers (in practice rational numbers to some suitable level of accuracy).

*BOOLEAN* is the set {true, false}.

From these we can construct a number of further types:

*CHAR*(20) is the set of all sequences of *CHAR*s of length less than or equal to 20.

*CHAR@*(20) is the set of all sequences of *CHAR* s of length less than or equal to 20

*DIGIT*(10) is the set of all sequences of *DIGIT*s of length less than or equal to 10.

*LETTER*(20) is the set of all sequences of *LETTER*s of length less than or equal to 20.

To relate the data values to the screens that they are associated with we introduce a Screen/Data table (Table 2.1). The names in the table will be used in the definition of the *customer* X-machine.

Now, in many approaches to design, one might be expected to carry out a data analysis which could culminate in the development of a relational data model in a suitable normal form. We will not do this here for a number of reasons. We question whether the benefits are worth the effort: as mentioned before, the improvements in speed and storage probably mean that the benefits are marginal, with the possible exception of massive distributed databases [46], which need special treatment anyway!

But another reason is the need to keep the model sufficiently simple to allow for its updating – the business is going to change frequently and so the business model will also change. It has been noted in many places that

**Table 2.1.** A Screen/Data table for the customer screen.

| Reference | Name | Type | Conditions | Screens |
|-----------|------|------|-----------|---------|
| < 1.0 > | Customer_name | CHAR(20) | N/A | 1, 3 |
| < 1.1 > | Customer_code | DIGIT(10) | length = 10 | 1, 3 |
| < 1.2 > | Customer_address | compound | N/A | 1 |
| < 1.2.1 > | number_and_street | CHAR(20) | N/A | 1 |
| < 1.2.2 > | town | LETTER(20) | N/A | 1 |
| < 1.2.3 > | county | LETTER(20) | N/A | 1 |
| < 1.2.4 > | postcode | CHAR(20) | N/A | 1 |
| < 1.2.5 > | country | LETTER(20) | N/A | 1 |
| < 1.3 > | phone | DIGIT(20) | N/A | 1 |
| < 1.4 > | fax | DIGIT(20) | N/A | 1 |
| < 1.5 > | e-mail | CHAR(20) | only one | 1 |
| < 1.6 > | account | CHAR(20) | N/A | 1 |

the key to success in the modern world is the ability to manage change effectively. The world is a highly dynamic, if not chaotic, organism and the ability to update our models simply and effectively is vital if we are not to build obsolescence into our methods and systems.

Our data model is as follows:

$$STORAGE =$$
$$CUSTOMER\_STORE \times PRICES\_STORE \times ORDERS\_STORE$$

where:

$$CUSTOMER\_STORE =$$
$$<1.0> \times <1.1> \times <1.2> \times <1.3> \times <1.4> \times <1.5> \times <1.6>$$

and

$$<1.2> = <1.2.1> \times <1.2.2> \times <1.2.3> \times <1.2.4> \times <1.2.5>$$

We will reserve a special value of this type: blank_customer_store, to represent a blank form on the screen for a new customer. The other components are:

$$ORDERS\_STORE =$$
$$<1.0> \times <1.1> \times <3.1> \times <3.2> \times <3.3> \times <3.4> \times <3.5>$$

(Similarly, blank_order represents a blank orders screen) (see Figure 2.4 for details) and *PRICES_STORE*, which will not be considered further here.

Suppose that we have to revise the data model in a significant way at a later date, for example the customer component may have to record whether the company was registered for sales tax. It is a simple matter to update the model and the screen to allow for a new parameter to represent this information. We just append to the product set of *CUSTOMER_STORE* the appropriate data type to cater for the new requirement. This is a simple example which does not create a major problem but more complex changes can also be dealt with in a similar manner without having to comprehensively redesign the relational or object data model of the business. For example, a more drastic change may occur if the client company decides to expand into exporting its products and the treatment of overseas customers requires different procedures and records. Perhaps a new screen for exports could be designed and accessed from the MAIN state, which would then be interfaced with the current system and the current database in a simple way, an issue we shall examine shortly.

The next stage is to assemble an X-machine description of the system. If we look at the top-level model state diagram (Figure 2.3) we can identify six states: OFF, MAIN, CUSTOMERS, HELP_CUST, PRICES, ORDERS. The processing functions are: **open, cust, close_cust, help_cust, prices, orders, edit_cust, edit_price, edit_order, close_price, close_order, close_help_cust.** The question we have to answer now is how do we define these functions?

Each function has a declaration, which must be of the form:

**function:** *Memory* × *Input* → *Output* × *Memory*

where *Memory, Input* and *Output* are defined suitably.

The *Input* set is relatively simple to define: we need to ask what are the inputs that make sense when considering the state diagram.

There is an input which corresponds to loading the program – let us denote that by the label *on*.

There is an input corresponding to the pressing of the QUIT button to close the program; we call this input *off*.

There is an input corresponding to pressing the CUSTOMERS button, and we will call that input *1*.

There is an input corresponding to pressing the PRICES button, which we will denote by *2*.

Similarly, we have inputs: *3, help_cust, close_1, close_2, close_3, cust_details, edit_price, edit_order, help, close_h.*

The **edit_cust, edit_order** and **edit_price** business processes will not be described in detail until we reach the next level of the design. They are considered as "atomic" operators at this stage.

So:

INPUTS =
  {*1, 2, 3, off, on, close_1, close_2, close_3, cust_details,*
    *edit_price, edit_order, help, close_h*}

What is the memory at this stage? We will construct the memory from two components – *STORAGE* and *SCREENS*, the latter component being used primarily to refresh the outputs. This is necessary because the stream X-machine model does not allow for outputs to be used as an input parameter by a processing function.

The *STORAGE* component has been described above and comprises a set of linear records describing the customers, the prices and the orders organised as a linear collection of linear records.

The *SCREENS* component is made up of the five screen displays with associated *slots* for presenting output information the data types associated with the screens. We will call these, for the time being, *screen*(CUST), *screen*(PRICES), *screen*(MAIN), *screen*(HELP_CUST), *screen*(ORDERS) and deal with the data output later. So:

SCREENS~ = {*screen*(CUST), *screen*(PRICES), *screen*(MAIN),
      *screen*(HELP_CUST), *screen*(ORDERS)}

where the notation ~= indicates an incomplete definition. Thus:

$$MEMORY = STORAGE \times SCREENS$$

The outputs will be *SCREENS* × *DATA* where *DATA* describes the format of the printed output from screens such as the ORDERS screen.

Now we can define the functions. Recall the notation we use:

**function_name**(*memory, input*) = (*output, memory'*) or in this case:

**function_name**((*storage, screens*), *input*) = ((*screens, data*), (*storage', screens'*)) and the convention that " – " is used as a "leave alone" symbol when the component is a memory value and Λ is a null output.

A diagrammatic notation like that shown in Figure 2.6 may be preferred. Thus:

> STATE-0 FUNCTIONS
> **open**((-, -), *on*) = ((*screen*(MAIN), Λ), -);

The **open** function simply sets up the system and displays the MAIN screen.

> **cust**((-, *screen*(MAIN)), *1*) ~ =
> ((*screen*(CUST),Λ), (*blank_customer*, *screen*(CUST)));

The **cust** function responds to the *customers* menu selection, the input *1*, and displays the blank CUSTOMERS screen with the database ready to accept the details input.

> **orders**((-, *screen*(MAIN)), *3*) ~ =
> ((*screen*(ORDERS),Λ), (*blank_order*, *screen*(ORDERS)));

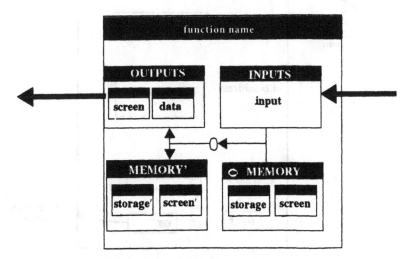

**FIG. 2.6.** Schematic for describing basic functions.

The **orders** function responds to the *orders* menu choice (input 3) and causes the ORDERS screen to be displayed ready for the input of an order.

> **prices** $((\text{-}, \textit{screen}(\text{MAIN})), 2) \sim =$
> $((\textit{screen}(\text{PRICES}), \Lambda), (\textit{blank\_price}, \textit{screen}(\text{PRICES})));$

The **prices** function does the same for the prices subsystem.

> **help\_cust** $((\text{-}, \textit{screen}(\text{MAIN})), \textit{help\_cust}) \sim =$
> $((\textit{screen}(\text{HELP\_CUST}), \Lambda), (\textit{blank\_help}, \text{screen}(\text{HELP\_CUST})));$

The **help\_cust** function displays the HELP\_CUST screen. Other help functions could be defined in a straightforward way, if required.

> **close**$(( \text{-}, \text{-} ), \textit{off}) \sim= (( \text{-}, \text{-}), \text{-})$

This function closes the system.

We cannot yet develop the other functions that loop back to their states until more details of the state screens are available. We can therefore look at the **edit\_cust** function as representing the overall operation of the CUSTOMERS screen, etc.

The next stage is to develop the state diagram for these screens. We will present the diagram for a slight simplification of the CUSTOMERS screen as an example (some of the data entry variables have been removed to prevent the process seeming too complicated at this stage).

The diagram of the simplified screen in Figure 2.7 has a number of features that should be commented upon. The address data entry has been described at a higher level since it needs to be broken down into five

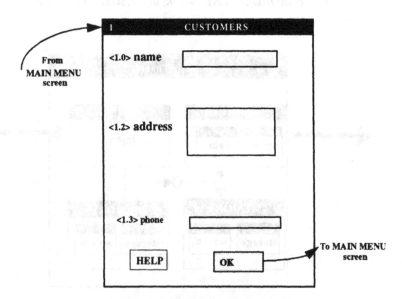

**FIG. 2.7.** The simplified CUSTOMERS edit screen.

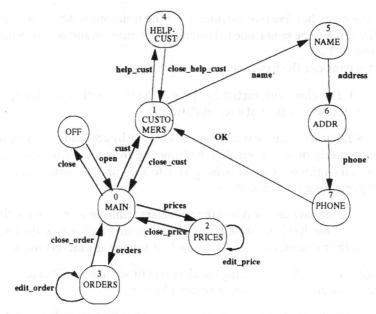

FIG. 2.8. A view of the Estimator system with edit_crust refined into a submachine.

specific data entry actions. This can be done through the expansion of the **address_edit** function as a subsidiary X-machine with five states in a similar manner to the way we decomposed the **edit_cust** function.

In Figure 2.8 we have expanded part of the system to reflect the activity in the CUSTOMER state. This is an example of model refinement, which we will look at in Chapter 4.

## 2.5 ANOTHER EXAMPLE OF A BUSINESS PROCESS AND ENTERPRISE MODEL

The previous system was based on a simple office process. The next model introduces the issue of time. We will consider a simple electronic alarm clock, illustrated in Figure 2.9. There are two modes of behaviour, user-independent time display and the user-dependent setting of the current time or the alarm time. These correspond to the four business processes described as follows.

FIG. 2.9. An alarm clock.

The clock has five buttons, one to set the time, one to set the alarm, one to increment the hours, one to increment the minutes and one to switch the alarm bell off.

We consider the basic scenarios or processes.

2.5.1 The clock automatically updates the time each second, displaying the current time at each update.

2.5.2. The user sets or resets the current time by accessing the time setting mechanism (by pushing the "time" button) and setting the hours and the minutes, then switching back to automatic timekeeping mode by releasing the "time" button.

2.5.3. The user sets or resets the next alarm time by accessing the time setting mechanism through the "alarm" button and setting the hours and the minutes, then switching back to automatic timekeeping mode.

2.5.4 The clock, on reaching the alarm set time, rings until the user cancels the alarm by pressing a suitable button.

These are the processes we have to integrate into an enterprise model. Note that one of these processes (2.5.1) involves a regular or *periodic* process, namely the updating of the clock at each "tick". Such a periodic process usually needs to be synchronised with all the other processes. Another similar example, that of a video cassette recorder, can be found in [39].

We need to consider, as before, the inputs, the outputs and the memory associated with these processes.

We will need to identify a data type to represent the time, which will be represented at this level by integers, and could be defined at a lower level by a model of the 24-hour clock.

So we define *TIME* as the basic type to represent time. The main operation that we can apply to this type is to increment it by one second according to the laws of the 24-hour clock, so we indicate the increment by $x + 1$.

For the inputs we have to have buttons that allow the user to access the different modes of the clock. Thus there is the time setting mode (call this T_SET), which is accessed when the input *time_button_on* occurs; the alarm setting mode (A_SET), accessed when the *alarm_button_on* event occurs; the actual time changing process, which involves feeding in a new time that will be any value $x$ in the set *TIME*; the button that cancels the alarm bell, the *cancel_alarm event*; together with an *on* switch and an *off* switch.

It also turns out that we need to inform the clock of when we have finished setting the time and the alarm. These will be *time_button_off* and *alarm_button_off* events (inputs). Finally, the passing of time, the ticking of the clock, must be represented by an automatically generated action or input called *tick*. This will update the memory and the display, and cause the alarm to sound when appropriate. So:

$INPUTS =$
$\{time\_button\_on, alarm\_button\_on, cancel\_alarm, on, off,$
$time\_button\_off, alarm\_button\_off, x \mid$
where $x$ is any value of $TIME$ $\}$

The outputs are the display (in hours and minutes) of the current time and the display of the set alarm time and the alarm ringing. We write $display(x)$ to indicate that the time value $x$ from $TIME$ is displayed on the clock face. So:

$OUTPUTS = \{display(x), alarm \mid$ where $x$ is any value of $TIME\}$

The memory needs to keep a record of the current time and the set alarm time. Thus:

$$MEMORY = CURRENT\_TIME \times ALARM\_TIME$$

where $CURRENT\_TIME = TIME$ and $ALARM\_TIME = TIME$. So:

$MEMORY = \{(x, y) \mid$ where $x$ and $y$ are any values of $TIME$

The top-level state diagram is shown in Figure 2.10.
The functions are defined in the following format:

**function_name** $(memory, input) = (output, memory);$

That is:

**function_name** $((x, y), input) = (output, (x', y'));$

Some specific examples are:

**time**$((x, y), tick) = (display\ (x + 1), (x + 1, y));$

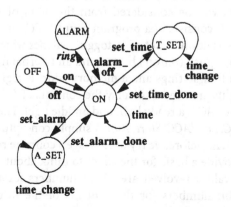

**FIG. 2.10.** Alarm clock top-level state diagram.

The passing of time is modelled by the time function, which is driven by the tick event.

$$\text{set\_time}((x, y), time\_button\_on) = (display\ (x + 1), (x + 1, y));$$

The time setting mode is accessed by the *time_button_on* event, and this is assumed to operate over a period of one second.

$$\text{time\_change}((x, y), x') = (display\ (x'), (x', y));$$

The time setting operation is achieved, once we are in the T_SET mode, by inputting the correct time $x'$. This is also assumed to take a second – an assumption that can be relaxed when the lower level details of this operation are considered.

$$\text{set\_time\_done}((x, y), time\_button\_off) = (display\ (x + 1), (x + 1, y));$$

The conclusion of the time setting process is modelled by the release of the time set button, i.e. the event *time_button_off*.

The other functions can be defined in a similar way.

## 2.6   A MICROPROCESSOR EXAMPLE

A common example of a simple microprocessor is the system described by Gordon [56]. We will show how this same system can be specified very simply using X-machines – see Bogdanov *et al.* for further details [57]. Harman and Tucker [58] also looked at this example and describe an alternative model based on synchronous algorithms and stream functions.

The approach taken in [57] went through a series of refinements, an issue that we will consider in a later chapter. Here we will describe the process model requirements and consider an initial model.

The system will be considered from the point of view of the micro-programmer. It consists of a program counter, *PC*, an accumulator, *ACC*, a set, *OP*, of instructions, a set of 16 toggle switches which define the data to be processed, a push (on/off) button and an internal memory store. There is a dial with four settings and a memory address register, *MAR*. A collection of 13 lights are used to display the contents of *PC*, 16 lights to display the contents of *ACC*, a ready light and an idle light. The dial has four positions: *LoadPC, LoadACC, Store, Run*. A simple, conceptual diagram is shown in Figure 2.11. As before, we try to envisage a concrete representation of the system to provide a basis for the client to think about the model.

The data values involved are 13 bit numbers for the contents of the *PC* and 16 bit numbers for the contents of the *ACC* and the memory store.

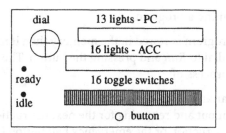

**FIG. 2.11.** A simple microprocessor control panel.

The *LoadPC* dial setting causes, when the push button is pressed, the binary value represented by 13 rightmost toggle switch settings to be stored in the *PC*. The *LoadACC* setting places the 16 values from the switches into the *ACC* when the button is pressed. The *Store* setting replaces the contents of the memory location specified by the *PC* with the contents of the *ACC* when the button is pressed. The *Run* setting starts the execution of the program at the memory location specified by the *PC* when the button is pressed.

There are a number of instructions carried out by the computer as described in Table 2.2.

There are two main business processes involved: (i) writing a program and storing it in the memory and (ii) running a stored program. When the machine is switched on the dial can be set to a value and the toggle switches operated.

The scenarios:

Part A: Writing a program. This is achieved by setting the toggle switches and then using these and the dial functions to place values in suitable places.

2.6.1 If the dial is set to *LoadPC* then the value represented by the toggle switches is placed in the *PC* when the button is pressed.

2.6.2 If the dial is set to *LoadACC* then the value represented by the toggle switches is placed in the *ACC* when the button is pressed.

2.6.3 If the dial is set to *Store* then the value represented by the toggle switches is placed in the PC.

**Table 2.2.** The microprocessor's instructions.

| Instruction | Code | Effect |
| --- | --- | --- |
| HALT | 000 | Stops execution |
| JMP L | 011 | Jumps to memory location L |
| JZERO L | 010 | Jumps to memory location L if ACC is zero |
| ADD L | 011 | Adds contents of memory location L to ACC |
| SUB L | 100 | Subtracts contents of memory location L from ACC |
| LD L | 101 | Loads contents of memory location L into ACC |
| ST L | 110 | Stores contents of ACC in memory location L |
| SKIP | 111 | Skips to next location |

Part B: Running a program.

2.6.4  If a program is stored in the memory then it may be executed by setting the dial to *Run* and pressing the button. The process then goes through a process of:

- fetching an instruction;
- carrying it out and returning for the next instruction; until it reaches the halt instruction or the emergency halt button (*B_halt*) is pressed.

A simple first-stage enterprise model is illustrated in Figure 2.12.

In this model we have slightly expanded process 2.6.4 to show some extra internal structure which describes the basic fetch–execution cycle of the system since this was detailed in the process description.

The process functions can be defined once we have specified appropriate *Input, Memory* and *Output* sets.

$$MEMORY = PC \times ACC \times READY \times IDLE \times MAR \times MEM \times OP$$

where *PC* is the set of 13 bit words giving the contents of the program counter; *ACC* is the set of 16 bit words, the accumulator contents, l(*acc*) means the three leftmost bits of the word *acc* and r(*acc*) is the 13 rightmost bits of *acc* $\in$ *ACC*; *OP* is the set of 3 bit words representing instructions; *READY* = {0, 1} where 1 means the ready light is on and 0 means it is off; *IDLE* = {0, 1} where 1 means the idle light is on and 0 means it is off; *MAR* is the set of 13 bit words which can be put in the memory address register; *MEM* is the set of functions from *MAR* to *ACC*.

$$INPUT = SWITCHES \times DIAL \times BUTTON$$

where *SWITCHES* is the set of 16 bit words obtained from the 16 switches on the console; *DIAL* = {1, 2, 3, 4} with 1 meaning *Load-acc*, 2 *Load-pc*, 3 *Store* and 4 *Run*; *BUTTON* = {0, 1} where 1 signifies that the button is pressed and 0 that it is not pressed.

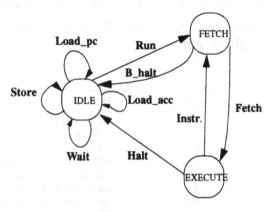

**FIG. 2.12.** A microprocessor.

$$OUTPUT = PC \times ACC \times ROUT \times IOUT$$

where *ROUT* describes the appearance of the *READY* light and *IOUT* that of the *IDLE* light.

Two sample process functions are given next, one related to the activity of writing a program and the other describing how a specific operation will work when a program is executed.

**Load_pc**$((pc, acc, 1, 1, addr, mem, op), (sw, 2, 1)) =$
$((r(sw), acc, 1, 1), (r(sw), acc, 1, 1, addr, mem, op));$

Thus, the **Load_pc** function takes the rightmost 13 values from the switch input and places them in the *PC*, with the rest of the memory unaffected, and outputs the information through the lights.

**Sub**$((pc, acc, 0, 0, addr, mem, SUB), (sw, d, 0)) =$
$((pc+1, acc\text{-}mem(r(mem(addr))), 1, 0),$
$(pc+1, acc\text{-}mem(r(mem(addr))), 1, 0, pc, mem, SUB))$

The **Sub** function takes the value of the memory at the address given by the 13 rightmost digits obtained from the element of memory at the address given by *addr* and subtracts this from the current value of the *ACC*, placing this new value in the *ACC*. The program counter is incremented by one.

## 2.7  IMPLEMENTATION

The effort made to construct a formal computational model of the system is not in vain. We will understand the business processes and the potential solutions much better once this has been done. We also have a precise statement of what the system should be, something that will be invaluable when it comes to establishing the correctness of any implementation. Not only can we use it as a reference point for evaluating particular implementations but, as we shall see in the next chapter, this description can be used as the basis for a powerful testing strategy. In fact, the complete test sets can be generated automatically from the X-machine description.

That is not all, however. The specification can also be turned into a operational implementation very easily. Eventually it will be possible to build a suite of tools that can be used to create and edit X-machine specifications, generate complete functional test sets for the specification and generate executable implementations automatically. (In fact, prototype tools already exist to do this.) If we examine how an implementation can be built we will see how valuable it was to think about algorithms at an early stage. Depending on the programming language chosen, the task of developing the code can be straightforward.

If the implementation is in a standard imperative language such as Pascal, the basic functions can be implemented more or less directly from the function definitions as procedures that produce the required outputs and memory updates. The states are implemented as procedures with IF statements corresponding to the transitions from that state.

In an object-oriented language such as C$^{++}$ the memory is implemented as a set of global variables accessible by all the basic functions. These, also, were simply implemented using the definitions. The explicit control structure of the model allows for a straightforward architecture which can be built with little effort and a very high level of confidence.

A number of systems have been built using the technique in several different languages. The effort required to complete the implementation, given the specification, was quite slight. In Chapter 5 we will look at one of these case studies in more detail. The system described there was built and installed for a client's business. A high quality user interface was required and a very robust system was developed in a relatively short time.

# 3 Testing, Testing, Testing!

*Summary. Testing, correctness, quality-oriented testing, when test-ing is done, finite state machine testing, X-machine testing, design for test, the fundamental theorem, reflections and conclusions.*

All software systems are subject to testing – for some of them testing is the major activity in the project. Testing, however, rarely gets the attention it deserves from researchers and developers, partly because its foundations are very weak and ill-understood. The principal purpose of testing is to detect (and then remove) faults in a software system. A number of techniques exist for carrying out testing, and in particular for the generation of test sets. Many sophisticated (and expensive) tools are available on the market and many look to these to provide a solution to the problems of building fault-free systems. We consider the problem of fault detection and note that few, if any, of the existing methods address the real issues. In particular, no methods allow us to make any statement about the type or precise number of faults that remain undetected after testing is completed. Thus we cannot really measure the effectiveness of our testing activities in any rigorous way. However, by considering testing from a straightforward, theoretical point of view we demonstrate that a new method for generating test cases can provide a more convincing approach to the problem of detecting *all* faults and allows us to make sensible claims about the level and type of faults remaining after the testing process is complete.

## 3.1 WHAT IS TESTING?

The purposes of software testing have been discussed in a number of places and we will consider a few of the interesting statements and claims that have been made about testing.

Myers [8] states that the purpose of testing is to *detect* faults and the def-inition of a good test is one that *uncovers* faults, the implication clearly being that a test that fails to uncover any existing faults is inadequate in some sense. This emphasis on the finding of faults could lead one to assume that the more faults detected, the better the test. However, one could argue that a test that uncovers a single serious fault might well be more successful than a test that uncovers a number of trivial faults. This immediately leads us into the vexed question of what is a "serious fault" and how these might be defined and identified.

Dijkstra [59] pours scorn on the whole concept of testing, stating that "Program testing can be used to show the presence of bugs, but never to show their absence!" This is true of most of the testing methods currently in use and is clearly a major drawback. Dijkstra's belief, shared by many in the formal methods community, is that formal verification, that is mathematical proofs that the system meets all the conditions required of it, is the only solution. However, the massive complexity of today's applications seems to be beyond the capability of these techniques. Researchers have not demonstrated that formal verification is "scalable" and practical in the context of current needs. It is also clear from a number of surveys that many of the notations, techniques and concepts of formal methods are regarded as very difficult to use. The quality of many tools to support the methods is often poor. Furthermore, some example systems that have supposedly been formally verified have been shown to have faults as a result of testing (see [60]).

There is another issue, if we are really interested in building correct systems. The clients and users need to be able to confirm that the specification is correct. This is impossible if it is written in a complex mathematical notation that they do not understand. If the specification is wrong, no amount of formal verification will deliver a correct system.

## Types of Testing Strategy

Testing techniques can be summarised as falling into three main categories: *functional testing, structural testing* and *random testing.* In a sense these are distinguished by the sort of information that is used to generate a test set. A test set is a set of input sequences, or test vectors, that can be applied to the system to establish its behaviour. Given such a test set, it is necessary to have some idea of what the correct response of the system should be. Thus testing, in its simplest form, involves applying the test vectors to the implementation and deciding if the resulting behaviour is what is required. This process needs to be support supported by a variety of test tools in a suitable environment, so test generation tools have to be used alongside test application systems, test oracles and test evaluation tools.

Functional (or black box) testing (see, for example, [61]) should start with a functional specification or description of how the desired system should behave. The test set is then constructed on this basis and the result of applying the test set is evaluated and compared with the desired result deduced from the specification. It is difficult to construct test sets from informal specifications it has to be done by hand. Some attempts have been made to use formal specifications, for example written in Z [62, 63], VDM [64] and OBJ [65], as a basis for automatically generating test sets but without a great deal of success. It seems reasonable to assume, however, that basing testing on functional testing using a precise formal specification is likely to be the most effective and trustworthy approach.

Structural (or white box) testing (see [66]) is based on the design of the implementation. If one has to use a tool to generate a very large set of test vectors it necessitates the use of a formal description of the system that can be input into the test generation tool. In the absence of a formal specification the only thing available is the source code of the application under test. This can also be used for static analysis, a process which can provide a lot of information about the construction and behaviour of the implemented software [67]. Structural testing techniques usually involve the analysis of the flow of activity in the program and can be based on finding suitable test vectors that will exercise different parts of the code in various ways, such as ensuring that every decision point is visited at least once, that every procedure is called at least once etc. The coverage of the test is then calculated on the basis of this type of analysis. The fundamental objection to this type of method is that it assumes that the code is sufficiently close to the requirements that it it can detect enough faults to provide some confidence that the system is correct. However, it is not possible to make this final deduction: there is no inductive link between the code and the specification; in fact, there is no detailed specification in most cases, just informal language descriptions of desired behaviour.

Random testing proceeds on a different basis [68]. The input domain is specified as best as it can and the random test generation tools then generate test vectors in a random way. It is possible to finesse the method if knowledge of the probability distribution of the likely inputs is available. The test evaluation process is then based on evaluating the program behaviour on the basis of an informal specification.

A number of experiments have been carried out to try to establish which of these methods is the most effective – in the complete absence of any theoretical foundation which might predict this. Typically the experiment will involve a small piece of code which is seeded with known faults, and the success of the different methods in detecting these faults is measured. Further analysis could be done on the type of faults each method was good or poor at detecting. Faults are classified for this purpose in a number of categories. Results from this type of survey can be useful in establishing the relative strengths and weakness of different, specific methods of test set generation. However, the situation is essentially artificial and it is not clear what can be said in general. The method is unable to prove, for example, that either approach is better at detecting naturally occurring or unseeded faults (the seeded ones may not be typical of real faults), or to identify conditions under which a method detects all faults. Thévenod-Fosse and Waeselynck [69], for example, concluded that the most successful approach involved the use of a combined functional and statistical approach. Reid [70] demonstrated that boundary value testing (a type of functional testing) was the most successful. We will comment on some of our experiments later in this chapter.

## 3.2   FUNDAMENTAL ISSUES OF CORRECT SYSTEM DESIGN

There is a case for hoping that building systems from *dependable components* will overcome some of the problems of building correct systems, and it may be possible that current testing or formal verification methods can be used *together* to provide the foundation for a scientifically based engineering approach to software development. At present, however, there is little sign of this happening. The software engineering industry is spending more and more time on testing in the hope of ensuring quality and yet real scientific evidence that they are being successful is minimal.

The subject of reuse and object-oriented design methods are areas where great hopes have been expressed for a genuine component-based approach to software construction. The libraries of classes that have become available, however, have often been a disappointment. It is hard to establish what the specifications of the components in these libraries are; worst still, the software extracted often behaves in an unpredictable way when integrated into a new system. These object-oriented methods are often held to be a great advance in the pursuit of quality software because of their supposed foundation on the principle of software or code reusability. However, it is pointed out in Binder [15] that, far from obviating the need for so much testing, the object-oriented methods require very substantial amounts of effort devoted to the task. Inheritance and dynamic binding provide many opportunities for introducing faults, the large numbers of interfaces between objects and the loose state control environment also compound the problem. Binder states "the hoped for reduction in object-oriented testing due to reuse is illusory". In fact, many new testing issues are raised by this paradigm. As a result the need for testing will undoubtedly grow and the industry will become more and more dependent on the successful pursuit of this activity.

One could argue that our current testing methods are not based on a firm scientific approach or theory; they tend to be methods that have evolved, informal *ad hoc* approaches that have been rationalised after the event rather than carefully constructed engineering methods based on a defensible, well-founded strategy. We test because we need to but we do not demand from testing the sort of rigour that the product demands. Testing must be made more to do with reassuring *clients* and *users* than with reassuring *testers, designers* and their *managers!* We must focus on *test effectiveness* rather than test *effort*.

One of the claims made here and elsewhere is that this will not be possible unless there is a more integrated approach to the design process, and until the testing methods used satisfy some fundamental requirements dictated by a careful investigation of the nature of software systems.

Although it might appear that we are belittling the achievements of software testing as a process, this is not the intention. Clearly the application of existing testing methods has resulted in the identification and subsequent removal of many important faults in software systems. However, the question remains about what faults are left undetected until the system is in service. It is to try to address this issue that we now turn.

One of the most successful approaches to scientific understanding is the *reductionist* philosophy. This entails the reduction of one problem to the solution of simpler ones or to the understanding of a lower level, perhaps more microscopic, situation. Since the current popular design methods in software engineering tend to emphasise the construction of systems from modules, objects and other simpler components one might hope that a similar reductionist approach to testing might be possible. This is not addressed by the different techniques of unit test and system/integration test or the test management process; it is much more fundamental than that. In such a reductionist approach we would consider a system and produce a testing regime that resulted in the *complete* reduction of the test problem for the system to one of looking at the test problem for the components or reduced parts. However, few testing methods support this view since we would have to be able to make the following statement:

> the system $S$ is composed of the parts $P_1,..., P_n$; as a result of carrying out a testing process on S we can deduce that S is fault-free *if* each of $P_1,..., P_n$ is fault free.

Here we define fault-free in the natural sense – that is, the system completely satisfies the behavioural requirements as detailed in the specification. A prerequisite is that the specification should be available as some formal, mathematical description to ensure that we can actually establish what the requirements are in an unambiguous sense. The exercising of tests on the system $S$ involves the testing of the complete system, its internal and external interfaces as well as the components $P_i$.

A corollary is that the approach could be applied to each component $P_i$, thus enabling the reductionist method to be continued downwards for as far as is appropriate and feasible. Ultimately we might end up at a point where the components in question are *tried and trusted*, having been extensively analysed and used over a number of years and thus having survived through a process of "natural selection".

## Fault Detection

For this approach to work we need to find some mechanism whereby we can establish that if all the components are free from fault then so is the complete system. This is something that is quite beyond most current

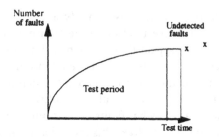

**FIG. 3.1.** The relationship between fault detection and test time.

testing methods. The claim "the system/component is fault-free" is not sustainable. In practice, all we can usually say is that we have uncovered a number of faults over a period of testing effort and the graph of the number of faults against the period or amount of testing, measured suitably, indicates that the *growth rate* is reducing (see Figure 3.1).

The trouble is, we do not know that *no* further faults are in the system at any particular time. Also, in general we cannot assert that the only faults remaining are located in a specific module or component. A general formula for this curve is not known. If one existed it would probably depend on the type of system, on the type of test methods and perhaps on the people doing and managing the testing as well as wider issues relating to the management of the design project, the attitudes of the clients, the implementation vehicle, the design methods and so on. High quality empirical results obtained over a very long period would be needed to make proper use of this approach. Even then, it is less than ideal. The work of Littlewood and Strigini [71] provides some statistical approaches to the question of software reliability but in some senses it is used as substitute because of the failure of software testing to deliver methods able to provide precise answers to the question "what faults are left?".

## Probable Correctness

Hamlet [72] introduced the idea of "probable correctness". Essentially, he considered the question of what we can say once a system has "passed" all the tests applied to it. He argued from a simple probabilistic point of view about the way in which a value could be placed on the likelihood of faults remaining in the system. This is an attractive idea that deserves more research. Hamlet's discussion was based on a number of very restrictive assumptions about the distribution of faults in the system and there is no discussion of the type and seriousness of faults. After all, if the likelihood of any faults remaining was quite small, say $1.0 \times 10^{-5}$, then we may or may not be satisfied but it would be so much more reassuring if we could say that the likelihood of a *serious* fault was $1.0 \times 10^{-10}$, however we define serious – perhaps we might identify certain safety considerations that must be met and orient our tests towards uncovering faults that cause these to be violated. We may not mind too much if a screen display omitted a full-stop in some text. On the other hand, if the display was giving instructions on medical dosage to paramedics a missing full-stop (decimal point) could be disastrous. So the importance of a fault depends on the application and the working environment. Treating all faults as of equal import is an unsatisfactory basis for this type of argument.

## A Simple Theory of Testing

Goodenough and Gerhard [73] introduce an outline theory for testing. They treat a software system as a (partial) function from an input set to an output set, and the testing process consists of constructing "revealing domains" that expose faults in this function – in other words, they are looking for values for which the specified function and the implemented function differ. This is a very general and abstract approach which provides a useful set of simple concepts and terminology for the discussion of some aspects of testing without giving too many clues as how to construct effective testing strategies.

We claim, therefore, that few of the existing testing methods measure up to our demands and the main theoretical attempts are inadequate for the purpose that we explained above – the philosophy of reductionist testing.

## When Testing is Done

Eventually the test phase must end and the product be released. When should this be and what will we be able to say about the quality of the system that we deliver once testing has ended? If our core objective is that the system we are releasing has as few faults as possible then we need to be able to have some estimate of the number and type of faults that may remain once testing has ended. Suppose that we have applied our test process to the product with the result that the system has passed all of the tests in the final test phase. We would like to claim that the system is now fault free but this is going to be very hard to justify. We might try to estimate this important quality of the product – that is, its freedom from faults – by measuring some attribute of the test process – typically its coverage. However, the relationship between test coverage and the location of faults is complex and unclear. It is possible to have a high test coverage which fails to detect crucial faults, faults which could be detected using a test strategy with a much lower coverage. In the absence of a detailed and precise functional specification the tests may not be detecting crucial functional faults anyway, since we may not have a clear idea of what these are! So we are faced with a number of dilemmas: we need to plan our testing strategy so that we can produce software of sufficient quality in an economic way and we need to know when we have achieved this quality target. In other words, we need to be able to decide whether our test strategy is adequate and when our testing can end – but how can we relate this to our quality aspirations?

Most decisions on the test strategy to be used in a project are based on the available information we have about the system under test and on the tools that are to hand. Under these conditions decisions on when to terminate testing will be made on the basis of: time running out (delivery pressures); money running out (economic pressures); personnel becoming unavailable (management pressures) and so on. None of these are a suitable basis for quality-oriented decisions. Quality-oriented testing is testing that relates to the issue of what faults remain after testing and where they may be located. We may try to rationalise the situation by collecting data on the detection of faults during the test process and use some rough reliability model for estimating the number of remaining faults but it is rare that these are accurate and we will not know anything about the severity or location of the faults remaining. This must compromise the quality of our product. The "saving grace" is that it is the same for everyone and so our competitive edge is not threatened, since other companies do not have access to test methods that can overcome these problems. Or do they?

## 3.3   AN APPROACH TO QUALITY-ORIENTED TESTING

### Some Practical Considerations

Let us try to identify the sort of approach that might break through these limitations. First we have to define what the system we are testing is supposed to do. In other words, we need a precise and complete statement of its functional requirements. This is hard enough but without it we are already in trouble. If the information we are putting into the testing process is incomplete then the outcome cannot compensate for this weakness. In other words, if we do not know what a system is supposed to do how can we establish whether it does it?

Formal specification languages, the academics' solution to this problem, have promised much and delivered little, primarily due to their unusability and their inability to scale up to industrial problems. It is possible to develop formal descriptions from the popular diagrammatic techniques if they are annotated suitably – see, for example, Chantatub and Holcombe [74] – and purely visual versions of the formal language Z have been developed with powerful and user-friendly tools [75].

The next requirement is a method for generating complete functional test sets from this specification. Most attempts at doing this, such as those based on Z, VDM and OBJ, still fail under the requirement of being able to say something about the faults that remain when testing stops since they are based on techniques such as category-partition and similar approaches (when generating test sets we have to make random or at best statistics driven choices, which cannot guarantee that all faults have been covered). The test generation process can be continued indefinitely without any guarantee that the fault detection capability of the test set is increasing in a commensurate manner. We may know what the system is supposed to do but we cannot say anything about when to stop testing and what faults may remain using these techniques.

The next issue is that of refinement. Most systems are constructed from components, and in the brave new world of Java these may be applications, applets, objects, classes etc. chosen from a variety of sources and integrated, possibly at run time, into a complete, dynamic software system. Some of these components may be highly reliable – tried and trusted – and to all intents and purposes can be regarded as fault free under suitable conditions. We would like to have a testing strategy that exploited this situation, which detected *all* possible faults in the integration (top-level system) and which had a clear termination. Subsequent testing of the components is then carried out in an appropriate way – if a particular component is not tried and trusted then it can be broken down into simpler components and its integration fully tested, with the subcomponents themselves being tested separately and so on. If a genuine market in components emerges and enough information about the reliability (correctness) of these components is available – together with a formal description of their functionality – then this will represent a major advance in the quest for software quality at an economic cost. The next chapter considers these issues further.

Finally, we need to develop an approach that is not too intrusive in terms of the in-house methods and tools used. One of the weaknesses of academic research into software engineering is that it usually comes up with a novel series of methods, involving new and often difficult languages, which have little relationship with what industry currently does and uses, and supported, if at all, by poorly built and conceived tools. The expectation is that industry will see the benefits of the new, untried, methods and will completely reorganise, retrain and retool to utilise them. Unfortunately this is a high-risk strategy and is unlikely to be a serious option. The expense, disruption and risk associated with such a strategy would deter even the most adventurous company.

## 3.4 TESTING BASED ON A COMPUTATIONAL MODELLING APPROACH

The process of software design, including within that activity all phases of requirements capture, specification, design, prototyping, analysis, implementation, validation, verification and maintenance, is one that is oriented, or should be, around the construction of computational solutions to specific problems.

## A Fundamental Strategy

When we are constructing a software system (this also applies to hardware) we are attempting to construct something that will, when operating, carry out some computable function. Consequently it is worth considering what this means. Essentially, computable functions have been identified as the functions computed by Turing machines. The only assumption we will make is that whatever implementation we produce, it can be considered to behave like a Turing machine that halts. In other words we will not try to deal with those systems that regress into an infinite loop from which no output emanates. For our purposes these systems will be deemed to be unacceptable anyway. A way to establish that a system is not of this form is to identify a period of time which is the maximum that the system can run without producing any detectable output. We will also assume that the specification of the system is also of this form, namely a Turing machine that halts under its intended operating conditions. Real-time systems are covered by this definition since we require that the specified system does have detectable behaviour under all conditions. This is a kind of *design for test* condition that we will see more of later.

We then have two algebraic objects, the Turing machine representing the specification of the desired system and the Turing machine representing the complete implementation. A testing method would then try to ascertain if these two machines computed the same function. This is a basic strategy that we will develop, although not in the context of a Turing machine, which is too low level and unwieldy, but in the context of a more useful, elegant and equivalent model.

In so doing we will quote some important theoretical results that justify what we are doing. It is important to stress that the method of finite state machine testing proposed by Chow [76], and developed by a number of other authors since, e.g. [77], is based on a similar sort of philosophy, the difference being that they have to make very strong assumptions about the nature of the implementation machine. However, their work did act as an important inspiration for our own.

## Finite State Machines Revisited

Finite state machines have been a popular and effective way of specifying and designing a number of different types of system. For example, simple control systems and real-time systems are often described in this way, as are hardware devices – particularly sequential systems and some aspects of microprocessors. The ease with which finite state machines can be used to convey the dynamics of user interaction in elementary menu systems has been exploited in many examples. The definition of a number of protocols for communications systems as finite state machines is also standard practice. The control structure of simple software systems can also be described using this modelling technique, and automatic generation of executable code is possible in some simple cases. Often these machines are used in conjunction with other methods, for example in systems analysis they are often combined with data modelling techniques.

Some of the advantages of finite state machines as a specification language are:

- they are intuitive, being based on a simple, dynamic model of computation;
- they can be represented in convenient ways such as diagrams and tables;
- a lot is known about the theory of these machines;
- many people have met them in university courses.

There are a number of disadvantages, which we will discuss later.

We begin with a restatement of a basic definition.

### Definition 3.4.1

A *finite state machine with outputs* consists of:

- A finite set $Q$, of internal states;
- An initial state, $q_0$;
- A finite set *Input*, of inputs;
- A finite set *Output*, of outputs;
- A next state function $F: Q \times Input \rightarrow Q$;
- An output function $G: Q \times Input \rightarrow Output$.

Typically, finite state machines are described using diagrams or tables.

We will sometimes say $\mathcal{M} = (Q, Input, Output, F, G, q_0)$ is a finite state machine with outputs.

### Example 3.4.1

Consider a simple machine with four states (Figure 3.2).

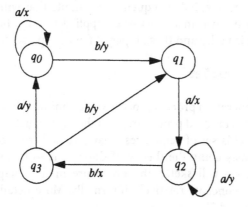

**FIG. 3.2.** A simple finite state machine.

Let $Input = \{a, b\}$ and $Output = \{x, y\}$

Recall from Chapter 1 the convention in the diagram where the arrows and their labels indicate the functions **F** and **G**. For example, the arrow labelled by $b/y$ from state $q_0$ to $q_1$ tells us that:

$$F(q_0, b) = q_1$$
$$G(q_0, b) = y$$

We might regard $q_0$ as an initial state, perhaps corresponding to an idle or off state in a system.

If the system is started in state $q_0$ and supplied with an input of $a$, the machine outputs $x$ and remains in $q_0$; if presented with an input $b$ while in state $q_0$ it moves to state $q_1$ and outputs $y$, and so on.

Putting in a stream of inputs, say $a::b::a::b::a::b$, the result is a transversal of the diagram to state $q_1$ producing, along the way, the output stream $x::y::x::x::y::y$. If there is a state where a given input produces no result the machine will halt, e.g. $a::b::b$ starting from $q_0$ halts in state $q_1$ after the second input is read.

## Testing Based on Finite State Machines

The basic idea is that we have a specification described in terms of a finite state machine. We also have an implementation which we wish to establish is correct with respect to the specification. If we can assume that the implementation is also a finite state machine then we reduce the verification problem to establishing whether the two finite state machines – the specification and the implementation – behave in an identical manner.

There is some theory that can assist in this task [76]. The essential ideas are based around deriving sequences of inputs that can detect whether there are any extra states or missing states in the implementation, whether there are any faulty or missing transitions and so on. The method proceeds by constructing suitable sequences of inputs that will produce different outputs in the two machines when applied to them both – if the implementation is faulty and these types of fault are present.

## Constructing a Test Set

The test generation process proceeds by examining the state diagram, minimising it (a standard procedure) and then constructing a set of sequences of inputs. This set of sequences is constructed from certain preliminary sets, the basis being the theory of Chow. It is to this work that we must now turn. We will sketch the procedure in this chapter, introducing a number of concepts relatively informally. More details can be found in Chapters 6 and 7.

## Definition 3.4.2

Let $L$ be a set of input sequences, and $q, q'$ two states, then $L$ is said to *distinguish* between $q$ and $q'$ if there is a sequence $k$ in the set $L$ such that the output obtained when $k$ is applied to the machine in state $q$ is different to the output obtained when $k$ is applied when it is in state $q'$. If the two states $q$ and $q'$ are not distinguished by $L$ we say that they are *L-equivalent*.

## Definition 3.4.3

A machine is called *minimal* if it does not contain redundant states. The formal definition is Definition 7.1.6.

There are algorithms that produce a minimal machine from any given machine. The minimal machine has the same behaviour in terms of input–output as the original.

## Example 3.4.2

In the machine shown in Figure 3.3 states $q_1$ and $q_2$ can be *merged* to form a machine with fewer states and the same input–output behaviour.

Let us consider, from now on, a minimal finite state machine.

## Definition 3.4.4

A set of input sequences, $W$, is called a *characterisation set* if it can distinguish between any two pairs of states in the machine.

## Example 3.4.3

In the machine in Example 3.4.1 $W = \{a, b\}$ is a characterisation set (the machine is minimal).

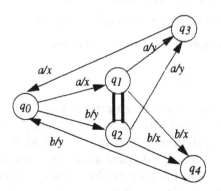

**FIG. 3.3.** A simple finite state machine which is not minimal.

*Definition 3.4.5*

A *state cover* is a set of input sequences $L$ such that we can find an element from $L$ to get into any desired state from the initial state $q_0$.

$L = \{< >, b, b::a, b::a::b\}$ is a state cover for the machine in Example 3.4.1; $< >$ represents the null input.

*Definition 3.4.6*

A *transition cover* for a minimal machine is a set of input sequences, $T$, which is a state cover and is closed under right composition with the set of inputs *Input*, so we can get to any state from $q_0$ by using a suitable sequence $t$ from $T$ and for any input $a$ in *Input* the sequence $t::a$ is in $T$.

Here $T = \{< >, a, b, b::a, b::b, b::a::a, b::a::b, b::a::b::a, b::a::b::b\}$ is a transition cover for Example 3.4.1.

There are algorithms for constructing all of these sets for specific machines.

## Generating a Test Set

We first need to estimate how many more states there are in the implementation than in the specification. Let us assume that there are $k$ more states and let $W$ be a characterisation set.

We construct the set:

$$Z = Input^{\,k} \bullet W \cup Input^{\,k-1} \bullet W \cup .... \cup Input^{\,1} \bullet W \cup W$$

Recall that if A and B are sets of sequences from the same alphabet then A$\bullet$B means the set of sequences that are constructed from a sequence from A followed by a sequence from B. Thus the set $Z$ is formed from a collection of sets where we first form the set of sequences obtained by using all input sequences of length $k$ followed by sequences from $W$, then add to this collection the sequences formed using input sequences of length $k-1$ followed by sequences from $W$, and continue building up a set of sequences in this way.

The final *test set* is: $T \bullet Z$ where $T$ is a transition cover.

The basic theorem (Chow) is given below.

*Theorem 3.4.1*

If we have two minimal finite state machines, $\mathcal{M}$ and $\mathcal{M}'$, one with initial state $q_0$ and the other with initial state $q_0'$, and $T$ is a transition cover and $W$ a characterisation set for one of these machines then they are isomorphic (behave identically) if $q_0$ and $q_0'$ are $T \bullet Z$-equivalent. This means that if they produce the same outputs when the sequences from $T \bullet Z$ are applied then they are equivalent machines.

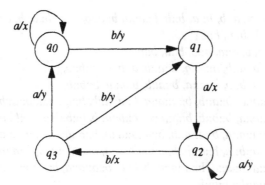

**FIG. 3.4.** A simple machine.

Note that $T \bullet Z$ is a *finite set of finite sequences*. We can therefore say something quite strong about the second machine, the implementation. If it behaves as the specification requires on *all* the input sequences from the test set $T \bullet Z$ it is then correct in the sense that for *every circumstance* defined by the specification the implementation produces the expected result.

*Example 3.4.4*

A simple machine is shown in Figure 3.4.

Figure 3.5 represents an implementation with one extra state, a missing transition and a faulty transition label.

The value of $k$ is assumed to be 1 for this example, then $Z = Input \bullet W \cup W = \{a, b\} \bullet \{a, b\} \cup \{a, b\} = \{a, b, a::a, a::b, b::a, b::b\}$ and the test set $T \bullet Z$ is thus:

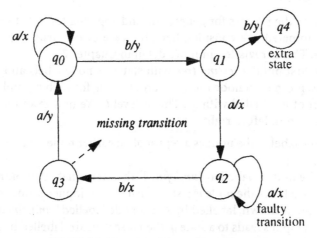

**FIG. 3.5.** A faulty version of the machine in Figure 3.4.

$T \bullet Z = \{<>, a, b, b::a, b::b, b::a::a, b::a::b, b::a::b::a, b::a::b::b\} \bullet \{a, b, a::a, a::b, b::a, b::b\}$

$= \{ a, b, a::a, a::b, b::a, b::b,$

$a::a, a::b, a::a::a, a::a::b, a::b::a, a::b::b,$

$b::a, b::b, b::a::a, b::a::b, b::b::a, b::b::b,$

$b::a::a, b::a::b, b::a::a::a, b::a::a::b, b::a::b::a, b::a::b::b,$

$b::b::a, b::b::b, b::b::a::a, b::b::a::b, b::b::b::a, b::b::b::b,$

$b::a::a::a, b::a::a::b, b::a::a::a::a, b::a::a::a::b, b::a::a::b::a, b::a::a::b::b,$

$b::a::b::a, b::a::b::b, b::a::b::a::a, b::a::b::a::b, b::a::b::b::a, b::a::b::b::b,$

$b::a::b::a::a, b::a::b::a::b, b::a::b::a::a::a, b::a::b::a::a::b, b::a::b::a::b::a,$

$b::a::b::a::b::b,$

$b::a::b::b::a, b::a::b::b::b, b::a::b::b::a::a, b::a::b::b::a::b, b::a::b::b::b::a,$

$b::a::b::b::b::b\}$

$= \{a, b, a::a, a::b, b::a, b::b, a::a::a, a::a::b, a::b::a, a::b::b, b::a::a, b::a::b,$

$b::b::a, b::b::b, b::a::a::a, b::a::a::b, b::a::b::a, b::a::b::b, b::b::a::a,$

$b::b::a::b, b::b::b::a, b::b::b::b, b::a::a::a::a, b::a::a::a::b, b::a::a::b::a,$

$b::a::a::b::b, b::a::b::a::a, b::a::b::a::b, b::a::b::b::a, b::a::b::b::b,$

$b::a::b::a::a::a, b::a::b::a::a::b, b::a::b::a::b::a, b::a::b::a::b::b,$

$b::a::b::b::a::a, b::a::b::b::a::b, b::a::b::b::b::a, b::a::b::b::b::b\}$

on removing repetitions.

The extra transition is exposed by the input $b::b$ which produces an output $y$ in the specification and $y::y$ in the implementation; the missing transition is exposed by $b::a::b::b$ and the faulty transition by $b::a::a$.

The transition cover ensures that all the states and transitions of the specification are present in the implementation and the set $Z$ ensures that the implementation is in the same state as the specification after each transition is used. The parameter $k$ ensures that all the extra states in the implementation are visiare visited.

## An Algorithm for Determining the Transition Cover

Much of the process for generating and applying test sets to real cases can be automated. We consider, here, the case of constructing the transition cover. This is revisited in more detail in Chapter 7.

We first build a *testing tree* with states as node labels and inputs as arc labels. From each node there are arcs leaving for each possible input value. The root is labelled with $q_0$. This is level 0. We now examine the nodes at level $m$ from left to right:

if the label at the node is a repeat of an earlier node then terminate the branch;
if the node is labelled "*undefined*" then terminate that branch;
if the label at the node is a state such that an input s is not defined then an arc is drawn, labelled by $s$, to a node labelled "*undefined*";
if an input s leads to a state $q'$ then insert an arc, labelled by $s$, to a node labelled $q'$.

*Example 3.4.5*

Figure 3.6 shows the testing tree for the machine is Figure 3.4. The labels of all partial paths in the tree form the transition cover.

Various authors have devised improved methods based on the use of fewer input sequences in the test set or by combining test sequences together to improve efficiency. Usually, the gain in obtaining a smaller test set is partly offset by the increased complexity of the process of generating it. These issues are revisited in Chapter 7.

## An Evaluation of Finite State Machine Testing

Unfortunately, Chow's method is only directly applicable to finite state machines and not to more complex machines involving explicit data processing and internal memory. It is often difficult to model many systems using finite state machines alone in a compact manner. The method can be used to test the control structure of some complex systems, with the data structure and processing functions being tested in some other way. This last method is unrealistic except in very special cases since the control is rarely independent of data state. By expanding the state space massively it is possible to construct better models but they rapidly become unusable. The assumption in the theorem that the implementation is a minimal machine can be removed easily. The assumption that the implementation is a finite state machine (that is, there is no hidden memory) is very doubtful in practice. In some cases, for example, in communications protocol testing, very strong assumptions are typically made, e.g. $k = 0$ is required for some of the methods for generating more efficient test sets to work.

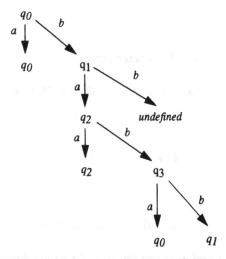

**FIG. 3.6.** The testing tree for the machine in Figure 3.4.

The use of statecharts [31] has improved the capability of finite state machine modelling at the expense, however, of a coherent semantics. Statecharts also lack a convenient method for describing the semantics of the individual transitions. Some extensions have been introduced [33], which provide a more powerful modelling language. Using these extended versions of statecharts, some considerable progress has been made on developing a powerful testing method; see Bogdanov and Holcombe [78].

## 3.5  STREAM X-MACHINES AND THE FUNDAMENTAL THEOREM OF TESTING

### Stream X-machines (Recap)

The results that we will discuss are based on the class of stream X-machines. These represent a very wide class of systems and can, essentially, describe all feasible computing systems.

Recall that a stream X-machine has an *input* set, an *output* set, a *memory* set, a set of *states* and a collection of *transitions* labelled by basic (or processing) *functions* that are dependent on the input and the memory.

Each transition function removes the head of the input stream and adds an element to the rear of the output stream, and, furthermore, no transition is allowed to use information from the tail of the input or any of the output. $m_0$ is the *initial* state of the memory.

For a stream X-machine to be *deterministic*, there must be a single start state and the set of basic functions F must be such that given any state and any input value and any memory value there is only one function that can be applied. Formally this is expressed as in Definition 3.5.1.

*Definition 3.5.1*

A stream X-machine, $\mathcal{M}$, is *deterministic* if

$$\forall \phi, \phi' \in \Phi, \text{if } \exists\, q \in Q, m \in M, in \in Input$$

such that

$$(q, \phi) \in \text{domain F}, (m, in) \in \text{domain } \phi$$

and

$$(m, in) \in \text{domain } \phi', \text{then } \phi = \phi'.$$

(Here domain $f$ refers to the domain of a partial function $f$.)

So each computation from the initial state to any other state is completely determined by the input sequence and the initial memory value. A deterministic stream X-machine will compute a partial function $f: Input^* \to Output^*$.

We proceed now with some general strategic remarks. The theory of finite state machines, as we have seen from Section 3.4, includes a result that describes how to test whether two finite state machines are isomorphic. Isomorphism means that they are algebraically similar and if we wish we can convert from one to another by using a "renaming" which respects the algebraic structure and the behaviour of the machines. Under these conditions their behaviour is the same. We can convert an X-machine into a finite state machine by treating the elements of $\Phi$ as abstract input symbols. We are, in effect, "forgetting" the memory structure and the semantics of the elements of $\Phi$. If we call this the *associated automata* of the X-machine we have the following result.

*Theorem 3.5.1*

Let $\mathcal{M}$ and $\mathcal{M}'$ be two deterministic stream X-machines with the same set $\Phi$ of basic functions, $f$ and $f'$, the functions computed by them, and let $\mathcal{A}$ and $\mathcal{A}'$ be their associated automata. If $\mathcal{A}$ and $\mathcal{A}'$ are isomorphic then $f = f'$. Proof: See [79].

Now proving that the two functions computed by the two stream X-machines, one the specification and the other the implementation, are equal is precisely what we want. If we can do this with a finite test set we will have a very powerful method indeed. This is our aim. To achieve this we need to consider how to prove that the associated automata of two stream X-machines are isomorphic.

Drawing on the techniques used in state machine testing will enable us to progress with this aim. We need some further terminology for stream X-machines.

## Design for Test Conditions

It turns out that if we wish to get the most from our testing strategy there are certain constraints that must be observed. In hardware design the idea of design for test is well understood. If the designer ignores the fact that the system will eventually need testing he or she can create a design that is very hard, if not impossible, to test thoroughly. The same is true for software. The following conditions represent a formalisation of the idea of design for test. They are conditions that must be satisfied if the complete test set we will be introducing is to be constructed. They do not result in any limitation since any stream X-machine can be made to satisfy these conditions – at the cost of including some extra test-based functionality.

Now consider any basic function $\phi \in \Phi$, so $\phi: M \times Input \rightarrow Output \times M$. Suppose that $m$ is any memory value that can be attained, is it possible to find an input $in \in Input$ that could cause this function $\phi$ to operate? This is motivation for the following definition.

## Definition 3.5.2

A type $\Phi$, is called *test-complete* (or *t-complete*) if $\forall \ \phi \in \Phi$ and $\forall$ $m \in Memory, \exists \ in \in Input$ such that $(m, in) \in$ domain $\phi$.

This condition prohibits "dead-ends" in the machine. We can turn an X-machine into one which is t-complete by introducing special test inputs and extending those functions that are not t-complete by defining them to behave suitably when these special test inputs are applied. The test inputs are not used during normal operation.

Now consider the case when a basic function has operated in a given state with a memory value and an input. We observe an output. What caused this output? We know it was a basic function, but which one? We cannot see these directly, only through their effect on the output, and so we must ensure that there is no other basic function which could have produced the same output under identical conditions. This leads to our other condition.

## Definition 3.5.3

A type $\Phi$ is called *output-distinguishable* if:

$$\forall \ \phi_1, \phi_2 \in \Phi, \text{if } \exists \ m \in M, in \in Input$$

such that

$\phi_1(m, in) = (out, m_1')$ and $\phi_1(m, in) = (out, m_2')$ with $m_1', m_2' \in M$, $out \in Output$, then $\phi_1 = \phi_2$

What this is saying is that we must be able to distinguish between any two different processing functions in an X-machine by examining outputs. If we cannot then we will not be able to tell them apart. So we need to be able to distinguish between any two of the processing functions (the $\phi$s) for all memory values. The mechanism for achieving output distinguishability is by introducing some special test outputs that are used in those cases where two functions would not normally be distinguishable. So some of the functions are augmented with these special indicator outputs that are only used in testing. In normal usage they will never appear.

These two conditions are required of our specification machine: we shall refer to them as *design for test* conditions. They are quite easily introduced into a specification by simply extending the definitions of suitable $\Phi$ functions and introducing extra output symbols. These will only be used in testing. As we will see in Chapter 7, these definitions only require checking with respect to *attainable* memory, the subset of memory that can be reached from the initial state.

Now we consider how test sets can be constructed that will show that the two associated automata are isomorphic. Consider the associated automata of the X-machine, $\mathcal{M}$. This is a finite state machine $\mathcal{A}$ with the basic function labels from the set $\Phi$ labelling the machine transitions. We now apply the Chow method of generating a test set using these labels instead of inputs. So we create a transition cover and a characterisation set in exactly the same way and form a test set as in Section 3.4. We have constructed a set of sequences of elements from $\Phi^*$ that will be the basis for our testing process, a set that will establish whether the two stream X-machines compute the same function. If $T$ and $W$ are a transition cover and a characterisation set, respectively, of the associated automaton $\mathcal{A}$ of $\mathcal{M}$ and we put:

$$Z = \Phi^k \bullet W \cup \Phi k^{-1} \bullet W \cup ... \cup W$$

where $k$ is the estimated number of extra states in the implementation compared to the specification, then $T \bullet Z$ is the set we have constructed to act as the test set for the associated automata.

However, this set is not really very convenient – we really want a set of *input* sequences from *Input*\* rather than a set of basic function labels from $\Phi^*$. We thus need to convert sequences from $\Phi^*$ into sequences from *Input*\*. In some cases there is a one to one correspondence between the basic functions and the inputs. Then the transformation of the set of function sequences into sets of input sequences is immediate. We do this transformation, in the general case, by using a fundamental test function, $t: \Phi^* \rightarrow Input^*$, defined recursively with reference to the specification machine. This is defined next. Note that the test function is not uniquely determined; many different possible test functions exist and it is up to the designer to construct it. There is an issue of choosing one which is of maximal efficiency, a subject that we have yet to investigate. However, it is very likely that a test function could be constructed and evaluated automatically.

## The Test Functions

What we have to do is replace the test sequences of function labels with sequences of machine inputs that will cause these sequences of functions, i.e. paths in the X-machine, to operate. This is done by constructing a function $t: \Phi^* \rightarrow Input^*$ that carries out this translation.

Consider a sequence of basic functions $\phi_1::...::\phi_{n+1}$ either this represents a path in the machine starting at the state $q$ with memory value $m$.

$$q \xrightarrow{\phi_1} q_2 \xrightarrow{\phi_2} q_3 \cdots q_{n+1} \xrightarrow{\phi_{n+1}} q_{n+2}$$

or there is no such path.

In the former case we look at the function $\phi_1$ and choose an input $in_1$ with the property that this input together with the memory value $m$ is in the domain of $\phi_1$ (that is, $in_1$ causes $\phi_1$ to operate in this state q and memory value $m$). The t-completeness of $\Phi$ ensures that this is possible. Now we look at the next function in the sequence, $\phi_2$, and repeat the process, and so on.

If the sequence of basic functions does not represent a path then we have two possibilities. Consider the sequence with the last element removed. If this does represent a path then we choose an input as above and terminate the process. We now have a sequence of inputs that exercises the path up to the penultimate element, then the final input causes the operation to halt as there is no transition triggered by that input. If the sequence with the last element removed still does not represent a path we remove the last element of the sequence and obtain a sequence $\phi_1 :: ... :: \phi_n$ and repeat the procedure until we have a path, then proceed as above.

This process of converting sequences of basic functions into sequences of inputs can be represented by a (recursively defined) function $t_{q,m} : \Phi^* \rightarrow Input^*$ (see Chapter 7). Then $t_{q,m}$ is called a *test function* of $\mathcal{M}$ with respect to $q$ and $m$. If $q = q_o$ and $m = m_o$, $t_{q,m}$ is denoted by $t$ and is called a *fundamental test function of M*.

If:

$$q \xrightarrow{\phi_1} q_2 \xrightarrow{\phi_2} q_3 .... q_n \xrightarrow{\phi_n} q_{n+1}$$

is a path in $\mathcal{M}$, then $s = t_{q,m}(\phi_1 ... \phi_n)$ will be an input string which, when applied in $q$ and $m$, will cause the computation of the machine to follow this path. If there is no arc labelled $\phi_{n+1}$ from $q_{n+1}$, then $t_{q,m} (\phi_1 ... \phi_n \phi_{n+1}) = s :: in$, where $in$ is an input which would have caused the machine to exercise such an arc if it had existed (i.e. therefore making sure that it does not exist). Also, for all $\phi_{n+2},..., \phi_{n+k} \in \Phi$, $t_{q,m}(\phi_1 ... \phi_n \phi_{n+1} ... \phi_{n+k}) = t_{q,m} (\phi_1 ... \phi_n \phi_{n+1})$ (i.e. therefore only the first non-existing arc in the path is exercised by the value of the test function).

We can say that a test function tests whether a certain path exists or not in $\mathcal{M}$ (hence the name).

Once all of this mechanism is in place we can generate a test set mechanically. Thus we construct explicitly **T** and **W** the transition cover and the characterisation set, respectively, of the associated automaton of the specification and then generate the set:

$$Z = \Phi k \bullet W \cup \Phi^{k-1} \bullet W \cup ... \cup W$$

and form the set of input strings $t(T \bullet Z)$, where $t$ is the fundamental test function as described above. This is the test set we are seeking. The value of k is chosen to represent the difference between the known state size of the specification and the (unknown) state size of the implementation. In practice this is not usually large; for especially sensitive applications one can make very pessimistic assumptions about k at the cost of a large test set.

Thus the test set is t(T • Z) and this is a set of input sequences that will be applied to any implementation of the specification that we are trying to validate.

The fundamental theorem of testing [79] (see Chapter 7) allows us to conclude that if all the tests are passed then the implementation is correct subject to the assumption that the basic functions have been correctly implemented in the implementation. We will examine the consequences later in this section.

## Testing the Estimator Example

The Estimator example considered in the previous chapter (Figure 3.7) satisfies the design for test conditions and so we can apply the test generation method immediately since the machine is deterministic and minimal.

The Estimator test set, where Φ = {close, open, cust, close_cust, edit_cust, help_cust, close_help_cust, prices, edit_price, close_price, orders, edit_order, close_order}

*State cover:* {< >, close, cust, help_cust, cust, prices, orders}

W consists of five sequences: {close, open, close_cust, close_help_cust, edit_price}.

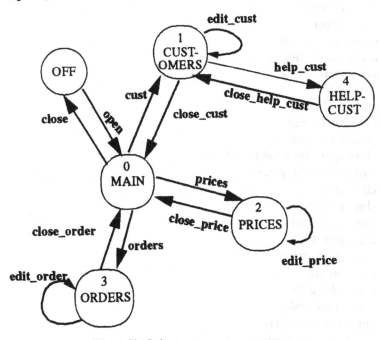

**FIG. 3.7. The Estimator:** top-level system design.

## Fundamental test set: 105 sequences

close close
open
close_cust
close_help_cust
edit_price
close open close
close close_cust
close close_help_cust
close edit_price
cust close
cust open
cust close_cust close
cust close_help_cust
cust edit_price
edit_cust
help_cust
prices close
prices open
prices close_cust
prices close_help_cust
prices edit_price close
close_price
orders close
orders open
orders close_cust
orders close_help_cust
orders edit_price
edit_order
close_order
close open open
close open close_cust
close open close_help_cust
close open edit_price
close cust
close edit_cust
close help_cust
close prices
close close_price
close orders
close edit_order
close close_order
cust help_cust close
cust help_cust open

```
cust help_cust close_cust
cust help_cust close_help_cust close
cust help_cust edit_price
cust help_cust cust
cust help_cust edit_cust
cust help_cust help_cust
cust help_cust close_help_cust open
cust help_cust close_help_cust close_cust
cust help_cust close_help_cust close_help_cust
cust help_cust close_help_cust edit_price
cust help_cust prices
cust help_cust close_price
cust help_cust orders
cust help_cust edit_order
cust help_cust close_order
cust cust
cust close_cust open
cust close_cust close_cust
cust close_cust close_help_cust
cust close_cust edit_price
cust edit_cust close
cust edit_cust open
cust edit_cust close_cust
cust edit_cust close_help_cust
cust edit_cust edit_price
cust prices
cust close_price
cust orders
cust edit_order
cust close_order
prices cust
prices edit_cust
prices help_cust
prices prices
prices edit_price open
prices edit_price close_cust
prices edit_price close_help_cust
prices edit_price edit_price
prices close_price close
prices close_price open
prices close_price close_cust
prices close_price close_help_cust
prices close_price edit_price
prices orders
prices edit_order
```

prices close_order
orders cust
orders edit_cust
orders help_cust
orders prices
orders close_price
orders orders
orders edit_order close
orders edit_order open
orders edit_order close_cust
orders edit_order close_help_cust
orders edit_order edit_price
orders close_order close
orders close_order open
orders close_order close_cust
orders close_order close_help_cust
orders close_order edit_price

In this list, which was generated by a test generation tool developed for this method, **open close_help_cust** means **open :: close_help_cust.** From this set of function sequences we can generate the complete test set by replacing the functions by their corresponding inputs. Thus **open** is replaced by *on*, **cust** by *1*, **close_cust** by *close_1* etc.

The example examined above was such that there was a one-to-one correspondence between inputs and basic functions. This is not always the case, and then the construction of the test functions is more complicated. Some examples of these cases will be found in Chapter 7.

## Reflections on the Test Generation Method

For the method to work we must make the following further assumptions:

1. The specification is a deterministic stream X-machine;
2. The set of basic functions $\Phi$ is output-distinguishable and t-complete;
3. The associated automata are minimal;
4. The implementation is a deterministic stream X-machine with the same set of basic functions $\Phi$.

Of these assumptions the first three lie within the capability of the designer. An algorithm for ensuring that a stream X-machine satisfies condition 2 is given in Ipate and Holcombe [80]. Any stream X-machine can be replaced by a machine satisfying condition 2. We refer to these conditions as "design for test" conditions – without them it is going to be difficult to test a system properly; there may be hidden behavioural faults in the implementation which cannot be exposed. The procedures are quite straightforward and intuitive.

Condition 3 requires some comment. It is clear that the designer can arrange for the associated automata of the specification X-machine to be minimal; standard techniques from finite state machine theory are available. The problem remains with the requirement that the implementation's associated automata is minimal. Since we do not have an explicit description of the implementation as an X-machine we cannot analyse its associated automata to see if it is minimal. We do know, however, that there is a minimal automata with the same behaviour as the automata of the implementation. It is this that will feature in the application of the fundamental theorem. Thus we have a test set that determines whether the behaviour, that is the function computed, by the specification equals the function computed by the implementation – providing that both implementation X-machine and the specification X-machine have the same basic function set $\Phi$.

The final condition is the most problematic. Establishing that the set of basic functions, $\Phi$, for the implementation is the same as the specification machine's has to be resolved, however. In practice this will be done with a separate testing process, either an application of the method explained above, since the basic processing functions are computable and thus expressible as the computations of other, presumably much simpler, X-machines or by using some other testing method for testing simple functions – perhaps the category-partition method [61] or a variant. If the basic processing functions are tried and tested with a long history of successful use – perhaps they are standard procedures, modules or objects from a library – then their individual testing could perhaps be assumed done. If we assume that the $\Phi$s are implemented correctly this carries with it the consequence that the implementation is a stream X-machine since these functions are the processing functions of a stream X-machine by construction.

What sort of restriction is this? It is quite legitimate to assume that the implementation is a deterministic stream X-machine because of the computational generality of this class of machines. This does not mean that all Turing machines can be represented as a stream X-machine, but that there exists a hierarchy of stream X-machines with progressively more complex basic functions which will approach the generality of the Turing model. In likely applications of the method we will successively apply the test method to the hierarchy of stream X-machines that are created when we consider the basic functions $\Phi$ at each level. Thus, testing a specific function $\phi$ will involve considering it as the computation defined by a simpler stream X-machine and so on. This is illustrated in Figure 3.8.

Ultimately, at the bottom level we need to test the basic functions in some suitable way – or assume that they are implemented correctly.

In many of the case studies that we have looked at, the basic functions that need to be used are typically very straightforward ones that carry out simple tasks on simple data structures, inserting and removing items from

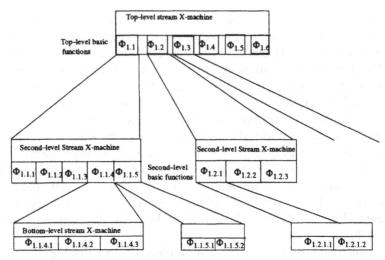

**FIG. 3.8.** Diagram illustrating how the basic functions can themselves be specified using simpler stream X-machines in a natural hierarchical manner.

registers, stacks etc., carrying out simple arithmetic operations on simple types and processing character strings in well-understood ways. There is probably little point in devoting a great deal of testing effort to this aspect of the problem. It may seem to be slightly dangerous to say so, but we know how to implement such simple operations correctly.

The benefits that accrue if the method is applied are that the entire control structure of the system is tested and *all* faults detected *modulo* the correct implementation of the basic functions.

## 3.6   DISCUSSION

Let us examine these results in the context of the issues raised in the earlier part of the paper. In particular, does this new method really deliver a principled method of testing? We now can say something about any faults remaining after the successful application of the full test set generated by the method (assuming that the specification X-machine satisfies all of the requirements). Any such faults are restricted to the basic processing functions. This approach does satisfy the reductive requirement that we expressed at the start. We no longer need to consider test coverage issues since we have full coverage with respect to faults – outside of the set of basic functions $\Phi$.

Recall that the reductionist philosophy means that we can replace the problem of testing for all faults in a stream X-machine to one of detecting faults in something simpler – namely the processing functions $\Phi$. These, themselves, can be represented as the computations of even simpler stream

X-machines if desired and the reduction continued further. Alternatively, these may be functions obtained from a library of dependable objects that the designers are confident are essentially fault-free.

The main point from all of this is that if this testing method is used and the implementation passes all of the tests in the test set then it is known to be free of faults, *providing the Φs have been implemented in a fault-free fashion.*

One could argue that all we are doing is shifting the major part of the testing burden onto testing the $\phi$ functions. This is not the case, however. The method involves a gradual process of testing based on the hierarchy of the design whereby, at each level in the hierarchy, the functions utilised at that level are assumed to be fault free. The testing at that level then focuses on the correct integration of these functions.

Another important issue concerns the estimate required for the number of states in the implementation. This can be done in a number of ways. If the implementation has been based on the structure of the specification then, providing the transformations into the implementation language have been done systematically and transparently, it should be possible to make this estimate accurately. It is always possible to overestimate the number of states at the expense of a larger than necessary test set. This may be economically justified if the application is of a critical nature.

Alternatively, assuming that the code has been developed in an *ad hoc* nature and the specification is only used as a reference point for compliance, then it is possible to analyse the code and to construct its X-machine model from this information by analysing the control flow and the memory (both global and local variables) involved. In fact, recent investigations into extracting a detailed X-machine specification from industrial safety-critical Fortran code has indicated that the process can be substantially automated.

The final question that needs to be addressed is concerned with the practicality of the method. For example, how complex is the test generation algorithm? This is considered in Chapter 7. The test sets generated by the method for all the case studies we have considered are manageable, as is the test application process. Clearly the method has to be supported by automated systems and suitable tools, which are under development.

In [81] we proposed the use of X-machines as the foundation of a completely integrated design, verification and test methodology. Because the approach lends itself to a rigorous refinement-based development process, it is possible to construct test sets for intermediate versions of the implementation, providing that they satisfy all the design for test conditions. At subsequent stages, after the model has been refined, perhaps by expanding some of the processing functions and reducing the abstraction in a coherent way, the refined machine may be tested in a way that utilises test information from the earlier version together with tests generated from the components used to carry out the refinement succinctly.

We have described a new approach to the testing of software systems which is reductionist in the sense that the approach provides a method for generating a finite test set which will detect *all* faults in the system *providing that the basic processing functions are implemented correctly*. The complexity of the test sets is better than that of a number of existing methods. The precondition for the application of the method is a formal specification of the system as a stream X-machine, a method that we and colleagues have introduced recently and evaluated with case studies drawn from a wide variety of different applications.

The scope of the method is quite general and is relevant for real-time applications as well as traditional information system applications. It is independent of the nature of an implementation also. The recent interest in object-oriented systems and the urgent need to develop effective testing methods for them provides a new and exciting opportunity. The fact that objects are computational phenomena means that we can identify them with suitable classes of X-machines. Representing the control structure more explicitly by way of the rich semantics of the X-machine model will provide a firm basis for the development of a principled testing method for object-oriented software.

## Refinement and Components

We have seen that the process of developing the specification incrementally and hierarchically is a convenient and manageable process. It also enables us to distribute the testing effort so that we can test components corresponding to suitable partitions (the submachines defined by the lower level diagrams and functions) and then test their integration using the method applied at the top level. This is more economic, too, as will be shown in Chapter 8 (see also a less general approach in [82]). At some point the developer will be able to use modules, classes and routines from a library (provided that their specification and the environment under which they can be used are known). If these are dependable – perhaps they have been used over a long period and proved reliable, perhaps they have been formally verified correct – they will form the basis of our testing as well as our implementation. In other words, we will assume that they are correct. This will then enable us to make conclusions about the correctness of the systems and subsystems that we build with them.

## Application of the Method

This method of testing has been used in a number of different situations. The system described in Chapter 5 was built using the complete X-machine specification and testing method. The process was done incrementally, testing the various submachines and their integration as separate processes. This exposed a number of faults which were corrected. Beneath it all was the assumption that the low-level functions in Access 2.0 etc. were correct. A very robust and sophisticated system was developed over a short period of time. The way in which the method was able to capture the client's real requirements in a simple and effective way, the simple nature of the formal language used in the specification and the powerful test generation method are all important strengths of the approach. Using modern software development tools (4GLs and a proprietary database system) adds to the attractions and practical nature of the method. The test generation process was done by hand, but tools have now been developed to automate this. So far the client has reported no faults and is entirely satisfied with the system. His company is now totally dependent on it.

A number of experiments have also been carried out using the method to specify simple but complete systems, and to generate test sets. The systems were then implemented fully and a number of different faults *seeded* into the applications. The faulty systems were then tested using the test sets and in all cases *all* of the faults were detected. Although the systems were small, between 500 and 1000 lines of code in Pascal, they included time-related ones – an alarm clock, a vending machine, a set of traffic lights and a calculator example. Furthermore, where faults were also seeded into the basic functions, these were detected by the test set also. Thus the test sets can identify faults in the basic functions, although this area needs further research.

## Conclusions

The issue of quality-oriented testing was addressed by insisting on a complete formal specification so that we knew what it was we were trying to deliver. The recognition that software construction is component based and needs to be functionally tested is the motivation for the hierarchical, refinement approach that we have developed. The issue of finding all faults has been addressed through the method by the realisation that if the components are dependable and the implementation passes all the tests then it has the same functional behaviour as the specification – provided that the specification has been augmented to ensure that it satisfies the design for test conditions. It is thus fault free.

Ultimately, at the bottom level we need to test the basic functions in some suitable way – or assume that they are implemented correctly. In many of the case studies that we have looked at the basic functions that need to be used are typically very straightforward ones that carry out simple tasks on simple data structures – inserting and removing items from registers, stacks etc., carrying out simple arithmetic operations on simple types and processing character strings in well-understood ways. The benefits that accrue if the method is applied are that the entire control structure of the system is tested and all faults detected modulo the correct implementation of the basic functions. The reductionist philosophy means that we can replace the problem of testing for all faults in a stream X-machine to one of detecting faults in something simpler – namely the processing functions F. These, themselves, can be represented as the computations of even simpler stream X-machines if desired and the reduction continued further. Alternatively, these may be functions obtained from a library of dependable objects that the designers are confident are essentially fault-free.

The main point from all of this is that if this testing method is used and the implementation passes all of the tests in the test set then it is known to be free of faults, providing the basic functions (the $\Phi$s) have been implemented in a fault-free fashion. If all the basic functions have been formally verified then the total method is one of formal verification; if one basic function has only been validated through testing then the overall process is one of testing.

A further consideration is the cost of this method. It is important that high-quality tools are available to support the specification and test generation process. Even so, there is no doubt that the method generates quite large sets, but the benefit from the method is based on what can be deduced if all the tests are passed. Quality does not always come cheap!

Our final conclusion is that if the aim is one of delivering quality systems, and we can construct a specification in the manner described that satisfies the design for test conditions, and if, further, we are confident that our bottom-level components are correctly implemented, then the test set will find all functional faults. If the system passes all the tests we can stop testing with confidence that the system is as good as its basic components allow.

# 4 Building Correct Systems

*Summary. Refining correct solutions, components, an integrated design and test strategy, a simple refinement example, testing refinements, conclusions.*

The approach that we have taken so far has been illustrated with simple, small examples of systems. In reality systems are large and complex. How can the ideas be translated to a more realistic scale? The question is not easily answered, and no software development method has really proved successful in this respect. One of the problems is that existing techniques tend to be programmer centred or at best analyst centred rather than oriented around the process of establishing requirements and transforming these in a consistent way into a complete design and test process. Creating a process that can adapt to possible changes in the business and its requirements is also hard to achieve. So the problem of building correct systems is made more difficult. Attempts have been made to introduce a more formal approach to the refinement of a specification or a design into a more complete representation of the system, ultimately leading to an implementation. Wirth [83] and Parnas [84] discuss refinement as a principle. Jones [17] looks at the issue of reification in the context of the transformation of a formal specification in VDM into a more concrete representation. Morgan [85] also introduces a formal mechanism for developing specifications in Z. These approaches are essentially procedures for transforming abstract notations, with or without possible machine support, and sit uncomfortably with the preferences of many software designers for a less symbolic and more diagrammatic way of describing systems.

In this chapter we will try to maintain the link with the client view and at the same time recognise that systems are large and complex, need to be designed in stages and, from time to time, redesigned. We will also look closely at the issue of components. It has been suggested in many places that a *software components approach* to design would overcome some of the real quality problems that afflict the field. Taking inspiration from the practice of many other types of engineering, it is believed that if we could develop libraries of robust and well-tested software components and build complete systems by composing these together in suitable ways to form complete solutions we will have taken a major step to solving the software crisis. Furthermore, if the requirements change then it may be possible to either add new components or replace some with others to swiftly achieve a re-engineered system. So far attempts at doing this have been failures. The idea of software reuse that lies at the heart of this approach is often used as a motivation for object-oriented languages and methods. However, reusing classes and objects from a library or from other systems will not necessarily result in an improvement over current practice because of the extra testing that is required. The widespread belief that well-tested classes and objects from other applications will not require retesting is a fallacy: the testing effort has been redistributed, not reduced. Furthermore, software designers tend to "interfere" with their "solutions". In other words, unlike other types of engineering, there is no fabrication phase whereby the design is handed over to a technical team for turning into a concrete artefact. Up to a few minutes before the software is installed and goes "live" the programmer can make changes to it. This has been the cause of many problems in the past and is inevitably the result of either failing to capture the requirements properly or failing to understand them, or just building and testing the system poorly.

## 4.1   REFINING CORRECT SOLUTIONS

Let us recall what a correct system solution is:

   a correct model of the requirements + a complete implementation

   + a complete and successful test strategy

We identify the client's needs through his or her perception of their business processes and the integration of these into enterprise solutions. There are a number of ways in which this process could be scaled up to more complex systems. We could begin with a very top-level view of the business and a possible solution which would emphasise the way in which the system was constructed from several smaller systems, which communicate with each other in particular ways. These system components would then be further decomposed until a point was reached where the components were sufficiently small that they could be analysed and built using the techniques described earlier. In this approach what is important is that the integration of the components – that is, the *communication model* – is precise and understood, is preserved during the design process and tested thoroughly throughout. The integration testing of any system is vital and can be an area where massive effort has to be applied. The framework for this approach should also allow for the inevitable changes that will occur to the requirements during the course of the project. Although requirements change there will usually have to be a point where they are frozen to prevent *requirements creep* and to enable a solution to be built. What is important is that the specification and the design are fully defined in such a way that later changes might be made and verified easily.

An alternative strategy might be to look at the available components and to see if these could be composed in some way to construct a possible solution, the problem then being that the verification of the constructed solution against a (possibly rather vague) requirement, is a major task. This bottom-up strategy seems to be the main approach to implementing systems using an object-oriented programming language where the integration and control of the components is distributed throughout the system.

The approach discussed here will incorporate both strategies. It will involve the top down decomposition based approach integrated into a refinement oriented method that allows the test strategy to develop with the requirement specification model and which is able to utilise the combination of trusted components into a complete and fully tested solution. We now turn our attention to trying to identify what a *component* might be.

## 4.2   COMPONENTS

What is a component? Is it a procedure, a module, a function, an object, a class or what?

How will we describe the detailed behaviour of the components? How can we put components together so that the resulting system has a predictable and desirable behaviour? Is it the case that poor quality components will lead to a poor quality system? These are some of the questions that we will be trying to address in this chapter.

A component is some *coherent* part of the system which has some intrinsic *common property*, something which has an *identifiable* and *consistent behaviour* or *structure* which makes it meaningful to treat it as an entity in some sense. The problem with this definition is that it is too general and there can be many ways in which it could be satisfied. We will try to address the issue through our approach to systems using computational models. So we make the following tentative definition.

*Definition 4.2.1*

A *component* for a system is a business process function or a stream (or enterprise) X-machine.

This brings with it a recognition that a component must have:

1. An interface comprising a definition of what inputs can be applied to the component and what outputs it can produce.
2. An internal control structure that determines how the component is organised dynamically.
3. An internal memory store that can be updated as the component operates.
4. An explicit functional description, which defines what the component does under all possible circumstances.

These ingredients are the classic elements of a stream X-machine. The internal control structure can be of a trivial nature in some cases, whereby they can be regarded as basic processing functions. Later on we will consider the issue of a *configurable* component, which will offer a convenient basis for system development.

Thus the process of decomposing an enterprise model into components is one of breaking it up into communicating networks of stream X-machines, essentially a top-down approach. We could build a system from components by integrating into a coherent X-machine a collection of simpler X-machines. This might be regarded as a bottom-up approach. From the point of view of building correct solutions it is then possible to distribute some of the verification and testing effort. This means that we might be looking at determining whether the components were correct at a different time, perhaps in a different place, to the verification of the complete system. Thus we could separate the testing of the components from the testing of their integration in a systematic way. This, of course, happens already, to some extent: systems are often built in parts, the parts being tested and then put together, and then the integration of the parts being tested separately. When this is done it is quite likely that the description of the functionality of the components is incomplete, the way they interact and interface with the rest of the system can be poorly understood and so much of the testing effort may well be misplaced. The goal of a library of well tested, tried and trusted components that can be integrated easily into complete solutions that need a minimal amount of testing is not going to be achieved under these conditions.

There is another general problem. We noted above that there were two broad approaches to designing systems – top down and bottom up. Life is never that simple, however, and we need to examine how a model is built and revised through an iterative process which could, like some theories of evolution, involve major generational mutations and changes as we traverse the development cycles.

## 4.3   AN INTEGRATED DESIGN AND TEST REFINEMENT STRATEGY

A proposed integrated approach is illustrated in Figure 4.1. In this scheme we develop the initial formal specification from the requirements specification. Outline proof obligations and testing strategies are defined at a high level of abstraction based on the requirements analysis and a hazard analysis, where appropriate. It may be possible at this stage to construct outline proofs and to generate outline test scripts based on the detail available at that level of the specification. The refinement process applied to the specification will extend the functionality or reduce the abstraction of the model and provide further opportunities for the description of verification conditions and test strategies at this level of detail. If we can identify the refine-

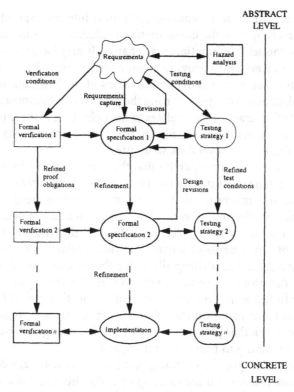

ABSTRACT
LEVEL

CONCRETE
LEVEL

**FIG. 4.1.** An integrated approach to the design, verification and testing of systems.

ment transformations in a formal way we could attempt to refine the proofs
and test scripts from the higher level to save repeating these activities where
this is not needed. Thus we can transform the model in a controlled and
logical way until we reach an implementation, dragging proofs and tests sets
with the design. Figure 4.1 provides a simplified schematic of what might
be possible. First, the study of the intended application area would include
some appropriate hazard analysis, an identification of potential hazards that
the system may endure and an initial set of conditions and properties that
the system must satisfy. This is a complex and difficult task which cannot
be automated easily. It is beyond the scope of this book but it is included
to emphasise the point that there may be overriding conditions imposed
on the development of the system that would influence the verification
and testing that is to be carried out. For example, if the system was specified as an X-machine it may be possible to identify states that should
not be entered under certain conditions of input and memory. These for-
bidden state/input/memory combinations should be *ensured* by making the
design compliant with these requirements.

A word about the idea of formal verification and proof obligations is
now pertinent. Each machine defines a computational function which

transforms some set of sequences of inputs into corresponding sequences of outputs subject to the initial memory value. As we refine and develop the machine model this function may change. It may have its domain (that is, its scope) extended to provide greater functionality in the system. It may be redefined so that it is defined in terms of a related, but not necessarily identical, domain of inputs. During the process of refinement we may reduce the level of abstraction as it relates to the definition of the input set, the output set or the memory. We may increase the number of states in order to control these lower level data structures.

The mathematical properties that the computational function of a solution X-machine must specify will be called *proof obligations*. Demonstrating that a given X-machine satisfies a set of proof obligations is the subject of *formal verification* or *model checking*. This is not the major emphasis of this work, but we have tried to recognise the fact that the proof obligations of a series of refinements of a machine will be related. Thus our philosophy of computational modelling allows for the precise analysis of the computational functions of the set of refined machines, thus providing a foundation for future work on refining formal verification proofs in tandem with the refinement of the model. The benefit is that we would only have to verify or check that part of the model that has changed, which will ease the burden of having to prove everything again.

Our main emphasis is refining test sets. Here there are definite savings to be made. As we will see in Chapter 8, the theory allows us to construct test sets in parallel with the refinement process and to distribute the testing into smaller chunks, with major cost and time savings. Since we are also interested in a genuine component-based approach to design we can also fully utilise the prior testing of these components safe in the knowledge that the results from this will be precisely related to our overall testing strategy.

## 4.4   A FIRST SIMPLE REFINEMENT

Our refinement strategy is to take an existing stream X-machine and to alter it in some useful way to produce a new machine that includes the relevant behaviour of the original machine together with some desired further properties. Thus we might have a machine which is presented in a very abstract way with little detail of some of the basic functionality or structure and create a new machine, based on the old one, but with more detail exposed. By doing this in a coherent and consistent way we can then utilise some of the testing strategies that have been developed and produce an integrated design approach that allows testing to be refined alongside the specification. This will lead to a number of savings in the complexity of the testing process and to considerable reductions in effort.

Now we consider the ways in which we can refine machine models. Let us start with a stream X-machine model and look at a transition and its associated basic function. The trigger for this transition will be a set of input-memory pairs. Suppose that we wish to replace this transition with a new stream X-machine. This could be the case if the input trigger to the original transition was of a compound type and we wished to decompose it into a sequence of simpler type values. In Figure 4.2(a) we start with a simple machine that captures the **name** input (a sequence of characters) and stores this in some parameter slot of the memory and then captures the **address** input (also a sequence of characters) and stores this in another part of the memory. To refine the **name** function to a lower level of detail we have to replace it with a machine that takes as inputs characters and allows for a sequence to be built up incrementally. This could be the machine in Figure 4.2(b), which we call a *refining machine for state A* in the original machine. The final stage is to insert or substitute the second machine into an appropriate place in the original machine to obtain a *refined machine* as in Figure 4.2(d). This is done by identifying or merging states as shown in Figure 4.2(c).

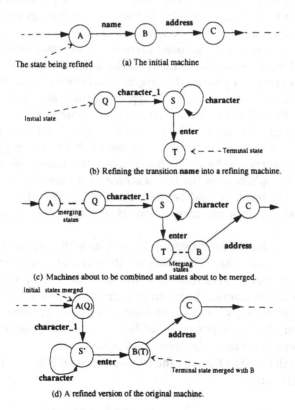

(a) The initial machine

(b) Refining the transition **name** into a refining machine.

(c) Machines about to be combined and states about to be merged.

(d) A refined version of the original machine.

**FIG. 4.2.** A simple refinement of a stream X-machine.

Now, the problems that we might find include upsetting the semantics of the original machine in undesirable ways and introducing nondeterminism. In the original machine, for example, the user types in a name, leaves the state A and then types in an address. There is no means of getting back to state A directly after the name has been typed in, to type in another name, for example. If there was a transition from T to Q in the refining machine then there would be a transition from B(T) to A(Q) in the refined machine, which could mean that the user could type in a name and then type in another before going on to the address. This disturbs the semantics of the machine in an unsatisfactory way. Another reason for avoiding transitions leaving from terminal states in refining machines is that we may have the possibility that doing this sort of operation could disturb the deterministic nature of the original machine. For example, if the refining machine included a transition from state T back to state Q then it is possible that there was a nondeterministic situation in the state B(T) caused by the domains of the functions on the transitions leaving that state intersecting in a non-trivial way. To avoid this in general we only allow refining machines to have a single terminal state (with no transitions leaving it).

The construction described could be repeated with other transitions from the same or other states. These also could cause problems if done in an incorrect way. Thus we require that when several states are being refined that the refining machines do not share states.

Once a refinement has been carried out we want to ensure that the original machine and the refined machine behave in a suitably related way. So, for example, a path in the original machine which is traversed when a suitable sequence of inputs is applied should correspond to a suitable path in the refined machine. Naturally, the input sets may have changed and this may mean that the path in the refined machine is longer and its output sequence may not exactly match that of the original machine. This means that we have to define a clear relationship (function) between the input alphabets of the two machines, between the output alphabets of the two machine and between their memories. Then the paths can be compared in a meaningful way as illustrated, in a general sense, in Figure 4.3.

Suppose that we have a stream X-machine with state set $Q$, and input set *Input*, output set *Output*, memory set *Memory* and basic functions $\Phi$. Let $q \in Q$ and suppose $\phi$ is a transition that leaves the state $q$. We wish to refine this transition from $q$. The refining machine for this will have a state set $R_q$, and input set *Input'*, output set *Output'*, memory set *Memory'* and basic functions $\Phi_q$. The input set *Input'* is likely to include sequences of inputs that correspond to single elements of *Input*.

The relationship between the two input sets will then be described by a partial function:

$$u: seq(Input') \rightarrow Input$$

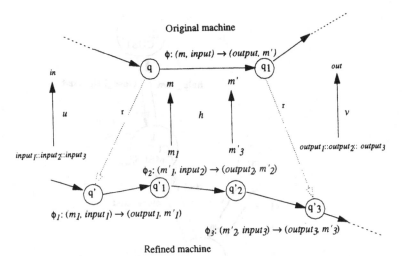

**FIG. 4.3.** Comparing the behaviour of the refined machine at a state with that of the original machine.

In a similar way the sequences of outputs of the refining machine may relate to a single output of the old machine so there needs to be a partial function $v$: seq($Output'$) → $Output$.

There is a partial function h: $Memory'$ → $Memory$.

We call the functions $u$, $v$ and h the *translation functions of the refinement*.

For the case where there is only one transition leaving $q$ in the original machine we can proceed as follows. The refining machine will have one terminal state with no transitions leaving it. The set of states of the refining machine is denoted by $R_q$. The terminal state is $t_q$.

Now we paste the refining machine into place by removing the arc $\phi$ in the original machine and fitting the refining machine in its place. The new machine will have a set of states that comprises all of the states of the original machine except $q$ together with the new states of the refining machine with $t_q$ identified with the target state of the $\phi$ transition and $q$ identified with the initial state of the refining machine.

We define a function r: $Q$ → $K$ to make these relationships explicit. $K$, the set of *key states*, is a copy of the states of $Q$ and the function $r$ maps $Q$ onto them. In some cases we will have $K = Q$, as in the following examples.

The situation is slightly different if the state $q$ has several transitions leaving it. In this case we must make sure that our refining machine has as many terminal states as there are transitions leaving $q$. Furthermore, none of these terminal states can have transitions leaving them. In this case the pasting of the refining machine into the original machine must be done in such a way that the transitions from the state $q$ in the first machine are replicated by transitions in the refining machine and the merged machine is such that the corresponding terminal states in the refining machine, are combined with the relevant states in the original. The next example illustrates this.

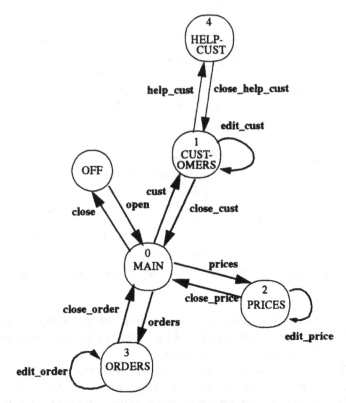

**FIG. 4.4.** A top-level view of the Estimator system.

Consider the Estimator example from Chapter 2 illustrated in Figure 4.4 and the process of introducing the CUSTOMERS screen. At the top level we have a state with a rather general and at present incompletely defined function, **edit_cust** defined at the state CUSTOMERS. The purpose of the refinement is to introduce the detailed description of this function and to relate it to a slight simplification in Figure 4.5 of the CUSTOMERS screen derived in Chapter 2. It is a simple matter to alter things to include the full details of the original screen. We have removed some of the input details to make the later analysis clearer. So we will build a refining machine for CUSTOMERS and then paste it into the original machine to produce a refined machine.

The approach is to use a type of refinement that is discussed, from a detailed theoretical point of view, in Chapter 6.

The state in the original machine that we are refining is CUSTOMERS. We need to construct a refining machine and then relate or insert it into the original machine to obtain the refinement. This process requires us to define a number of functions that will indicate how the states in the machines are related, and functions to translate between the old and new inputs and output sets.

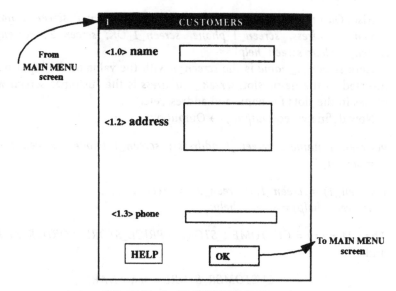

**FIG. 4.5.** The simplified CUSTOMERS edit screen.

The set of key states in this case is the original state set – {OFF, MAIN, CUSTOMERS, ORDERS, PRICES, HELP_CUST}.

We also let *Input* = {*1, 2, 3, off, on, close_1, close_2, close_3, cust_details, edit_price, edit_order, help, close_h*}, as before, and introduce the new input events associated with a simplified version of the CUSTOMERS screen, *Input'* = {*1, 2, 3, off, on, close_1, close_2, close_3, name, address, phone, OK, edit_price, edit_order, help, close_h*}.

The next stage is to relate these two input alphabets using a function defined on certain sequences of the CUSTOMERS screen. The former input that causes the edit_cust function to operate, *cust_details*, has been replaced by the inputs *name, address, phone* and *OK* in the new screen.

So we put *u*: seq(*Input'*) → *Input* by defining:

$$u(name::address::phone::OK) = cust\_details.$$

$$
\begin{aligned}
u(1) &= 1, u(2) = 2,... \\
u(close\_3) &= close\_3, \\
u(price\_details) &= price\_details,... \\
u(close\_h) &= close\_h
\end{aligned}
$$

A similar function is needed to relate the outputs of the old, unrefined, machine and the new. We must identify the output sets for the two machines first.

Let *Output* = {*screen_1, screen_2, screen_3, screen_0, screen_1', screen_2', screen_3', screen_0, clear, screen_help*}.

So *screen_1* consists of the customer screen with the slots blank; *screen_1'* is the same screen with all the values in the slots.

Also, $Output' = \{screen\_1, screen\_2, screen\_3, screen\_0, screen\_1\_name,$ $screen\_1\_address,\ screen\_1\_phone,\ screen\_1\_OK,\ screen\_2',\ screen\_3',$ $screen\_0, clear, screen\_help\}$

Here $screen\_1\_name$ is the $screen\_1$ with the value of the input name inserted in the name slot, $screen\_1\_address$ is the customer screen with values in the slots for name and address, etc.

Now define $v$: seq($Output'$) $\rightarrow$ $Output$ by:

$v(screen\_1\_name :: screen\_1\_address :: screen\_1\_phone :: screen\_1\_OK)$
  $= screen\_1'$

$v(screen\_1) = screen\_1, v(screen\_2) = screen\_2, \ldots,$
  $v(screen\_help) = screen\_help.$

Then $Memory = CUSTOMER\_STORE \times PRICE\_STORE \times ORDER\_STORE$, and:

$$\begin{aligned}
CUSTOMER\_STORE &= \text{seq}(CHAR), \\
PRICE\_STORE &= \text{seq}(CHAR), \\
ORDER\_STORE &= \text{seq}(CHAR),
\end{aligned}$$

whereas the new machine memory is:

$Memory' = CUSTOMER\_NAME \times CUSTOMER\_ADDRESS$
  $\times CUSTOMER\_PHONE \times PRICE\_STORE \times ORDER\_STORE$

with

$CUSTOMER\_NAME \times CUSTOMER\_ADDRESS \times CUSTOMER\_PHONE$
  $= \text{seq}(CHAR) \times \text{seq}(CHAR) \times \text{seq}(CHAR)$

We have to relate the memory sets of the two machines so we define h: $Memory' \rightarrow Memory$ by h($a, b, c, d, e$) = ($a :: b :: c, d, e$) where $a \in CUS\text{-}TOMER\_NAME$, $b \in CUSTOMER\_ADDRESS$, $c \in CUSTOMER\_PHONE$ and $a :: b :: c \in CUSTOMER\_STORE$, $d \in PRICE\_STORE$, $e \in ORDER\_STORE$. The functions are defined as follows:

**cust**$((-, -, -), cust) = (screen\_1, (-, -, -))$;
**close_cust**$((cust\_details, -, -), close\_cust) = (screen\_0, (cust\_details, -, -))$;
**edit_cust**$((-, -, -), cust\_details) = (screen\_1', (cust\_details, -, -))$
**open**$((-, -, -), open) = (screen\_0, (-, -, -))$;
**prices**$((-, -, -), prices) = (screen\_2, (-, -, -))$;
etc.

The inputs like $cust\_details$ are being treated as a high-level abstraction. In the refined machine such inputs are decomposed into lower level abstractions such as $name$, $address$, etc. These can, at a later refinement stage, be refined into strings of a given type.

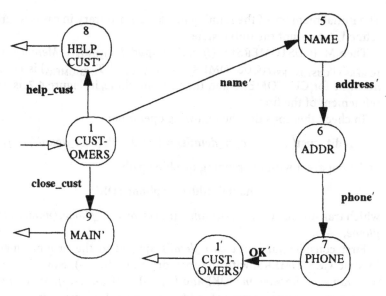

**FIG. 4.6.** A refining machine for CUSTOMERS.

In Figure 4.6 the new functions are:

**name'**$((-,-,-,-,-), name) = (screen\_1\_name, (name,-,-,-,-))$;
**address'**$((name,-,-,-,-), address)$
   $= (screen\_1\_address, (name, address,-,-,-))$;
**phone'**$((name, address,-,-,-), phone)$
   $= (screen\_1\_phone, (name, address, phone,-,-))$;
**OK'**$((name, address, phone,-,-), OK)$
   $= (screen\_1\_OK, (name, address, phone,-,-))$;
etc.

We are restricting the user somewhat into typing in the customer details in a fixed order, namely *name, address, phone* and *OK*. This is simply for the sake of keeping the model simple.

Here $R_{CUSTOMERS}$ = {CUSTOMERS, NAME, ADDRESS, PHONE, MAIN',
                         HELP_CUST', CUSTOMERS'},
$T_{CUSTOMERS}$ = {CUSTOMERS', MAIN', HELP', PHONE},
$K$ = {MAIN, PRICES, ORDERS, CUSTOMERS, HELP_
                         CUST, OFF}, i.e. the set of states of the initial
                         machine.
$L$ = {MAIN', PRICES', ORDERS', CUSTOMERS', HELP_
                         CUST', OFF'}, i.e. all states are primed.

r is the identity.
$d(q) = q'$ for all states of $K$.

The initial memory of the refining machine is arbitrary in cases where the refined state is not the initial state.

Then $M'$ (CUSTOMERS) = ($Input'$, $Output'$, $R_{CUSTOMERS}$, $Memory'$, $\Phi_{CUSTOMERS}'$, $F_{CUSTOMERS}$, $r$(CUSTOMERS), $m_{CUSTOMERS}'$, $T_{CUSTOMERS}$) is a refining machine for CUSTOMERS and the third machine, in Figure 4.7, is a state refinement of the first.

To check this consider the following operation:

**edit_cust**( (-, -, -), $cust\_details$) = ($screen\_1'$, ($cust\_details$, -, -))

and compare it with the refining machine path:

**name'; address'; phone'; OK'**

which transforms ((-, -, -, -, -), $name$) into ($screen\_1\_phone$, ($name, address$, $phone$, -, -)).

First consider an input $cust\_details$ applied to the original machine in state CUSTOMERS, with the memory value (-, -, -). Now $cust\_details$ = $u$($name::address::phone::OK$) and ( -, -, -) = h(-, -, -, -, -). Also $screen\_1'$ = $v$($screen\_1\_name :: screen\_1\_address :: screen\_1\_phone :: screen\_1\_OK$).

Therefore applying first the input sequence $name::address::phone::OK$ to the refining machine, $M'$ (CUSTOMERS) will yield the output–memory pair:

($screen\_1\_name :: screen\_1\_address :: screen\_1\_phone :: screen\_1\_OK$, ($name, address, phone$, -, -))

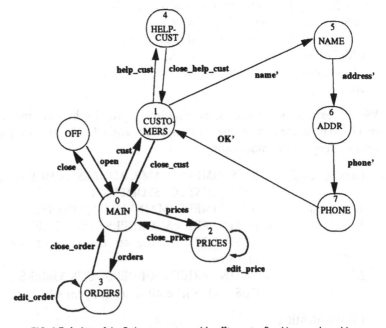

**FIG. 4.7.** A view of the Estimator system with **edit_cust** refined into a submachine.

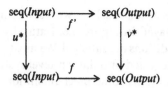

**FIG. 4.8.** Functional refinement.

which can be mapped onto (*screen_1'*, (*name::address::phone*, -, -) by applying *v* to the first component (the output) and h to the second (the memory).
Thus the desired result is achieved.

What can we say about this refined machine? Firstly, it has a precise relationship with the original machine in the sense that we can relate the
semantics clearly through the covering relations that hold between the
input and output alphabets and the memory. The theory in Chapter 6
demonstrates that the state refinement we have constructed is actually
a *functional refinement*. This relates the functions computed by the
machines in a transparent manner. If the original machine computes a
function $f$: seq(*Input*) $\rightarrow$ seq(*Output*) and the refined machine computes
the function $f'$: seq(*Input'*) $\rightarrow$ seq(*Output'*) then these are related by the
diagram in Figure 4.8, where $u^*$ is the sequential generalisation of
$u$ : seq(*Input'*) $\rightarrow$ *Input* and $v^*$ is the sequential generalisation of
$v$: seq(*Output'*) $\rightarrow$ *Output*. The diagram means that for any $x \in$ seq(*Input'*):

$$v^*(f'(x)) = f(u^*(x))$$

Once we have understood how to refine a state and an associated processing function, it is an easy matter to consider a more general refinement
process where we carry out several such refinements in one go. Naturally,
one has to be careful to keep the refining machines separate and to integrate the refinements in a consistent way. A complete definition of how this
can be done is covered in Chapter 6.

## 4.5   TESTING REFINED MACHINES

There is another benefit when we come to examine the test sets for the
refined machine. There are two possible strategies. We could generate the
complete stream X-machine after it has been fully refined and then apply
the complete functional testing method in one go. This will involve generating a single, and potentially very large, test set as we described in Chapter
3. The alternative approach is to generate test sets for the refining machines
separately, test them and then construct a testing strategy for the integration of these into the initial top level machine. The theory behind this
approach is explained in Chapter 8.

The procedure is as follows. First we test an implementation of the refining machine displayed in Figure 4.6. Naturally, we must ensure that the design for test conditions are satisfied. We must also consider how the component is to be integrated into the top-level system. It is necessary that the implementation contains some mechanism for indicating to the top-level machine whether it is in its terminal state. This is done through the use of *transfer variables*. What we do is define an extra basic function in the refining machine at its terminal state which is a loop transition that, when fired, indicates that the terminal state has been reached. The detailed definition and examples are in Definition 8.2.1 and Figure 8.2. The test set for this part is determined according to the method in Chapter 3. In the general case this loop transition augmentation has to be done in *each* refining machine.

Let us now assume that this has been done and this component (implementation of the refining machine) has passed the tests. We now proceed to testing the complete system. The complete system has been implemented using the components integrated into a complete implementation using the state refinement method. We thus have a potential implementation for the machine in Figure 4.7.

The complete test set that will be applied to this compete implementation is of the form:

$$Y_r = Y' \cup U_k,$$

where $Y$ is a test set of the original (unrefined machine) and $Y'$ is a set of input sequences in the refined machine that are constructed from $Y$, and $U_k$ is a special set of test inputs known as a k-distinguishing set of the refining set. We will explain how these are constructed in the case of the Estimator example, where MAIN is the initial state.

### 4.5.1. Step 1: generating Y:

$$Y \text{ is } t(X),$$

where $X = T \bullet (\Phi^k W \cup \Phi^{k-1} W \cup ... \cup W)$
Now, $S = \{< >, \textbf{close, orders, prices, cust, cust :: help\_cust}\}$ is a state cover of the original machine, thus $T = S \cup S \bullet \Phi$ hence:

$$T = \Phi \cup \{\textbf{close}\} \bullet \Phi \cup \{\textbf{orders}\} \bullet \Phi \cup \{\textbf{prices}\} \bullet \Phi \cup \{\textbf{cust}\}$$
$$\bullet \Phi \cup \{\textbf{cust :: help\_cust}\} \bullet \Phi$$

Now let $W = \{\textbf{edit\_order, edit\_price, edit\_cust, open, cust}\}$.
If $k = 1$ then

$$X = [\Phi \bullet W] \cup [\{\textbf{close}\} \bullet \Phi \bullet W] \cup [\{\textbf{orders}\} \bullet \Phi \bullet W] \cup [\{\textbf{prices}\} \bullet$$
$$\Phi \bullet W] \cup [\{\textbf{cust}\} \bullet \Phi \bullet W] \cup [\{\textbf{cust :: help\_cust}\} \bullet \Phi \bullet W] \cup [\Phi^2 \bullet W]$$
$$\cup [\{\textbf{close}\} \bullet \Phi^2 \bullet W] \cup [\{\textbf{orders}\} \bullet \Phi^2 \bullet W] \cup [\{\textbf{prices}\} \bullet \Phi^2 \bullet W]$$
$$\cup [\{\textbf{cust}\} \bullet \Phi^2 \bullet W] \cup [\{\textbf{cust :: help\_cust}\} \Phi^2 \bullet W]$$

Thus $Y = t(X)$ which is obtained, in this case, by replacing the functions by their corresponding input (button press event), so **orders** is translated into orders and so on. In general this may not be the case and the test function will have a more complex definition.

**4.5.2. Step 2: refining $Y$ to $Y'$.** This is done by replacing any occurrence of the input cust_details with the sequence name :: address :: phone :: **OK**.

**4.5.3. Step 3: constructing the k-distinguishing set.**

$S = \{<\ >, $ **close, orders, prices, cust, cust :: help_cust**$\}$ is a state cover of the original machine. If we take $k = 1$ then (see Chapter 8) we identify all the paths that start at the initial state of the original machine and which comprise either an element from the state cover or an element of the state cover followed by a basic function.

$P_1 = \{<\ >, $ **close, orders, prices, cust, cust :: help_cust, close :: open, orders :: edit_order, orders :: close_order, prices :: close_price, prices :: edit_price, cust :: edit_cust, cust :: close_cust, cust :: help_cust :: close_help_cust**$\}$

Also, we construct distinguishing sets (Definition 8.1.2) for the refining machines. These are sets of sequences of basic functions that will distinguish the initial state of the refining machine from the rest. In this case they are:

$$X_{CUSTOMERS} = \{\textbf{name}'\}$$

for the refining machine of Figure 4.6 and

$$\begin{aligned}
X_{MAIN} &= \{\textbf{close}\} \\
X_{OFF} &= \{\textbf{open}\} \\
X_{PRICES} &= \{\textbf{edit\_price}\} \\
X_{ORDERS} &= \{\textbf{edit\_order}\} \\
X_{HELP\_CUST} &= \{\textbf{close\_help\_cust}\}
\end{aligned}$$

for the others since all the refining machines except one are trivial.

Now we can build $U_1$. Consider a path from the set $P_1$ and let $q$ be its end state. The path defines a sequence of inputs $s^*$ from $\Phi$ through the application of the fundamental test function for the top-level machine. There is a sequence $s^{*\prime}$ of inputs in the refining machine that are mapped by $u$ onto $s^*$. We will combine this input sequence with the sequences obtained by applying the test function of the initial state of the refining machine to the distinguishing sets for each state in the original machine to create $U_1$.

$U_1 = \{cust :: name :: address :: phone :: OK :: t_{CUSTOMERS}(\textbf{name}'),$
$\qquad cust :: help\_cust :: t_{HELP\_CUST}(\textbf{close\_help\_cust}),$
$\qquad prices :: edit\_price :: t_{PRICES}(\textbf{edit\_price}),.........\}$

$\quad = cust :: name :: address :: phone :: OK :: name,$
$\qquad cust :: help\_cust :: help\_cust,$
$\qquad prices :: edit\_price :: edit\_price,.........\}.$

What we are doing here is exercising paths in the completed system which connect the component machines to the top-level machine. In other words, we are testing the integration of the component. Hence the path defined by the input sequence (for any initial memory value).

*cust* :: *name* :: *address* :: *phone* :: *OK* :: *name* is accessing the component, moving through it to exercise the refined path (function), returning to the main machine and then accessing the component initially again. The other input sequences in $U_1$ are exercising the rest of the original machine to establish that the CUSTOMERS component has not disturbed the functionality of the rest of the machine. In a more complex refinement these paths would also be exercising the other refinements using other refining machines. So, for example, if we had refined ORDERS and PRICES in a similar way to CUSTOMERS we would have seen sequences representing the access and traversal of these components as well.

From the theory in Chapter 8 we see that the combination of testing the components separately and testing their integration in this way is sufficient to fully test the complete system.

## 4.6   COMPONENTS REVISITED

We mentioned, earlier, that a component would be regarded as a stream X-machine or a basic process function. In the refinement of the Estimator example we have seen the way in which a stream X-machine, the refining machine, was involved in the process of building a more complete solution. Here is an example of a potential component. Suppose that we were constructing the Estimator model and we wished to create the refinement which replaced the high-level function carried out by the **edit_cust** operation. We identified that the refining machine needed to have an alphabet that decomposed part of the original alphabet, and processing functions that extracted inputs of a suitable type and stored them in a suitable memory structure. The outputs were also related and involved the packaging of the user interface for this refining machine into a suitable screen layout and display. All of this could be *implemented* in a *local* package with the relationships between the original machine and the refining machine described by the translation functions *u, v* and h.

A component of this type consists of a stream X-machine with a specified input set, output set, memory set, basic processing functions and the state structure *together* with a well-tested implementation. The initial state and the terminal states must also be specified. Such a package could be available in many different programming and hardware description languages. The way that it was integrated into the original machine would be determined by the state being refined and the translation functions. It is a straightforward matter to implement a stream X-machine where the input and output sets are described in conveniently implementable data structures, as is the memory. The control structure of the machine provides the overall control architecture of the program and the basic functions are implemented directly from their definitions. A refinement will involve interfacing the refining machine or component to the master program by using the translation functions and replacing the original basic function calls by calls to the component.

Many components are likely to be very similar. We have seen the use of a component which extracted input information and stored it under the label of *name, address, phone*. Thus there were three data slots. Each slot was defined with respect to a specific data type, seq(CHAR). It would be quite feasible to have another component with the same basic structure but which stored the resultant input data under different labels, e.g. *reference_number, model_type, price* if the system was a sales record system. Thus the component could be reused if there was a simple way of changing the names of the data slots as well as the names displayed on the user interface screens.

We could take it further and envisage components which allowed us to define the number of slots that were available, the type of each slot and its name. A generic stream X-machine architecture could then be constructed which would amount to a *configurable component*. In this case the configurable component could be available as a software package with the information presented in a diagram something like Figure 4.9, together with definitions of the types and suitable algorithms or functional descriptions of the processing functions. Automatically configured test sets would be available for such components and the use of these would be integrated into the testing strategy of the refined system.

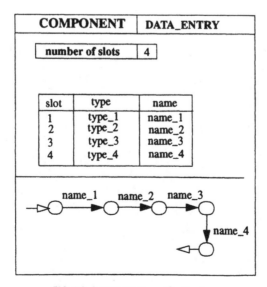

**FIG. 4.9.** A component specification box.

The idea of a configurable component can be taken much further. However, we must not compromise the complete description as a stream X-machine if we are to capitalise on the philosophy of correct system construction and the integrated design and test approach. The use of well tested and easily testable configurable components, which would be available as software modules with stream X-machine descriptions, is a natural direction for software and hardware engineering to take, rather than the seemingly unreliable world of classes, objects and other ill-defined "component" approaches.

# 5 A Case Study

*Summary. The stamp dealer's business background, a requirements statement, developing the specification, generating the test sets, developing the implementation, looking at the final system.*

In this chapter we look at a real case study, a system that was built for a real, commercial, client using the ideas described above. The background was of a small retail enterprise that wished to computerise its entire operations. The challenge was to deliver the correct system at the correct time to a high level of quality. This was achieved: it took three person months, was delivered on time and has run continuously for 16 months with no faults reported. This chapter is based on the work of Mohammed Al-Qaed.

## 5.1 AN EXAMPLE OF A STREAM X-MACHINE SPECIFICATION: BASIC BACKGROUND AND THE REQUIREMENTS CAPTURE PROCESS

A critical part of this project, like any other project, was that of identifying, *correctly*, the required system and this is an area where the integrated X-machine approach was very helpful. A number of discussions with the client took place, which could be summarised as follows:

- understanding the client's business and its environment;
- identifying the basic business processes and producing a business process model in simple English, which was approved by the client;
- translating the business process model into a sequence of specific activities defined around a number of user interface modes – essentially screens;
- formalising the top level interface structure using state diagrams;

- identifying the activity for each screen, the data to be input at appropriate points and the control buttons to move to other states of the system;
- checking with the client, through a number of simple non-functional prototype screen displays, that the correct information was available at the correct time and in the correct order during the proposed system operation.

Thus the outline structure of the system architecture was based on the identification of the main "superstates" of the user interface and of the type of data to be input to or output from these screens and their relative relationships – which screen led to which screen and so on (that is, the dynamics of the interface navigation). This is a very important and practical method since the client was able to see the relationship of the different parts of the system in a meaningful and concrete way at an early stage and was able to relate it to the business process model that he understood. The approach was intuitive for all concerned and yet produced, in a hierarchical and structured way, a *complete* formal specification to the level of abstraction that was required for an implementation. It is unlikely that traditional formal methods – Z [16], VDM [17], OBJ [18], CCS [38], CSP [86] – could be used in this way to the same effect. Yet the specification was entirely formal, was developed in a way that emphasised precision and conciseness and was used as a basis for the generation of a complete functional test set.

This case study is based on a real software development project undertaken by Mohammed Al-Qaed and one of the authors during June–September 1996. The client runs a postal philately business and wishes to computerise his operation. These notes describe the current business process and some initial outline requirements as captured by the software engineer during a number of discussions with the client. Later we will see a full formal development of this system using stream X-machines. The method is based around the identification of the structure of the user interface in consultation with the client and, eventually, the use of a visual programming language. The testing method was then applied, as discussed in a later chapter.

## The Current Business Environment

The dealer sells new (mint) and used postage stamps from any country to stamp collectors, who collect stamps out of interest or for investment. Some of the stamps are extremely rare and valuable. These stamps are categorised by *country* and every group of stamps from the same category is located on one or more *cards*. The cards are simply small albums of two sizes – the small ones are more expensive than the bigger ones. The *units* consist of one or more cards, and these are filed ready for sending to customers. Units are the smallest part in the system and they have an *identity number* with a *colour* to make the search easier. In the normal course of business, customers will indicate the type of stamps they are interested in and on a regular basis the dealer will send collections of stamps by post to customers for their approval, the customers retaining the ones they want and returning the rest with an appropriate payment. Currently the dealer stores all the information required in manual files and when he wants to send some units he adds all the data manually and ensures that the units to be sent have not been sent before to the same customer.

## Current Manual Procedures

5.1.1. The dealer categorises the stamps into groups and separates each group into units. Each unit contains a selection of stamps and all the stamps are from a specific country.

5.1.2. He then numbers each group using three digits and four colours to make the manual search easier.

5.1.3. All new stamps have to be categorised and numbered before they are added to the system.

5.1.4. The customer, initially, contacts the dealer and indicates that he or she wishes to buy some stamps.

5.1.5. The dealer replies with a list of categories available.

5.1.6. The customer chooses some categories of stamps and selects an appropriate time interval for receiving the stamps (for example, immediately, two weeks, one month or any other date).

5.1.7. The dealer will check if these categories are available or not. He will send some units from the categories requested (if all the categories requested are not available then he writes to ask the customer to choose others). He will write down the customer's name, address and the units to be sent.

5.1.8. The customer selects some stamps from the units delivered and keeps them. He or she returns the others to the dealer with the money for the stamps purchased and gives their next choice of categories and the date for receipt of another package of stamps.

5.1.9. The dealer writes down the cost of the stamps sold and puts the customer's name in the queue for the next order. This queue is subject to the choice of the customer for his or her next order date (a customer who does not give a next order date will be deleted from the system automatically).

5.1.10. Repeat steps 5.1.1 to 5.1.3 for new stamps to be added to the system.

5.1.11.  Repeat steps 5.1.7 to 5.1.9 for the process of selling the stamps (Steps 5.1.4–5.1.6 are for new customers only).

This is a simple business process model, which was confirmed by the dealer/client as representing the way he wished the proposed system to work. This activity was relatively straightforward, since there were no technical computing issues raised at that time.

## Elementary Data Modelling

We now start identifying some of the simple aspects of the system.

### Units and Customers

Description of the sale units:

The system consists of 300–400 units (maximum).

There are two types of units (big/small).

Each unit has the following fields:

Number: Identity number (unique) to distinguish between cards.

Colour: To make the search easy.

Number: Number of cards in the units.

Category: Country or region.

Description of the customers:

The system consists of 150 customers (maximum).

Each customer has the following fields:

Number: Identity number (unique).

Name: Customer's name.

Address: Customer's address.

Date of next order: Immediately, one week, two weeks or one month.

Categories: Stamps requested from specific categories.

Unit numbers: Which units were sent to the customer (could be more than one)?

Cost: How much has the customer spent?

### Basic Assumptions and the Operating Context

The system will be installed in a "standalone" computer and will be used by the dealer only, so no protections such as passwords are required by the dealer.

The dealer should have a basic knowledge of the Windows environment [87], and he must be able to run a suitable word processor application and be able to edit and print out texts.

The system must be easy enough to understand and use without a lot of training. The system will use the Windows environment and must provide appropriate help when needed at every stage.

A search facility is needed for customer numbers and names but not for addresses.

Only records of requests during the last six months are required to be stored in the system for each customer.

### Specific Constraints

The user owns an Intel Pentium PC with 8 MB of RAM, an 800 MB hard disk and 100 MHz processor.

The system was to be implemented using a Visual Basic [88] interface to a microsoft Access [89] database. This decision was made primarily on the basis of what was available to the developer but also to see if the specification and testing methods were suitable for such a commonly used language. The system must be reliable and fully documented and needed to be developed rapidly (three months at most).

## Informal Initial Requirements

Req. 1. To produce an application to automate the manual operations of the stamp dealer system. This application must do all the functions of the system that can currently be done manually and provide the necessary data for the user at the appropriate time. The application should be easy to use and the process must be faster and easier than the manual method.

Req. 2. The manual method consists of *units* and each unit consists of *cards* that contain many *stamps* of the same *category*. These units have *identity numbers* and *colours* to distinguish them. The user should be able to **edit** units' data (*unit number, colour, category, number of cards* and *type*). The units' data should be stored in the computer for use at the time fo sale (request and send orders process).

Req. 3. The maximum number of units in the system is *400* and there are four colours (*Red, Blue, Yellow, Green*). There should be no restrictions in permitted category names except the length, which is *30* characters maximum. The card type is either small or large, and the number of cards is not more than *20* and not fewer than *1*.

Req. 4. *Customer names* and *addresses* need to be **stored** in the computer database, so *identity numbers* are important in order to identify each customer. There will be no more than 200 customers in total, so three digits could be enough for the identity numbers.

Req. 5. The dealer should be able to **add** new units or customers to the system. He should be able to **modify, browse** or **delete** the existing ones.

Req. 6. The dealer could **send** existing units to existing customers at any time. This process is done in two steps: in the first, the customer **requests** to see some stamps from a particular country (category) and gives a preferred date for receiving these stamps. The dealer **opens** a request transaction for the customer and **notes** the categories needed, with the date. If this is not the first request for the customer, then the dealer notes the cost of previous stamps sold to the customer to provide a check on the customer's usual purchasing habits.

Req. 7. When the dealer wants to **send** stamps to customers the system should suggest the first order to be done. The suggestion comes from the first due date of the requests, but the dealer should also be able to **examine** the order and **select** any request from the list.

Req. 8. The system should be able to **display** a customer's record (number, name and address). Some useful information must be displayed with the customer record: the total number of orders the customer has made previously and the total value of stamps purchased by the customer. This will give an indication about the customer's previous purchasing record to allow the dealer to send a suitable number of units.

Req. 9. The system should **suggest** the units to be sent to the customer, which should be different from those sent during the last six months' transactions with that customer. These units should, naturally, be available from stock and also from the same category requested by the customer. This suggestion will assist the dealer in sending suitable units that have not been sent before to the customer. This must be flexible and allow the dealer to select from the units sent to the customer before if he prefers.

Req. 10. The **replies** from a customer with his or her next request and the **send** to customer process should be repeated until the dealer **deletes** the customer from the system.

### Additional Requirements (Identified after installation of Version 1)

NewReq. 1. *After* **selecting** some units in (step Req. 9), the dealer should be able to **print** a *ready* letter (edited beforehand) to the customer including the unit numbers which will be sent and the category names. A *special offer message* must be printed in the same letter if the customer has recently purchased more than 10 (or some other suitable number) collections of stamps over a given period.

NewReq. 2. If the customer **fails to return** the units sent on approval, then the dealer should be able to **send** a letter requesting **return** of the unwanted items. This letter must include the units with the date of dispatching the stamps to the customer.

## 5.2   DEVELOPING THE SPECIFICATION

The first outline interface specification (identification of the top level control states) is shown in Figure 5.1. This diagram presents the top-level control structure of the proposed user interface. It presents to the client a series of forms that will implement, in outline, the processes identified in the requirements. The labels on the arcs represent functions which will be defined formally later; at this level these functions represent events such as clicking on a menu button to select a new state. The **MM** functions represent the return to the main menu, either at the end of an action or through an explicit "MainMenu" button click. In this particular example, prototype forms were implemented (using Visual Basic), to provide the client with a realistic simulation of a system.

Many of the states were then refined by introducing subsidiary states to reflect the "subfunctionality" of the state; thus, we extend the Customer-DataEntry state to include a display and select operation, in other words the

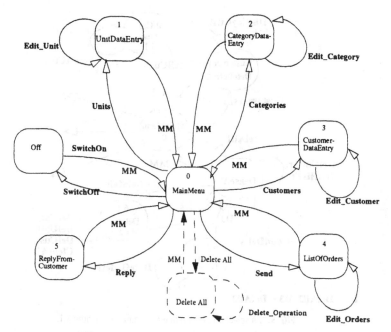

**FIG. 5.1.** An X-machine specification: first version (level 1).

**Edit_Customer** function in the CustomerDataEntry state was refined by a suitably designed refining machine. Other states were introduced to cater for functions that were not in the original model, after discussion with the client. For example, the client wished to have a screen where various types of deletion operation could be carried out. This meant that the new top-level diagram had an extra state, indicated by the dotted area of Figure 5.1. This is an example of changing requirements being managed in a simpn a simple and intuitive way. Having done this the **Delete_Operation** function could be refined, which involved introducing a DeleteAll state and refining the diagram as shown in Figure 5.2.

Thus a number of refinements involving the refining of functions on specific states have been carried out. These can be refined further to allow for the full description of the functionality of the system down to the level of the basic Access functions described later in this section. It was thus possible to move to a full specification of the system in a few refinement stages. We present some of the details.

## Developing the Input/Output

The input for this system is of two types: constants (lower case characters) and variables (upper case characters). These two categories correspond to control inputs which will cause, in general, a change of the control state, and data entry inputs. The first are simply the mouse clicks over the objects on

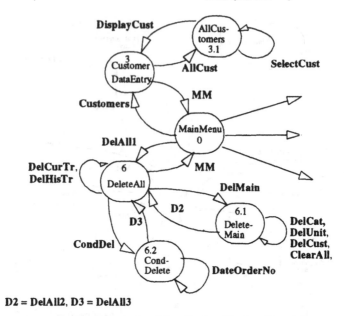

**D2 = DelAll2, D3 = DelAll3**

**FIG. 5.2.** A selection of the refined machine from Figure 5.1.

the displayed screens, and the second are the details of the form entry values. These second inputs must be of the correct type and lie within the range of valid values.

Y = {*on, off, data_maint, unit_data_entry, category_data_entry, customer_ data_entry, all_units_list, all_customers_list, select_unit, select_customer, reply_from_customer, send_to_customer, list_of_orders, delete_ all_menu, delete_main, cond_delete, delete_cats, delete_units, delete_ custs, delete_cur_tr, delete_hist_tr, clear_all, main_menu, next, previous, delete, modify, add, save, cancel, ok, apply, change_order, yes, no, show_hide, select, de_select, select_all, selection, other, print*} ∪ *CUST_NOS* ∪ *CUST_NAME* ∪ *ADDRESS* ∪ *UNIT_NOS* ∪ *CATEGORIES* ∪ *GROUP* ∪ *NO_OF_CARDS* ∪ *TYPE* ∪ *DATE* ∪ *COST* ∪ *ORDER_NO* ∪ *PERIOD*

where:

- *CUST_NOS* represents the set of all the valid customer numbers (i.e. 100 ≤ *CUST_NOS* ≤ 999).
- *CUST_NAME* represents a set string of characters, where the allowed length is between 1 and 50 characters.
- *CATEGORIES* represents a set of string of characters, where the allowed length is between 1 and 30 characters.
- *GROUP* represents a set of strings of characters, where the allowed length is between 1 and 30 characters.

- *NO_OF_CARDS* represents the set of numbers starting from 1 to 20. (i.e. $1 \leq NO\_OF\_CARDS \leq 20$).
- *TYPE* is the type of cards. There are only two types of cards (i.e. *TYPE* = {*big, small*})
- *DATE* is any valid date of the format (*dd'-mm'-yy'*),where *d, m, y, d', m', y'* ∈ *DIGIT*.
- *COST* is the cost of the purchased stamps. The *COST* could be any real number.
- *UNIT_NOS* is a character representing unit colour (*R, B, Y, G*) or mint (*M*) and a set of all the valid unit numbers (i.e. $100 \leq UNIT\_NOS \leq 999$), so *UNIT_NOS* are the combination of one letter with three digits.
- *ADDRESS* represents a set of strings of characters, where the allowed length is between 1 and 200 characters.
- *PERIOD* = {*Three months, Six months, One year, Two years*}.
- *ORDER_NO* is any integer number.

The output will be divided into two streams: $Z = Z_1 \times Z_2$.

$Z_1$ = {*MAIN_MENU, DATA_MAINT, UNIT_DATA_ENTRY, CATEGORY_ DATA_ENTRY, CUSTOMER_DATA_ENTRY, ALL_UNITS, ALL_CUS-TOMERS, REPLY_FROM_CUST, SEND_TO_CUST, LIST_OF_ORDERS, DELETE_ALL, DELETE_MAIN, COND_DELETE* }

$Z_2$ = {*LETTER1, LETTER2*} × *MESSAGES*

where:

- *MAIN_MENU* is the main menu screen, which contains five options to choose from [state 0].
- *UNIT_DATA_ENTRY* = *UDE_Screen* × *UNIT_NO* × *CATEGORIES* × *NO_OF_CARDS* × *TYPE* [state 1].
- *CATEGORY_DATA_ENTRY* = *CDE_Screen* × *CATEGORIES* × *GROUP* [state 2].
- *CUSTOMER_DATA_ENTRY* = *CuDE_Screen* × *CUST_NO* × *CUST_NAME* × *ADDRESS* [state 3].
- *ALL_UNITS* = *ALU_Screen* × *SeqOfUnit* (sequence of records), where each record contains (*UNIT_NOS* × *CATEGORY* × *NO_OF_CARDS* × *TYPE*) [state 1.1].
- *ALL_CUSTOMERS* = *ALC_Screen* × *SeqOfCust* (sequence of records), where each record contains (*CUST_NO* × *CUST_NAME*) [state 3.1].
- *REPLY_FROM_CUST* = *RFC_Screen* × *CUST_NO* × *CUST_NAME* × *RETURN_PRO* × *NEW_ORDER_PRO*, where:
  - *RETURN_PRO* = *LIST_UNITS* × *LIST_RET_UNITS* × *COST*
  - *NEW_ORDER_PRO* = *LIST_CAT* × *LIST_REQ_CAT* × *DATE* [state 5].
- *SEND_TO_CUST* = *STC_Screen* × *CUST_NO* × *CUST_NAME* × *ADDRESS* × *TOT_ORDER* × *TOT_COST* × *DATE* × *LIST_BIG_UNITS* × *LIST_SMALL_UNITS* × *UNIT_NOS* × *SEL_BIG* × *SEL_SMALL* [state 4.1].

- *LIST_OF_ORDERS = LOO_Screen × SeqOfOrd* (sequence of records), where each record contains (*CUST_NO × CUST_NAME × DATE*) [state 4].
- *DELETE_ALL* is the "delete all" screen, which contains five options to choose from [state 6].
- *DELETE_MAIN* is the delete main data menu, which contains five options to choose [state 6.1].
- *COND_DELETE = CD_Screen × PERIOD × ORDER_NO*, where *PERIOD* and *ORDER_NO* are introduced in the input alphabet [state 6.2].
- *LETTER1* represents a sequence of characters saved as a text file named **return_a.txt**, which contains a letter to customers who have failed to return the approvals sent to them. This letter requests the customer to return the approvals as soon as possible.
- *LETTER2* represents a sequence of characters saved as a text file named **send_apr.txt**, which contains a letter to customers including all the units sent to them.
- *MESSAGES = {msg1, msg2, msg3,…, msg92, No_Mess}*, where *msg1,…., msg92* are messages or sequences of messages displayed by the machine. These are four examples of the messages:
  ⇒ *msg1* = "Duplicate category.. Please try again."
  ⇒ *msg2* = "You must fill the category field."
  ⇒ *msg3* = "You must fill the group field."
  ⇒ *msg4* = "Are you sure you want to delete this category?"
  ⇒ *No_Mess* represents the blank message.

## The memory

The memory does not contain any screen formats or messages, but it stores the information needed at the execution process of the X-machine model. We will be wishing to access the underlying database records, and certain basic information is needed in the memory to do this conveniently. As described in the last section, the memory consists of:

$$M = \text{an array of global variables} \times Z_1$$

where: an array of global variables: *FLAG × UNIT_NOS × CUST_NOS*:

- *FLAG*, an integer, represents a flag and its valid values are *1* to *5*.
- *UNIT_NOS* is a character representing unit colour (*R, B, Y, G*) or mint (*M*) and a set of all the valid unit numbers (i.e. *100 # UNIT_NOS # 999*), so *UNIT_NOS* are the combination of one letter with three digits.
- *CUST_NOS* represents the set of all the valid customer numbers (i.e. *100 ≤ CUST_NOS ≤ 999*).

$Z_1$ was defined above.

The initial memory value *m0* = ( *InitMem*, ∧ ) where *InitMem* is the clear array of global variables (*0, ∧, 0*).

## The Processing Functions

In addition to the processing functions we require some other functions to manipulate the database functions or any other functions in the lower levels. The database used to develop the system is Access 2.0 [89]. We will require some functions to "write", "read", "find a record", "delete", "modify", etc. the database. Since these functions are available in the Access 2.0 database we will not be concerned about the way these functions are implemented within Access 2.0. We will also make an assumption that these functions are correct. There are also some other "system" functions available in Visual Basic [88], such as "select a cell", which we will assume to be available and correctly implemented.

These are some of the partial functions required in Level 1 of our X-machine, followed by descriptions of some of them as an example:

GetFirstUnit(UnitTable), GetFirstCat(CategoryTable), GetFirstCust (CustomerTable), GetAllUnits(UnitTable), GetAllCust(CustomerTable), GetUnitNo(SeqOfUnit), GetUnit(), SelUnit(SeqOfUnit), SelCust (SeqOfCust), GetRecords(TempTrans), SelRec(SeqOfOrd), GetCustNo (SeqOfOrd), GetCustData(CustomerTable, TempTransTable), GetRecords (TempTrans).

where:

- GetFirstUnit(UnitTable) retrieves the first record in the unit table and displays it on the screen if the table is not empty.
- SelRec(SeqOfOrd) selects the clicked record by highlighting it; once the record is highlighted it means that one of its attributes has changed. Since all attributes are kept in the memory, this function will change the memory.
- GetCustData(CustomerTable, TempTransTable) retrieves customer data from customer tables and the categories requested by the customer from TempTrans table.

The following is the complete set of functions, which have the effect of reading the input and current memory, moving to the next state, and altering the memory and the output.

$\Phi$ = {SwitchOn, SwitchOff, DataMaint1, MainMenu1, Units, DisplayUnit, AllUnit, SelectUnit, DataMaint2, Categories, DataMaint3, Customers, DisplayCust, AllCust, SelectCust, DataMaint4, Reply, MainMenu2, Send, MainMenu3, SelectRecord, Ok, List, MainMenu4, DelAll1, MainMenu5, DelCurTr, DelHisTr, DelMain, DelAll2, DelCat, DelUnit, DelCust, ClearAll, CondDel, DelAll3, Cancel, Date, OrderNo, Next1, Prev1, Delete1, Cancel1, Save1, NewUnit, IllegalUnitNo, UnitNo, Modify, IllegalCategory1, SelCategory1, IllegalNoCards, NoCards, IllegalType, Type, NewCategory, Cancel2, Save2, Next2, Prev2, Delete2,

IllegalCategory2, Category2, IllegalGroup2, Group2, NewCustomer, IllegalCustNo3, CustNo3, IllegalCustName3, CustName3, IllegalAddress, Address, Ok3, Modify3, Cancel3, Save3, Next3, Prev3, Delete3, IllegalCustData4, ChangeOrder, DeleteTrans, CustData, Cancel41, Cancel42, Save41, Save42, Select41, DeSelect41, Select42, DeSelect42, Apply41, Apply42, IllegalCost, Cost, IllegalDate, Date, NewOrder, ReturnUnits, No41, No42, Yes41, Yes42, PrintLet4, YesPr41, NoPr41, NoPr42, YesPr42, All41, Selection41, All42, Selectio42, Ok5, Next5, Prev5, Cancel5, Save5, Select5, DeSelect5, ShowHide, OtherSelect, UnitNo5, TryAgain, IllegalUnitNo5, Ignore, Apply5, NoPr5, YesPr5 }

Some examples of the definitions of these functions are given next. We have introduced the memory and the output stream, so (for the sake of simplicity) we will introduce the processing functions in the following format, $\phi: Y \times M \to M \times Z_2$. We will not have to mention $Z_1$, since it is part of the memory. These are some examples of the processing functions from Level 1, with brief descriptions for a selection of them:

- **SwitchOn**$(on, (InitMem, \wedge)) = ((InitMem, MAIN\_MENU), (\wedge, No\_Mess))$. The **SwitchOn** function starts at the initial memory (clear memory), removes the current input symbol $(on)$, and displays the *MAIN_MENU* screen. This function does not give any messages or printings. The *MAIN_MENU* screen will be kept in the memory.
- **SwitchOff**$(off, (InitMem, MAIN\_MENU)) = ((InitMem, \wedge), (\wedge, No\_Mess))$. The **SwitchOff** function can be applied from the *MAIN_MENU* screen only. It removes the current input symbol $(off)$, clears the memory and clears the output.
- **DataMaint1**$(data\_maint, (InitMem, MAIN\_MENU)) = ((InitMem, DATA\_MAINT), (\wedge, No\_Mess))$
- **MainMenu1**$(main\_menu, (InitMem, DATA\_MAINT)) = ((Init\_Mem, MAIN\_MENU), (\wedge, No\_Mess))$
- **Units**$(unit\_data\_entry, (InitMemory, DATA\_MAINT)) = ((Init\_Mem, (UDE\_Screen, GetFirstUnit(UnitTable))), (\wedge, No\_Mess))$

## 5.3   DATA DESIGN

The first version of the specification of the entities contained four entities only (*Unit, Category, Customer* and *Transaction*). Initially the customer entity consisted of three attributes but the user requested two additional ones, the total number of orders that a customer has placed and the total price of stamps bought by the customer, so these additional attributes were added after the first version of the product was installed. After the second version of the product was installed the user requested an additional requirement: the *special offer*. This new requirement can be provided by adding a counter

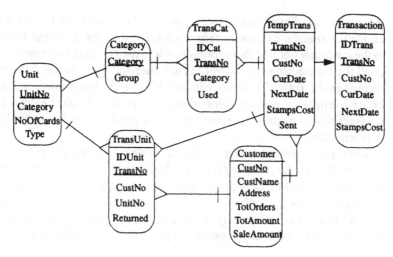

**FIG. 5.3.** Refined entity relationship (all relations are one-to-many).

attribute (*SaleAmount*). The four entities were normalised several times to resolve the one-to-one and many-to-many relationships as these are not accepted by the rules of the entity relationship model. The final entity relationship (the normalised one) is given in Figure 5.3, in which all relations are one to many.

## Some Comments about this Entity Relationship

The TempTrans entity was introduced to differentiate transactions in progress from completed transactions. When any transaction is processed completely it will be moved to the Transaction entity. This reduces the search time for current transactions and reduces the size of the TempTrans entity that is required to be used at every transaction.

The transaction entity is required only as a history at the conditional delete process, and the other attributes may be used in future for some addition requirements from the user (such as detailed transaction information about every customer).

The TempTrans entity is separated into three entities (TempTrans, TransCat and TransUnit) in order to resolve the many-to-many relationship. This normalisation reduced the database size significantly, as in the first model for every transaction we needed to repeat fields of the TempTrans entity for every category the customer requested (it may be more than 20 for an order) and repeat them again for every unit sent to the customer (possibly more than 7 for every order). We can imagine the database size for only 100 transactions.

The CustNo attribute is added to the TransUnit entity (this is not required by the normalization rules). This is done because every time the user requires to send some units to a customer the system must suggest units under the specific categories requested and those that have not been sent to the customer before. This process needs to read from the transaction entity all the transactions made by the customer and then search the matched records in the TransUnit entity with every record in Transaction entity. This process reduces the search time of the system as it should be done for all transactions, so adding only one attribute is much better than affecting the performance.

Since all the entities required by the system have been introduced, we need to choose the most appropriate database to be created and linked to the system. Visual Basic supports many types of databases. After a detailed investigation the final decision was in favour of Access 2.0. The relational data analysis was not strictly necessary, but it was convenient to do this because of the chosen implementation package for the underlying database.

## 5.4   TESTING

One of the main benefits of the X-machine approach is the existence of a complete functional testing theory and algorithms for generating these test sets. This is the next task, and tools would usually be used to construct the full test set. However, it is possible to illustrate some of the constructions with this example. It may seem strange that we are discussing the test generation process before we have looked at the design and implementation process. This is deliberate and is intended to emphasise the importance of thinking about testing at an early stage. Issues of test refinement in conjunction with specification refinement will be discussed elsewhere, and this relationship completes the essential link between specification and test that is one of the cornerstones of our approach.

The following is a small selection of the test set for the X-machine specification defined in Section 5.2. (The specification has to be augmented in the appropriate way so that the design for test conditions are satisfied; this is straightforward and we do not examine it in detail here.)

The first machine can be tested simply, because its input set is very small. All inputs of this machine are the clicks over different command buttons to move from one screen to another, so the complete test set can be constructed and applied in a reasonable time.

The test set for the top-level machine is constructed from the specification involving the following transitions:

$$\Phi = \{reply, MM, SwitchOn, SwitchOff, Units, Edit\_Unit, Categories, Edit\_Category, Customers, Edit\_Customer, Send, Edit\_Orders\}$$

The state cover is:

$$\{< >, Reply, SwitchOff, Units, Categories, Customers, Send\}$$

The W set is:

**{Reply, MM, Edit_Unit, Edit_Category, Edit_Customer, Edit_Orders}**

The complete test set for the top-level machine comprises 128 elements. As we discussed in Chapter 4, the process of testing a system implemented from a number of components involves transforming this test set and testing the implementations of the components separately. So, using the refinement testing method a series of further test sets can be generated, and the whole system tested incrementally.

These test sets were then applied to the implementation and were able to find all faults on the assumption that the basic underlying functions and the primitive Access functions were correct. In practice what happened was the implementations of the individual submachines, such as the CategoryDataEntry machine, were tested fully using the test sets generated, then the complete integration of these machines was tested with the test set formed using the method described in the previous chapter. The details of the refining machines are too lengthy to describe here but the process of constructing the test set for the integration of the components was quite straightforward.

## 5.5  IMPLEMENTATION

The role of the implementation is to translate the detailed design into a physical representation (code) using a programming language. The physical implementation should achieve the user's general and detailed requirements. In order to deliver a system meeting all the agreed client's requirements, which is easy to test and maintain, an appropriate method has to be applied during the development process.

### General Comments

All objects and screens should carry meaningful names, satisfied by the naming rules, and use the graphical power provided by Visual Basic as much as possible. The created screens will not be thrown away (it is not a prototype), so special attention must be given at the implementation of these screens to make them user friendly and easy to use. Copying the components of a well-implemented screen to any similar screens and then modifying the copied components is a good idea and could save time in the event of redesigning the new screens (e.g. UnitDataEntry and CustomerDataEntry).

### Level 1 of the X-machine State Diagram

We translate each state from the first-level X-machine state diagram into a *form* (each form can be considered as a separate screen) and link them as specified in the diagram. The implemented screens will represent Level 1 in the diagram and the arcs between any two states can be represented as an object (Command button) in the first screen (first state), which will unload the current screen and display (load) the second screen (second state) when clicked. This process will end with completed screens for those states that are not refined in the initial diagram (e.g. MainMenu).

## Level 2 of X-machine State Diagram

The second level (refined from some states in Level 1) can be implemented by adding some objects (Command boxes, Text boxes, etc.) to the designed forms. Then the new objects should be linked together in a similar way to the linking between the states in the refined screens. This is not as simple as implementing Level 1 by loading or unloading screens when applying the functions. The control movements this time are going to be done within the same screen between the objects, so we have to disable all the objects on the screen except those that are allowed to be used at that point in the process.

For example, the UnitDataEntry screen (Figure 5.4) implements the UnitDataEntry state (Figure 5.1), so all command buttons on the screen can be clicked (functions in the diagram) except **Save** and **Cancel**. The Text and Combo boxes cannot be accessed at this state. If the command button **NewUnit** is clicked then only the UnitNo text box and Cancel button should

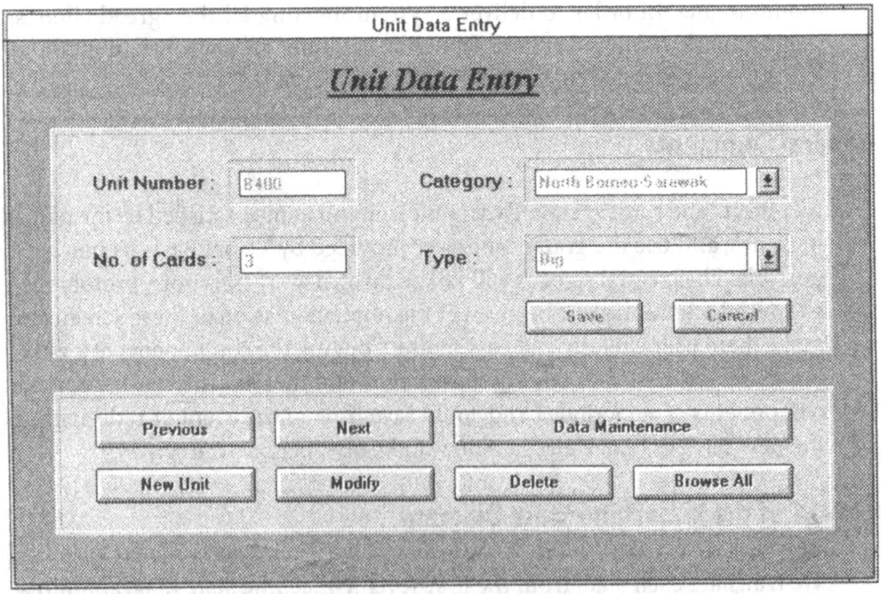

**FIG. 5.4.** UnitDataEntry screen.

be accessed and the others should be disabled. This is the way all the screens were implemented to make them similar to the states in the X-machine specification description. At this step the text boxes will allow any type or length of edited strings as we are not concerned with the data structure and types. At the end of this step we will have many missing functions from the diagram (e.g. Prev1, Next1, IllegalUnitNo), since these require the data structure.

Note: the implemented screens can be used as a prototype version to give the user an idea about the final product layout and how it will perform. This can be done during the requirements capture stage and provides a mechanism for the client to explore the designer's understanding of the business processes. Since the method addresses the client's business processes through screen displays based on forms and the type of data that the client is used to dealing with it turned out to be very productive in this case. The complete requirements must be confirmed at this step or as soon after as possible.

## Add the Conditions Required to Move Between States

At some states a string or number will be required to be edited. The state allows only a particular text, which meets a specific condition (e.g. WaitNoCards state is allowed only a numeric value within the range 1–20 to be inserted/edited in order to move to the next state, and if the input is not of this type the system should stay at the same state and give a message asking the user to edit a valid number within the range). At the end of this step all functions will be implemented except those that require physical data storage (database, file, printer, etc.). The system will provide a convenient environment for coding the main procedures and functions. The programmer should add codes to the objects when a specific event happens (click, key-press, etc.) and code the procedures and functions required.

## Create and Link the Database, Tables and Files

The database, tables and files can be created, because the complete requirements were given, thus the system should be designed completely (the feedback may cause some modifications). After creating the database it can be linked to the system. The link should be started from the basic data (unit, category, and customer entry screens). The product constructed from this stage is ready for the installation as a first version to take the final comments or modifications required by the user (the user may find some errors when using the system in the real environment, so this is an additional means of testing – no formal specification can easily capture all of the environmental conditions that affect the system; in particular, the client's machines may differ in subtle and undisclosed ways from the developer's).

Finally, a complete set of report/user messages and facilities were added and the final modifications made. The complete set of messages in the system was 92 messages, providing the user with a clear statement about the errors, invalid input, confirmation requests for risky functions, etc. Any additional facilities the programmer wishes to add to the system in order to improve the quality or to make the system easier can be added at this stage. The design of these is of great importance and should be discussed with the client.

## 5.6    A SUMMARY OF THE FACILITIES PROVIDED BY THE COMPLETED SYSTEM

The system provides many facilities, including:

5.6.1. It allows you to scroll through all the units' data in one screen and then to select the unit required for modification or deletion using a very simple and easy method (by clicking on the record only). This facility is available for the customers list as well.

5.6.2. It allows you to change the order of the units by unit number, category or type, which could help the user and save time significantly.

5.6.3. It allows you to change the order of customers' data by customer number or name.

5.6.4. During the daily transactions it is very important to provide the user with a powerful searching facility, which is required many times every day. The system provides the user at the time of requesting new orders or at the time of returning units (ReplyFromCustomers screen) with four different ways to find customers. The customers' numbers and names are combined in an ordered list (ordered by number), so the user just has to scroll through them to find the appropriate customer. The second way is by changing the order of the same list to be by customers' name and then make the selection. The third is by typing the customer number and the last is by typing the customer's name: the system will automatically retrieve the customer's information.

5.6.5. The user can delete any untidy/unsatisfactory transaction for a specific customer from the ReplyFromCustomer screen.

5.6.6. To select the requested categories the user has only to click on the categories required from the list and they will be selected, or click over the all Option button to select all the categories. The selection of the returned units can be done in a similar way.

5.6.7. The searching facilities are not required at the time when units are sent, so a list of requests made by all customers is provided (ordered by the sending date) to allow the user to select from it (just click over the record). Then the system will display the complete information about the customer (total number of orders, total stamps sold), which may help the user to decide what sort of customers this is (good, bad, etc.) and thus he can allow the appropriate units to be sent at the same time.

5.6.8. The system will automatically suggest the units to be sent to a customer, which must be units that are available and which have not been sent to the same customer previously. It provides some flexibility by allowing the user to add one of those units sent to the customer, or any units not from the requested categories. He could display the categories requested on the same screen, which helps in selecting the appropriate units.

5.6.9. To simplify the user's work the system displays the total number of big and small cards selected (each unit consists of one or more cards) because he will put them in an envelope and is therefore restricted to a maximum limit of cards.

5.6.10. When the selection is completed by default the system will ask the user to confirm the details in order to print a letter for the customer informing him or her of the units included. If the letter is not printed for some reason (e.g. if the printer is not ready), then the user can print it later from the ReplyFromCustomer screen. If any customer fails to return the units sent to him or her another letter can be printed (including detailed description of the units previously sent) requesting their return as soon as possible. Both letters can be edited or modified by the user, because they are saved as text files.

5.6.11. A complete set of delete facilities is available in the system (delete all units, delete all categories, delete all customers, clear the database, delete the transactions under process, delete the history transactions, or delete history transaction by two conditions: date and number of orders for every customer). All deletion functions will ask for confirmation before applying the delete process.

## Conclusions

A very robust and successful system was developed over a short period of time. The way in which the method was able to capture the client's real requirements in a simple and effective way, together with the user-friendly nature of the formal language used in the specification, were of considerable help in understanding the business processes involved. This precise information was then invaluable for constructing the code very rapidly and for generating the powerful test sets. These are all important strengths of the approach to building a *correct* system for the business. Using modern software development tools (a 4GL, Visual Basic and a proprietary database system, Microsoft Access) adds to the practical nature of the method.

So far the client has reported no faults and is entirely satisfied with the system. His company is now totally dependent on it.

# Part 2
# Theoretical Foundations

# 6 The Theory of X-Machines

*Summary. Basic theory of X-machines, stream X-machines and stream functions, functional refinement, state refinement, the fundamental theorem of refinement.*

The first part of this book concentrated on practical methods for designing a comprehensive formal model of a system in an integrated way that related naturally to the initial stages of requirements identification and capture and allowed for the generation of complete functional test sets. It was formulated on the development of models through a variety of levels of functionality and detail. In this chapter we look at some of the theory that underpins this approach. The philosophy is essentially one of the algebraic modelling of computation. This requires some previous knowledge of the theory of finite state machines [23] and of Turing machines [22], typically material taught in undergraduate computer science degree courses. The chapter begins by considering the formal definition of an X-machine and some of the basic terminology. In Section 6.2 we look at stream X-machines, the key model used in Part 1. The last section introduces the idea of machine refinement – the mechanism for developing a stream X-machine model into more complex models with extended functionality.

## 6.1 THE BASIC THEORY OF X-MACHINES

The Turing model [22] has been a cornerstone of the theory of computation for many years and the Chomsky hierarchy of machines a useful mechanism for categorising machines and languages of different capabilities. Despite their theoretical value, these computational models are not used by software engineers, the principal reason being that they are not readily amenable to traditional analysis and system development. Indeed, the data structures these machines use and process is much too restrictive and low level to be used in practical situations – in most cases such data structures are stacks or tapes and the operations allowed on these are fairly primitive; for example, not even the addition of two integers is straightforward to describe using such low-level models. Also, in practice, one would have the freedom to be able to choose the system data and the way it is processed that best suits the application in hand – as long as these can be implemented on a computer, of course.

One could argue that the development of any software system is a hierarchical process in which each level will use things that result from the previous levels. The depth of this process will depend on the tools that the current application will use; in most cases the bottom level will coincide with methods (functions, procedures, modules, etc.) from the libraries available to the implementation medium used.

Even though the existing computational models are of very little practical use, there is, however, a model, namely the X-machine, that easily accommodates this hierarchical approach and which could therefore be of great practical value. The X-machine is not a computational model itself; it is rather a general framework that abstracts the common features of the main existing models (i.e. finite state machine, pushdown machine, Turing machine and other standard types of machine) and can easily be adapted to suit the needs of many practical applications. The model was introduced in the first chapter; we will now provide a formal definition.

## Basic Concepts

The full and most general definition of an X-machine is our starting point. Such a machine has a finite set of states, $Q$, together with some arrows that link some states with some others. Each arrow is labelled with a function taken from a set of functions $\Phi$ (these functions are possibly partial functions). Each of these functions operates on a given data set, $X$. We identify a set, $I$, of initial states, so that the machine is always started off in one of these states. Usually there is a unique start state. There is also specified a set, $T$, of terminal or final states. In many cases this is the set of all states. In certain situations, however, we may wish to restrict what states can be terminal states and then we will be interested in the conditions under which the machine halts in such a state.

The main issue left is how such a machine would operate. It would need some stimulation and this will be by applying a series of inputs to it. The response of the system will be to create some visible output behaviour. So we postulate the existence of a set *Input* of all possible inputs to the machine and a set *Output* of all possible outputs. The way these inputs are applied to the machine is by an input function $\alpha$, which takes an input and interprets it as an element of $X$. Having supplied the machine with a starting value of $X$ and an initial starting state, it will try to start computing by searching for an arrow leaving that state which is labelled by a function $\phi$

from $\Phi$ which can process the initial value $x$ of $X$. Note that there may be none, one or many such functions such that the value $x$ lies within their domain. One of these functions (if any exist) is selected randomly, say $\phi$, and the new value $\phi(x)$ of $X$ calculated at the same time the machine moves to the state pointed to by the arrow labelled by $\phi$. The process then continues until no further processing is possible. Then we may interpret the value of X using an output function $\beta$ to obtain an output value.

*Definition 6.1.1*

An *X-Machine* is a 10-tuple $\mathcal{M} = (X, Y, Z, \alpha, \beta, Q, \Phi, \mathbf{F}, I, T)$, where:

1. $X$ is the *fundamental data set* that the machine operates on.
2. $Y$ and $Z$ are the *input* and the *output sets*, respectively.
3. $\alpha$ and $\beta$ are the *input* and the *output (partial) functions*, respectively, used to convert the input and the output sets into, and from, the fundamental set:

$$\alpha: Y \to X, \beta: X \to Z$$

4. $Q$ is the (finite) *set of states*.
5. $\Phi$ is the *type* of $\mathcal{M}$, a set of relations on $X$:

$$\Phi: \mathcal{P}(X \to X)$$

The type of the machine is the class of partial functions that constitute the elementary operations that the machine is capable of performing. $\mathcal{P}A$ denotes the power set of A and $(X \to X)$ denotes the set of all, possibly partial, functions from $X$ to $X$. $\Phi$ is viewed as an abstract alphabet. $\Phi$ may be infinite, but only a finite subset $\Phi'$ of $\Phi$ is used (this is because $\mathcal{M}$ has only a finite number of edges despite the infinite number of labels available).

6. $\mathbf{F}$ is the *next-state partial function*:

$$\mathbf{F}: Q \times \Phi \to \mathcal{P}Q$$

$\mathbf{F}$ is often described by means of a state-transition diagram.

7. $I$ and $T$ are the sets of *initial* and *terminal* (or *final*) *states*, respectively:

$$I \subseteq Q, T \subseteq Q$$

Before we continue, we make some simple observations. It is sometimes helpful to think of an X-machine as a finite state machine with the arcs labelled by functions from the type $\Phi$. As we shall define formally later, a computation takes the form of a traversal of a path in the state space and the application, in turn, of the path labels (which represent basic processing functions or relations) to an initial value of the data set X. Thus the machine transforms values of its data set according to the functions called during the state space traversal. The role of the input and output encoding relations is not crucial for many situations but it does provide a general interface mechanism that is useful in a number of applications.

Given an X-machine $\mathcal{M}$ as above, we can convert it into a finite state machine $\mathcal{A} = (\Phi, Q, F, I, T)$ by treating the elements of $\Phi$ as abstract input symbols. We are, in effect, "forgetting" the $X$ set and its structure and the semantics of the elements of $\Phi$. We call this the *associated automaton* of $\mathcal{M}$.

In a similar way to the case for a finite state machine, we can define an arc or a path of an X-machine. As one might expect, a path is a connected sequence of arcs through the machine starting from one state and ending at another (possibly the same one).

### Definition 6.1.2

If $q, q' \in Q$, $\phi \in \Phi$ and $q' \in F(q, \phi)$, we say that $\phi$ is the *arc* from $q$ to $q'$, represented thus:

$$\phi: q \to q' \text{ or } \quad q \quad \xrightarrow{\quad \phi \quad} \quad q'$$

### Definition 6.1.3

If $q, q' \in Q$ are such that there exist $q_1,..., q_{n-1} \in Q$ and $\phi_1,..., \phi_n \in \Phi$ with:

$$\phi_1: q \to q_1, \phi_2: q_1 \to q_2,..., \phi_n: q_{n-1} \to q'$$

we say that we have a *path* $p = \phi_1... \phi_n$ from $q$ to $q'$ and write $p : q \to q'$.

A *successful path* is one that starts in an initial state (in $I$) and ends in a final one (from $T$).

Unlike finite state machines, though, each path $p$ will give rise to a (partial) function:

$$|p| = \phi_n \cdot \phi_{n-1} \cdot ... \cdot \phi_1: X \to X$$

So we apply the functions labelling the path one after the other in the order specified by the path. It may be that the composition is not defined at some point, because the possible values of $X$ computed at that stage do not lie within the domain of the next function to be applied. Under these conditions the path will not be successful after that state.

The function $|\delta|$, corresponding to the empty path $\delta$, is the identity function on $X$.

The union of all the functions computed over successful paths will make up the behaviour of the machine. The behaviour is a process that converts values of $X$ into new values from $X$ but only using the successful paths and the compositions of the functions defined by these paths.

### Definition 6.1.4

$\mathcal{M}$ determines a machine relation $|\mathcal{M}|: X \leftrightarrow X$ in the following way:

$$x \, |M| \, x' \Leftrightarrow \exists \, q_i \in I, q_t \in T \text{ and } p: q_i \to q_t \text{ such that } |p|(x) = x'.$$

$|\mathcal{M}|$ is called the *behaviour* of $\mathcal{M}$.

So $x'$ is related to $x$ with respect to the machine $\mathcal{M}$ if we can find a path from an initial state to a terminal state such that the function defined by this path translates $x$ into $x'$.

To relate this idea to the overall operation of the machine as it relates to its environment – that is, its input and output functions – we proceed as follows. Given $y \in Y$, the operations of the X-machine $\mathcal{M}$ on $Y$ consist of:

1. Picking a path $p$, from a start state $q_i$ ($q_i \in I$), to a final state $q_t$ ($q_t \in T$), $p: q_i \rightarrow q_t$.
2. Applying $\alpha$ to the input to convert it to the internal type $X$.
3. Applying $|p|$, if it is defined for $\alpha(y)$. Otherwise, go back to step 1.
4. Applying $\beta$ to get the output.

Therefore, the operation can be summarised as $\beta(|p|(\alpha(y)))$. Note that in general the output may be nondeterministic in the sense that a set of outputs is produced from a given input.

### Definition 6.1.5

The composite relation $f$ given by $f = \beta \cdot |M| \cdot \alpha : Y \leftrightarrow Z$, i.e.:

$$ Y \xrightarrow{\alpha} X \xleftrightarrow{|\mathcal{M}|} X \xrightarrow{\beta} Z $$

is called the *relation computed* by $M$.

The X-machine model is sufficiently general to model most common types of machine from finite state machines (where the memory is trivial) to Turing machines (where the memory is a model of the tape); see [28].

### Example 6.1.1 (Eilenberg [28])

To demonstrate that the X-machine is a general model of computation we will show how Turing machines, pushdown automata and finite state machines are all special cases. First, we introduce some further notations. These allow us to define a number of very simple functions that add and remove, where possible, symbols from either end of a string.

Let $A$ an alphabet and let $s \in seq(A)$. Then we define (see [28]) the functions $L_s, R_s: seq(A) \rightarrow seq(A)$ by:

$$ L_s (x) = s :: x, R_s (x) = x :: s \ \forall \ x, s \in seq(A) $$

and the partial functions $L_{-s}, R_{-s}: seq(A) \rightarrow seq(A)$ by:

$$ L_{-s} (x) = s^{-1} x \text{ (i.e. domain } L_{-s} = \{s\} \bullet seq(A) \text{ and } L_{-s} (s :: x) $$
$$ = x \ \forall \ x \in \text{domain } L_{-s}); $$

$$ R_{-s} (x) = x :: s^{-1} \text{ (i.e. domain } R_{-s} = seq(A) \bullet \{s\} \text{ and } R_{-s} (x :: s) $$
$$ = x \ \forall \ x \in \text{domain } R_{-s}); $$

Obviously, $L_s$ composed with $L_t$, that is $L_s \, L_t$, equals $L_t :: s$, $R_s \, R_t = R_{s::t}$, $L_{-s} \, L_{-t} = L_{-t::s}$, $R_{-s} \, R_{-t} = R_{-s::t}$ $\forall \, s, t \in seq(A)$. We shall denote the identity function on $seq(A)$ by $1: seq(A) \to seq(A)$.

(i) *Turing machine*. Let $A$ be any finite alphabet. Let $X = seq(A) \times seq(A)$. We define the set of basic functions $\Phi$ to be a set of functions of the following forms:

$$L_s \times L_t \, ; \, L_{-s} \times L_t \, ; \, L_s \times L_{-t} \, ; \, L_{-s} \times L_{-t}$$

where s, t $\in seq(A)$. These functions correspond to the usual operations applied to the tape represented by X. The input code is:

$$\alpha: seq(A) \to X \text{ is defined as } \alpha(s) = (1, s), s \in seq(A).$$

(ii) *Pushdown automaton* [90]. Let $A$ and $B$ be any finite alphabets, the latter representing the values that can be stored on the pushdown stack. Let $X = seq(B) \times seq(A)$. The basic functions $\Phi$ will be a set of functions of the following forms:

$$1 \times L_{-s}, R_t \times 1, R_{-t} \times 1 \, ; \, s \in seq(A), t \in seq(B).$$

Also, $\alpha(s) = (<>, s), s \in seq(A)$, where $<>$ is the empty sequence.

(iii) *Finite state machine*. Let *Input* and *Output* be two finite alphabets. The set $X = seq(Input) \times seq(Output)$. The basic functions $\Phi$ will be a set of functions of the following forms:

$$L_t \times L_{-s}$$

where $s \in seq(Input), t \in seq(Output)$.
Also, $\alpha(s) = (<>, s), s \in seq(Input)$.

## Deterministic X-machines

A *deterministic* X-machine is one in which there is *at most one* possible applicable transition for any state q and any $x \in X$.

### Definition 6.1.6

An X-machine $\mathcal{M} = (X, Y, Z, \alpha, \beta, Q, \Phi, F, I, T)$ is called *deterministic* if the following are true.

1. F maps each pair $(q, \phi) \in Q \times \Phi$ onto at most a single next state, i.e.

$$F: Q \times \Phi \to Q.$$

1. A partial function is used because every $\phi \in \Phi$ will not necessarily be defined as the label to an edge in every state.

2. *I* contains only one element, i.e. $I = \{q_0\}$.

3. If φ and φ' are distinct arcs emerging from the same state:

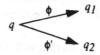

then domain φ ∩ domain φ' = ∅.

Note that requirements 1 and 2 in Definition 6.1.6 above are equivalent to saying that the associated automaton of the machine is deterministic.

In general, these conditions do not always ensure that $f = \beta \cdot |\mathcal{M}| \cdot \alpha$ is a partial function. However, this will be the case for the particular type of X-machines that this book focuses on.

## 6.2 STREAM X-MACHINES

A number of important classes of X-machines have been identified and studied; see [28, [36]. Typically the classes are defined by restrictions on the underlying data set $X$ and the type, $\Phi$, of the machines. In particular, the stream X-machines class has been found to be extremely useful in practice and most of the theory developed so far has concentrated on this class. This is the only class of X-machine that we consider here.

As suggested by their name, stream X-machines are those in which the input and the output sets are streams of symbols. The input stream is processed in a straightforward manner, producing, in turn, a stream of outputs and a regularly updated internal memory state. The power of this subclass of X-machines is considerable and they are able to model many practical computing situations. There are some natural restrictions that must be placed on the form of the processing functions φ to ensure that the machines behave in a sensible way. A formal definition is given next.

When considering sequences of inputs and sequences of outputs we will use seq($A$) to denote the set of finite sequences with members in $A$. $< >$ will denote the empty sequence and seq$_+(A)$ = seq($A$) − {< >}. The notation $a^* \in$ seq($A$) will denote a particular example of such a sequence, $a^* :: b^*$ the concatenation of sequences $a^*$ and $b^*$ and $(a^*)^n$ will denote the concatenation of $a^*$ with itself for $n$ times, $(a^*)^0 = < >$. For two sets $U, V \subseteq$ seq($A$), $U \bullet V = \{a^* :: b^* \mid a^* \in U, b^* \in V\}$.

Also $U^n = \{a_1^* ::...:: a_n^* \mid a_1^*,..., a_n^* \in U\}$, $U^0 = \{< >\}$.

*Definition 6.2.1*

An X-machine $\mathcal{M}$ is called *stream X-machine* if:

1. The type of the machine is of the form:

$$X = seq(Output) \times Memory \times seq(Input)$$

where *Input, Memory, Output* are sets of data; *Input* and *Output* are finite, *Memory* may be infinite. *Input* and *Output* are called the input and the output *alphabets* of the machine respectively, *Memory* is the machine's memory.

The processing functions that will form the set $\Phi$ will operate by reading the *current input* and the *current memory* value and then calculate a *new memory* value and an *output* value. The machine moves to a new state at the same time.

2. The overall inputs and outputs of the machine will be sets of input and output symbols, respectively, i.e.:

$$Y = \text{seq}(Input), Z = \text{seq}(Output)$$

3. The input code $\alpha$: $\text{seq}(Input) \to \text{seq}(Output) \times Memory \times \text{seq}(Input)$ will define the *initial memory value* $m_0 \in Memory$, i.e. $\forall s^* \in \text{seq}(Input)$:

$$\alpha(s^*) = (<>, m_0, s^*)$$

Thus $\alpha$ takes a sequence of inputs and transforms them into a value of $X$ by forming a triple with the empty output word and the initial memory value.

The output code $\beta$: $\text{seq}(Output) \times Memory \times \text{seq}(Input) \to \text{seq}(Output)$ will extract the output sequence of any data value in $X$ with empty input sequence, i.e. $\forall g^* \in \text{seq}(Output)$, $m \in Memory$, $s^* \in \text{seq}(Input)$:

$$\beta(g^*, m, s^*) = \begin{cases} g^*, \text{if } s^* = <> \\ \bot, \text{otherwise} \end{cases}$$

The symbol $\bot$ indicates that the function is undefined in these cases.

The output function just "prints" out the output string provided the computation has stopped with no further input waiting to be processed.

4. Each processing function $\phi \in \Phi$, $\phi$: $\text{seq}(Output) \times Memory \times \text{seq}(Input) \to \text{seq}(Output) \times Memory \times \text{seq}(Input)$ will process (and discard) an input symbol, produce an output symbol and may change the memory, i.e.:

$$\forall g^* \in \text{seq}(Output), m \in Memory \cdot \phi(g^*, m, <>) = \bot$$

and

$\forall m \in Memory, s \in Input \cdot$ either
$\quad \forall g^* \in \text{seq}(Output), s^* \in \text{seq}(Input) \cdot \phi(g^*, m, s :: s^*) = \bot$ or
$\quad \exists m' \in Memory, g \in Output$ (that depend on $m$ and $s$) $\cdot$
$\qquad \forall g^* \in \text{seq}(Output), s \in \text{seq}(Input) \cdot \phi(g^*, m, s :: s^*) = (g^* :: g, m', s^*)$

Thus each basic function $\phi$ is such that it reads the current memory value, reads the current input value and generates a new memory value and an output value at each operation. As a stream of inputs arrives the basic functions will operate one by one if, at each stage, the pair of memory and input values are in the domain of a basic function at that state. Otherwise the machine halts.

A stream X-machine will be denoted by a tuple:

$$\mathcal{M} = (Input, Output, Q, Memory, \Phi, \mathbf{F}, q_0, m_0, T).$$

Stream X-machines were first introduced by Laycock [35]. As pointed out in the first chapter, any processing function $\phi$ of a stream X-machine is completely determined by the values of $g$ and $m'$ above (if any), so, for the sake of simplicity, it will be referred to as:

$$\phi: Memory \times Input \rightarrow Output \times Memory$$

and defined in the form:

$$\phi(m, s) = (g, m')$$

So, starting the machine in a given initial state and an initial memory value and supplying it with a stream of inputs, it will generate a corresponding stream of outputs.

Using this notation, the (partial) function produced by a path $p = \phi_i... \phi_n$ of a stream X-machine can be written as:

$$|p|: Memory \times seq(Input) \rightarrow seq(Output) \times Memory$$

where

$$|p|(m, s^*) = (g^*, m') \Leftrightarrow \exists\, s_1,..., s_n \in Input,$$
$$g_1,..., g_n \in Output, m_2,..., m_n \in Memory$$

with

$$s^* = s_1 ::...:: s_n, g^* = g_1 ::...:: g_n \text{ and } \forall\, i = 1...n, \phi_i(m_i, s_i) = (g_i, m_{i+1})$$

where $m_1 = m$ and $m_{n+1} = m'$. The partial function corresponding to the empty path $\delta$ will be defined by $|\delta|(m, < >) = (< >, m)$, where $m \in Memory$.

The string of inputs will force the machine to traverse a path in a deterministic machine or halt at the first state where no basic function is defined for the current input and current state. As it traverses the path it will generate a string of (internal) memory values and a string of outputs.

In our description we will use the projection functions $\pi_1, \pi_2,..., \pi_n$, where:

$$\pi_1: A_1 \times A_2 \times... \times A_n \rightarrow A_1,$$
$$\pi_2: A_1 \times A_2 \times... \times A_n \rightarrow A_2,$$
$$\pi_n: A_1 \times A_2 \times... \times A_n \rightarrow A_n,$$

and $A_1, A_2,..., A_n$ are sets.

Thus if $|p|(m, s^*) = (g^*, m')$ then the output $g^*$ and the new memory value $m'$ can be referred to as $\pi_1(|p|(m, s^*))$ and $\pi_2(|p|(m, s^*))$, respectively.

Also, given an initial memory value $m_0$, the relation $f: seq(Input) \leftrightarrow seq(Output)$ computed by the machine can be defined by:

$$s^* f g^* \Leftrightarrow \exists\ q_i \in I, q_t \in T \text{ and } p: q_i \to q_t \cdot \pi_1(|p|(m_0, s^*)) = g^*$$

All transitions of the machine $\mathcal{M}$ can be fully described by a relation:

$$[\mathcal{M}]_0: Q \times Memory \times Input \leftrightarrow Output \times Q \times Memory$$

defined by:

$$(q, m, s)\ [\mathcal{M}]_0\ (g, q', m') \Leftrightarrow \exists \text{ an arc } \phi: q \to q' \cdot |\phi|(m, s) = (g, m').$$

Thus, the entire computation of the machine $\mathcal{M}$ can be described by a relation:

$$[\mathcal{M}]: Q \times Memory \times seq(Input) \leftrightarrow seq(Output) \times Q \times Memory$$

defined by:

$$\forall q \in Q, m \in Memory \cdot (q, m, <>) [\mathcal{M}] (<>, q, m)$$
$$\forall\ q, q' \in Q, m, m' \in Memory, s \in Input, s^* \in seq(Input),$$
$$g \in Output, g^* \in seq(Output)$$
$$(q, m, s :: s^*)\ [\mathcal{M}]_0\ (g :: g^*, q', m') \Leftrightarrow \exists\ q'' \in Q, m'' \in Memory \cdot$$
$$(q, m, s)\ [\mathcal{M}]_0\ (g, q'', m'') \text{ and } (q'', m'', s^*)\ [\mathcal{M}]\ (g^*, q', m')$$

In other words, $(q, m, s^*)\ [\mathcal{M}]\ (g^*, q', m')$ if and only if $\exists$ a path $p: q \to q'$ with $|p|(m, s^*) = (g^*, m')$.

$[\mathcal{M}]_0$ will be called the *transition relation* of $\mathcal{M}$ and $[\mathcal{M}]$ the *extended transition relation* of $\mathcal{M}$.

Thus, as far as the machine computation is concerned, a stream X-machine behaves identically to an infinite state machine with outputs whose state set is $Q \times Memory$. However, there is one important difference, which lies in their architecture: an X-machine is made up of a *finite* number of elements (the basic processing functions) which are combined by means of a *finite* state machine-like diagram. This feature will be of crucial importance when it comes to testing.

As defined previously, a deterministic stream X-machine will be one in which there is a single initial state (i.e. $I = \{q_0\}$ ) and there is at most one possible transition for any triplet $q \in Q, m \in Memory, s \in Input$, thus $[\mathcal{M}]_0$, $[\mathcal{M}]$ and $f$ will be (partial) functions rather then relations. This will almost always be the case in practical applications and will be the assumption we will be making throughout our theoretical discussion.

Two concepts that will be needed in our description will be those of *reachable state* and *attainable memory*. A state $q$ is called reachable if the machine can be brought into the state $q$ from the initial state and the initial memory value. An unreachable state can never occur if we always start the machine in the initial state with the initial memory value. All memory values that result from such a computation will be called attainable in $q$.

*Definition 6.2.2*

A state $q$ is called *reachable* if $\exists\ s^* \in$ seq(*Input*), $m \in$ *Memory*, $g^* \in$ seq(*Output*) and $p: q_0 \to q$ a path from the initial state $q_0$ to $q$ with $|p|$ $(m_0, s^*) = (g^*, m)$.

A machine in which all states are reachable will itself be called *reachable*. Clearly, if a state is not reachable it can be removed along with all arcs that emerge from or arrive to it without affecting the function computed by the machine.

*Definition 6.2.3*

Let $q \in Q$. Then $m \in$ *Memory* is called *attainable in* $q$ if and only if $\exists\ s^* \in$ seq(*Input*) and a path $p: q_0 \to q$ with $\pi_2(|p|(m_0, s^*)) = m$.

*Definition 6.2.4*

For any $q \in Q$ we define a subset of memory related to $q$ by:

$$Mattain_q(\mathcal{M}) = \{m \in Memory : \exists\ s^* \in seq(Input)$$

$$\text{and a path } p: q_0 \to q \text{ such that:}$$

$$\pi_2(|p|(m_0, s^*)) = m\}.$$

Thus $Mattain_q(\mathcal{M})$ is the set of memory values that can be taken by the machine whenever it is in state $q$.

Obviously, if $q$ is reachable then $Mattain_q(\mathcal{M})$ is not empty. The union of all sets $Mattain_q(\mathcal{M})$ will make up the attainable memory of the machine.

*Definition 6.2.5*

The subset of memory defined by:

$$Mattain(\mathcal{M}) = \bigcup_{q \in Q} Mattain_q(\mathcal{M})$$

is called the *attainable memory* of $\mathcal{M}$.

**Stream Functions**

The next section will provide a characterization of the (partial) function computed by stream X-machines.

*Definition 6.2.6*

Let $f:$ seq(*Input*) $\to$ seq(*Output*) be a (partial) function. Then $f$ is called a *weak (partial) stream function* if the following are true.

1. $\forall \, s^* \in$ domain $f$ such that length($f(s^*)$) = length($s^*$), where length($s^*$) denotes the number of elements of the sequence $s^*$.
2. $\forall \, s^*, t^* \in$ seq($Input$), if $t^*, t^* :: s^* \in$ domain $f$ then $\exists \, g^* \in$ seq($Output$) such that $f(t^* :: s^*) = f(t^*) :: g^*$.

Thus stream functions preserve the length of a sequence in the sense that the length of the resulting sequence equals the length of the sequence supplied to the function and it "respects" the concatenation operator in a natural way.

### Theorem 6.2.1

Let $f$: seq($Input$) → seq($Output$) be a (partial) function. Then $f$ is a weak (partial) stream function if and only if there exists a stream X-machine that computes $f$.

*Proof:*
(i) Suppose that we have a stream X-machine which computes $f$, then length($f(s^*)$) = length($s^*$) is obvious. Also, the second requirement is a result of the machine being deterministic.
(ii) Suppose that $f$ is a weak (partial) stream function. A two-state stream X-machine that computes $f$ can be constructed easily. This will have the state transition diagram as in Figure 6.1 and *Memory* = seq($Input$). $\phi_1$ will process all pairs $(t^*, s) \in$ *Memory* × *Input* for which $t^* :: s \in$ domain $f$ and $\phi_2$ those pairs for which $t^* :: s \notin$ domain $f$. $A$ will be the only terminal state of the machine. $A$ will also be the initial state of the machine if and only if $< > \in$ domain $f$.

Of special interest to us will be machines whose states are all terminal (i.e. $T = Q$). If this is the case then $f$ will be defined by:

$$f(s^*) = g^* \Leftrightarrow \exists \, q \in Q \text{ and } p: q_0 \to q \cdot \pi_1(|p|(m_0, s^*)) = g^*$$

or alternatively by:

$$f(s^*) = (\pi_1 \cdot [M \,])(q_0, m_0, s^*)$$

### Definition 6.2.7

Let $f$: seq($Input$) → seq($Output$) be a weak (partial) stream function. Then $f$ is called a *(partial) stream function* if:

$$\forall \, s^*, t^* \in \text{seq}(Input) \cdot \text{if } t^* :: s^* \in \text{domain } f \text{ then } t^* \in \text{domain } f$$

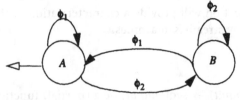

**FIG. 6.1.** A two-state stream X-machine computing a weak partial stream function.

**FIG. 6.2.** A single-state stream X-machine.

### Theorem 6.2.2

Let $f$: seq($Input$) → seq($Output$) be a (partial) function. Then $f$ is a (partial) stream function if and only if there exists a stream X-machine with all states terminal that computes $f$.

*Proof*:
(i)  If $f$ is computed by such a stream X-machine then it is obviously a stream function.
(ii) Suppose that $f$ is a stream function. It is easy to construct a single-state stream X-machine as in Figure 6.2 that computes $f$. If $Memory$ = seq($Input$) then $\phi_1$ will process all pairs $(t^*, s) \in Memory \times Input$ for which $t^* :: s \in$ domain $f$.

### Example 6.2.1

Suppose that $\mathcal{M}$ is a three state machine as shown in Figure 6.3 (the initial state is marked with an in-arrow).

$$Input = Output = \{0, 1\}, Memory = \{10, 11\} \text{ and } m_0 = 10$$

$\mathcal{M}$ has four processing functions, $\phi_1, \phi_2, \phi_3, \phi_4$, where:

$$\phi_1(10, 0) = (1, 11)$$
$$\phi_2(11, 0) = (1, 10)$$
$$\phi_3(11, 0) = (1, 11)$$
$$\phi_4(11, 1) = (0, 11)$$

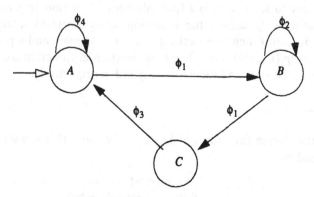

**FIG. 6.3.** A three-state stream X-machine.

It is easy to see that if $A$ is the only terminal state of the machine then $\mathcal{M}$ will compute the following partial function $f$:

$$f(<>) = <>$$
$$f(0 :: 0 :: 0 :: 0 :: 1^n) = 1 :: 1 :: 1 :: 1 :: 0^n, n \geq 0$$

On the other hand, if all states are terminal then $f$ will be of the form:

$$f(<>) = <>$$
$$f(0) = 1$$
$$f(0 :: 0) = 1 :: 1$$
$$f(0 :: 0 :: 0) = 1 :: 1 :: 1$$
$$f(0 :: 0 :: 0 :: 0 :: 1^n) = 1 :: 1 :: 1 :: 1 :: 0^n, n \geq 0$$

In the first case $f$ is a *weak partial stream function*; in the second case $f$ is a *partial stream function*.

*Aside*: When we consider the issue of testing in Chapter 7 we shall assume that all the states of the machine are terminal. Thus the set $T$ will be ignored unless it has a particular significance for our theoretical discussion. This means that all paths that emerge from the initial state will be successful so their corresponding outputs are observable to the user. This is particularly useful when it comes to testing since all outputs – even those that correspond to intermediate computations – are observable, thus providing more information about the system behaviour. Obviously the extra outputs can be filtered out once the system has passed all tests.

Before we go any further, we give one more definition.

### Definition 6.2.8

Let $f$: seq(*Input*) $\rightarrow$ seq(*Output*) be a (partial) function and let $t^* \in$ domain $f$. Then we can define a (partial) function $f$: seq(*Input*) $\rightarrow$ seq(*Output*) by:

$$f_{t^*}(s^*) = f(t^*)^{-1} :: f(t^* :: s^*), \text{ where } t^* :: s^* \in \text{domain } f$$

For $a^*, b^* \in$ seq($A$) if there exists $c^*$ with $a^* :: c^* = b^*$ then $a^{*-1} :: b^* = c^*$. It is easy to see that $f_{t^*}$ is a (partial) stream function. In terms of stream X-machines $f_{t^*}$ admits the following straightforward interpretation. If $t^* \in$ domain $f$ then there exist $q \in Q$, $m \in$ *Memory* and a path $p: q_0 \rightarrow q$ with $\pi_2(|p|(m_0, s^*)) = m$. Then $f_{t^*}$ is the (partial) function computed by $\mathcal{M}$ if the initial state and memory are $q$ and $m$ respectively.

### Example 6.2.2

For the stream function $f$ of Example 6.2.1 and $t^* = 0 :: 0 :: 0$ then $f_{t^*}$ is defined by:

$$f_{t^*}(<>) = <>$$
$$f_{t^*}(0 :: 1^n) = 1 :: 0^n, n \geq 0$$

## 6.3  STREAM X-MACHINE REFINEMENT

If stream X-machines are to be useful as a tool for specification, there needs to be some way of developing existing machines into more complex and more detailed versions without starting anew with each modification. The remaining part of this chapter will investigate the concept of refinement in the context of X-machines. Several types of refinement have been studied [57, 91, 92], but we will only present one of them, one that is potentially the most useful in practical applications.

When we say that a machine $M$ is a refinement of another machine $M'$ we mean that the new machine is more complex than the original but it preserves in some sense its functional properties. In other words, the refined machine will do everything that the original did plus some extra functionality. The internal structure of $M'$ may differ from that of $M$ in various ways. Obviously, we will be interested in methods of constructing $M'$ starting from the architecture of $M$, so that the internal structure of $M$ is preserved in some sense and the construction of the new model will not start anew with each modification.

The following two sections will define the concept of refinement in terms of the input/output behaviour of two machines. In general terms, given two stream X-machines $M$ and $M'$, we say that $M'$ is a *functional refinement* of $M$ if:

- each input (or output) sequence of $M$ can be mapped onto at least one input (or output (sequence) of $M'$;
- each input/output transformation of $M$ can be mapped onto at least one input/output transformation of $M'$.

In order to give a more rigorous interpretation of these two requirements we introduce some preliminary concepts.

### 6.3.1  Alphabet covering

*Definition 6.3.1.1*

Let $A$ be a set and $P$ a subset of $seq(A)$. Then $P$ is called a *prefix* if the following is true.

$$\forall\ a^*, b^* \in seq(A) \text{ such that if } a^*, a^* :: b^* \in P \text{ then } b^* = <\ >.$$

Obviously, if the empty sequence $<\ > \in P$ then $P = \{\ <\ >\}$. We will say that $P$ is a *non-trivial prefix* if $P$ is non-empty and $P \neq \{<\ >\}$.

*Definition 6.3.1.2*

Let $A$ and $A'$ be two alphabets and let $u: seq(A') \to A$ be a (partial) surjective function. If the domain of $u$ is a non-trivial prefix then we say that seq($A'$) *covers* seq($A$) with respect to $u$. Also, $u$ will be called an *alphabet covering* and the domain of $u$ the *domain of the covering*.

### Lemma 6.3.1.1

If $u$ is an alphabet covering, as above, then the following is true.

$$\forall\, a_1{}^*, a_2{}^*,..., a_n{}^*, b_1{}^*, b_2{}^*,..., b_m{}^* \in \text{domain } u$$
$$\text{if } a_1{}^* :: a_2{}^*::... :: a_n{}^* = b_1{}^* :: b_2{}^*::... :: b_m{}^* \text{ then } n = m \text{ and}$$
$$a_1{}^* = b_1{}^*, a_2{}^* = b_2{}^*,..., a_n{}^* = b_n{}^*.$$

*Proof:*
This follows by induction on $n$ since domain $u$ is a prefix.

Then we can define a partial surjective function $u^*$: seq($A'$) $\rightarrow$ seq($A$) by:

$$u^*(a^*) = \begin{cases} <>, \text{if } a^* = <> \\ u(a_1{}^*) ::..:: u(a_n{}^*), \text{if } \exists\, n \geq 1, a_1{}^*,..., a_n{}^* \\ \qquad \in \text{domain } u \text{ with } a^* = a_1{}^*::..:: a_n{}^* \\ \bot, \text{otherwise} \end{cases}$$

Clearly, domain $u^*$ = seq(domain $u$).
We illustrate the above concept with two examples.

### Example 6.3.1.1

Let $A \subseteq A'$ be two finite alphabets and let $u$: seq($A'$) $\rightarrow A$ be a surjective partial function with domain $u \subseteq$ seq($A' - A$) $\bullet$ $A$ that extracts the element of $A$ from any sequence for which $u$ is defined, i.e.:

$$\forall\, a \in A, b^{*'} \in \text{seq}(A' - A) \cdot \text{if } b^{*'} a \in \text{domain } u \text{ then } u(b^{*'} a) = a$$

We will call $u$ a *filter* of $A$ with respect to $A'$.
It is easy to see that the domain of $u$ is a prefix, seq($A'$) covers seq($A$) with respect to $u$ and that domain $u^* \subseteq$ (seq($A'$) $\bullet$ $A \cup \{<>\}$) and $u^*$ will extract all elements of $A$ from any sequence in the domain of $u^*$.
For example let $A = \{0, 1\}$ and $A' = \{0, 1, a, b\}$. Then $v$: seq($A'$) $\rightarrow A$ defined by:

$$v(s^* :: 0) = 0, s^* \in \text{seq}(\{a, b\})$$
$$v(s^* :: 1) = 1, s^* \in \text{seq}(\{a, b\})$$

is an alphabet covering.
Also, for any $k \geq 0$, $u_k$: seq($A'$) $\rightarrow A$ defined by:

$$u_k(a^n :: 0) = 0, n \geq k$$
$$u_k(b^n :: 1) = 1, n \geq k$$

are alphabet coverings.

*Example 6.3.1.2*

Let $A$ and $A'$ be two alphabets, $b \in A'$ and let $w: \text{seq}(A' - \{b\}) \to A$ be a (partial) surjective function. Then $\text{seq}(A')$ covers $\text{seq}(A)$ with respect to $u$, where $u$ is defined by:

$$u(a^*::b) = w(a^*), \; a^* \in \text{seq}(A' - \{b\}).$$

We illustrate this type of covering with the following practical application. Let CHARS be the set of all alphanumeric characters and $\text{WORDS}_n$ the set of all words of at most $n$ characters, i.e. $\text{WORDS}_n = \{\text{'}a_1\, a_2 \ldots a_j\text{'} \mid a_1, a_2, \ldots, a_j \in \text{CHARS}, 0 \le j \le n\}$. '$a_1\, a_2 \ldots a_j$' denotes the word composed of characters $a_1, a_2, \ldots a_j$. If $j = 0$ then '$a_1\, a_2 \ldots a_j$' = ' ', the empty word.

We assume that each such word can be entered from the keyboard as a sequence of characters followed by *enter* and that the keys available are all character keys, *backspace* and *enter*. If more than $n$ characters have been entered, then the rest will be ignored, unless one or more of the first $n$ characters have been deleted. This process can be described by a partial function

$$u_n: \text{seq}(\text{CHARS} \cup \{backspace, enter\}) \to \text{WORDS}_n$$

with domain $u_n = \text{seq}(\text{CHARS} \cup \{backspace\}) \bullet \{enter\}$ defined by:

$$u_n(enter) = \text{' '}$$

$$u_n(a^* :: backspace :: enter) = \begin{cases} \text{'}a_1 \ldots a_{j-1}\text{'} \text{ if } u(a^* :: enter) \\ \quad = \text{'}a_1 \ldots a_j\text{'} \text{ with } 0 < j \le n \\[2mm] \text{' '}, \text{ if } u(a^* :: enter) = \text{' '} \end{cases}$$

where $a^* \in \text{seq}(\text{CHARS} \cup \{backspace\})$.

$$u_n(a^* :: b :: enter) = \begin{cases} \text{'}a_1 \ldots a_j\, b\text{'} \text{ if } u(a^* :: enter) = \text{'}a_1 \ldots a_j\text{'} \\ \quad \text{with } 0 \le j < n \\[2mm] \text{'}a_1 \ldots a_j\text{'}, \text{ if } u(a^* :: enter) = \text{'}a_1 \ldots a_j\text{'} \\ \quad \text{with } j = n \end{cases}$$

where $a^* \in \text{seq}(\text{CHARS} \cup \{backspace\})$, $b \in \text{CHARS}$.

It is easy to see that $\text{seq}(\text{CHARS} \cup \{backspace, enter\})$ covers $\text{seq}(\text{WORDS}_n)$ with respect to $u_n$.

If there is no restriction on the number of characters that a word can have then the corresponding alphabet covering will result from the definition above for $n = \infty$.

## 6.3.2 Functional Covering

Our definition of refinement is aimed at meeting the two requirements stated above while being precise enough to be both meaningful and usable in examples. This is given next.

*Definition 6.3.2.1*

Let $f$: seq(*Input*) → seq(*Output*) and $f'$: seq(*Input'*) → seq(*Output'*) be two (partial) stream functions such that seq(*Input'*) covers seq(*Input*) with respect to $u$ and seq(*Output'*) covers seq(*Output*) with respect to $v$. Then we say that $f'$ is a *refinement of* $f$ with respect to $(u, v)$ if the following are true:

1. $f'$ (domain $u^*$) $\subseteq$ domain $v^*$
2. The following diagram commutes:

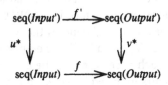

*Definition 6.3.2.2*

Let $M$ and $M'$ be two X-machines and $f$ and $f'$ respectively the functions they compute. Then we say that $M'$ is a *functional refinement* of $M$ with respect to $(u, v)$ if $f'$ is a refinement of $f$ with respect to $(u, v)$.

*Lemma 6.3.2.1*

$M'$ is a functional refinement of $M$ with respect to $(u, v)$ if and only if the following are true.

1. $\forall p'$ a path in $M'$ that starts in $q_0'$ with $\pi_1(|p'|(m_0', s^{*'})) = g^{*'}$:

   $s^{*'} \in$ domain $u^* \Leftrightarrow g^{*'} \in$ domain $v^*$.

2. $\forall s^* \in$ seq$_+$(*Input*) the following requirements are equivalent.
   (i) $\exists g^* \in$ seq$_+$(*Output*) and $p$ a path in $M$ that starts in $q_0$ with $\pi_1(|p|(m_0, s^*)) = g^*$
   (ii) $\forall s^{*'} \in u^{*-1}(s^*) \exists g^{*'} \in$ domain $v^*$ and a path $p'$ in $M'$ that starts in $q_0'$ such that $\pi_1(|p'|(m_0', s^{*'})) = g^{*'}$

   where $g^*$ and $g^{*'}$ above satisfy $v^*(g^{*'}) = g^*$.

*Proof:*
This follows from the definition of functional covering and that of the function computed by a stream X-machine.

Thus everything that is processed by $M$ can be processed by $M'$ with essentially the same result. For a discussion of related topics with respect to finite state machines see [25].

*Example 6.3.2.1*

Let *Input* = *Output* = {0, 1}, *Input'* = *Output'* = {0, 1, a, b} and let $f$: seq(*Input*) → seq(*Output*) be the stream function from Example 6.2.1, i.e.:

$$f(<>) = <>$$
$$f(0) = 1$$
$$f(0 :: 0) = 1 :: 1$$
$$f(0 :: 0 :: 0) = 1 :: 1 :: 1$$
$$f(0 :: 0 :: 0 :: 0 :: 1^n) = 1 :: 1 :: 1 :: 1 :: 0^n, \text{ where } n \geq 0$$

Then it is easy to see that for any $k \geq 0$, $f_k'$ is a refinement of $f$ with respect to $(u_k, v)$, where $u_k$ and $v$ are those of Example 6.3.1.1 and $f_k'$ is defined by:

$$f_k'(a^{j_1}) = b^{j_1}, j_1 \geq 0$$
$$f_k'(a^{j_1} :: 0 :: a^{j_2}) = b^{j_1} :: 1 :: b^{j_2}, j_1 \geq k, j_2 \geq 0$$
$$f_k'(a^{j_1} :: 0 :: a^{j_2} :: 0 :: a^{j_3}) = b^{j_1} :: 1 :: b^{j_2} :: 1 :: b^{j_3}, j_1 \geq k, j_2 \geq k, j_3 \geq 0$$
$$f_k'(a^{j_1} :: 0 :: a^{j_2} :: 0 :: a^{j_3} :: 0 :: a^{j_4}) = b^{j_1} :: 1 :: b^{j_2} :: 1 :: b^{j_3} :: 1 :: b^{j_4}, j_1 \geq k, j_2 \geq k,$$
$$j_3 \geq k, j_4 \geq 0$$
$$f_k'(a^{j_1} :: 0 :: a^{j_2} :: 0 :: a^{j_3} :: 0 :: a^{j_4} :: 0 :: b^{m_1}) =$$
$$b^{j_1} :: 1 :: b^{j_2} :: 1 :: b^{j_3} :: 1 :: b^{j_4} :: 1 :: a^{m_1}, j_1 \geq k, j_2 \geq k, j_3 \geq k, j_4 \geq k, m_1 \geq 0$$

........................

$$f_k'(a^{j_1} :: 0 :: a^{j_2} :: 0 :: a^{j_3} :: 0 :: a^{j_4} :: 0 :: b^{m_1} :: 1 :: ..... :: b^{m_{n-1}} :: 1 :: b^{m_n}) =$$
$$b^{j_1} :: 1 :: b^{j_2} :: 1 :: b^{j_3} :: 1 :: b^{j_4} :: 1 :: a^{m_1} :: 1 :: ..... :: a^{m_{n-1}} :: 1 :: a^{m_n},$$
$$j_1 \geq k, j_2 \geq k, j_3 \geq k, j_4 \geq k, m_1 \geq k, ...., m_{n-1} \geq k, m_n \geq 0, n \geq 0$$

Before we go any further we state two results that we will use in the following sections.

## Lemma 6.3.2.2

If $f'$ is a refinement of $f$ with respect to $(u, v)$ and $t^{*\prime} \in$ domain $u^*$ then the following are true.

1. $f'(t^{*\prime}) \neq \perp$ if and only if $f(t^*) \neq \perp$, where $t^* = u^*(t^{*\prime})$.
2. If $f'(t^{*\prime}) \neq \perp$ then $f_{t^*}$ is a refinement of $f'_{t^{*\prime}}$ with respect to $(u, v)$, where $t^* = u^*(t^{*\prime})$.

### Proof:
1. This follows from Definition 6.3.2.1
2. If $s^{*\prime} \in$ domain $u^*$ and $s^* = u^*(s^{*\prime})$ then $f(t^* :: s^*) = f(t^*) :: f_{t^*}(s^*)$ and $f'(t^{*\prime} :: s^{*\prime}) = f'(t^{*\prime}) :: f'_{t^{*\prime}}(s^{*\prime})$ hence $f(t^*) :: f_{t^*}(s^*) = v^*(f'(t^{*\prime})) :: v^*(f'_{t^{*\prime}}(s^{*\prime}))$

## Lemma 6.3.2.3

If $f'$ is a refinement of $f$ with respect to $(u, v)$, $t^{*\prime} \in$ domain $u^*$, $s^{*\prime} \in$ domain $u$ and $\mathcal{M}$ is a stream X-machine that computes $f$ then the following are true.

1. $f'(t^{*\prime}) \neq \perp \Leftrightarrow \exists\, q_1 \in Q$, $m_1 \in Memory$ and a path $p: q_0 \rightarrow q_1$ in $\mathcal{M}$ with $\pi_2(|p|(m_0, t^*)) = m_1$, where $t^* = u^*(t^{*\prime})$.
2. If $f'(t^{*\prime}) \neq \perp$ then:
   $f'_{t^{*\prime}}(s^{*\prime}) \neq \perp \Leftrightarrow \exists\, q_2 \in Q$, $m_2 \in Memory$ and an arc $\phi: q_1 \rightarrow q_2$ with $\phi(m_1, s) = (m_2, f_{t^*}(s))$, where $t^* = u^*(t^{*\prime})$ and $s = u(s^{*\prime})$ and $q_1 \in Q$, $m_1 \in Memory$ are those from 1.

### Proof:
Follows from Lemma 6.3.2.2

### 6.3.3   Construction of Refinement: State Refinement

Once the transformation has been defined in terms of the input/output behaviour of the two machines, we turn our attention to the construction of the refined machine $\mathcal{M}'$. Intuitively $\mathcal{M}'$ will have a larger state space and memory, which will enable it to perform the more complex functionality. On the other hand, since the functionality of the original machine $M$ will be preserved one would expect that it should be possible to find a systematic way of developing the architecture of $M$ into an architecture that will correspond to the refined input/output behaviour. The following result (Eilenberg [28]) provides us with a basic idea for our construction.

*Lemma 6.3.3.1*

Let $A$ be a set and $P \subseteq \text{seq}(A)$. Then $P$ is a non-trivial prefix if and only if $P$ is the behaviour of a (possible infinite) state machine that has a single final state $q_t$ and no arcs emerge from $q_t$.

So it appears that all we need to do is refine (in the sense of the commutative diagram of Definition 6.3.2.1) each arc of $\mathcal{M}$ to a stream X-machine with a single terminal state (i.e. this is computationally equivalent to an infinite finite state machine) and replace all arcs with their corresponding refining machine.

However, this idea, although straightforward, has no immediate application, the principal reason being that the construction could result in a nondeterministic machine. Suppose, for example, that $\mathcal{M}$ is a machine with *Input* = *Output* = $\{0, 1\}$ for which there are two arcs $\phi_1$ and $\phi_2$ emerging from the same state, where:

$$\phi_1(m, 0) = (0, m), m \in \text{Memory}$$
$$\phi_2(m, 1) = (1, m), m \in \text{Memory}$$

that *Input'* = *Output'* = $\{0, 1, a\}$ and that the alphabet refinements $u$ and $v$ are defined by:

$$u(a :: 0) = v(a :: 0) = 0$$
$$u(a :: 1) = v(a :: 1) = 1$$

Then $\phi_1$ and $\phi_2$ can be refined to $\mathcal{M}_1$ and $\mathcal{M}_2$ shown in Figure 6.4(a) and (b), with $\phi_3$ defined by:

$$\phi_3(m, a) = (a, m), m \in \text{Memory}$$

Thus the construction suggested above will lead to a nondeterministic machine (see Figure 6.4(c)).

However, there is a way around this problem: rather than replacing each arc with a machine with a single terminal state, we replace all the arcs that emerge from a state $q$ with a single machine that has a terminal state for each such arc (see Figure 6.4(d)). This idea will be pursued in what follows and will form the basis of the concept of *state refinement*.

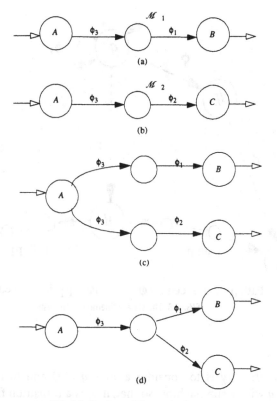

**FIG. 6.4.** Nondeterminism and refinement.

So we are going to construct a *refining* machine $\mathcal{M}'(q)$ for a given state $q$ whose state set will be denoted by $R_q$. This will consist of a *copy* of $q$ denoted by $q'$ together with some new states needed to act as intermediate states along the new paths that will be replacing the original transitions from $q$. We also add a *copy* of all the states that these transitions point at. This second set of new states will be our set of terminal states, $T_q$. Then, each arc labelled by a $\phi$ in the original machine that leaves the state $q$ will be replaced by a path in $\mathcal{M}'(q)$ that will correspond to the original transition *modulo* the covering relationships between the input and output alphabets. This is illustrated in Figure 6.5.

Notation: in our description, for $n$ (partial) functions $f_1: A_1 \rightarrow B_1,....,$ $f_n: A_n \rightarrow B_n, \{f_1,..., f_n\} : A_1 \times... \times A_n \rightarrow B_1 \times... \times B_n$ will be a partial function defined by:

$$\{f_1,..., f_n\} \, (a_1,..., a_n) = (f_1(a_1),..., f_n(a_n)), a_1 \in A_1,..., a_n \in A_n$$

First, we prepare the ground for our formal construction.

Let $\mathcal{M} = (Input, Output, Q, Memory, \Phi, F, q_0, m_0)$ be a stream X-machine. Let *Input'* and *Output'* be two alphabets so that seq(*Input'*) covers seq(*Input*) with respect to $u$ and seq(*Output'*) covers seq(*Output*) with respect to $v$. The

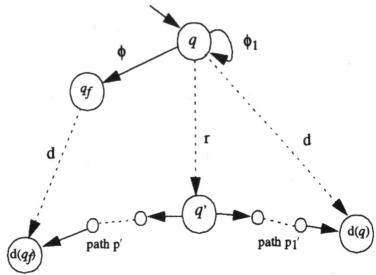

Path p′ is induced by $\phi$      Path p$_1'$ is induced by $\phi_1$

**FIG. 6.5.** The state refinement relationship.

essential strategy is to consider a state $q \in Q$ and to replace each arc leaving $q$ with a submachine, so that, if $\phi_1$ is a transition from $q$ to $q'$ then we introduce a set of states $q^1{}_1, q^1{}_2,\dots, q^1_{n_1}$ of the submachine with a path through them replacing $\phi_1$. We do this for each transition $\phi_i$ that leaves $q$. The states of the refining machine for $q$ will consist of all these states together with the state $q$. Of these states the states $q^i_{n_i}$ for each $\phi_i$ will be designated terminal states in the refining machine for $q$. We need to construct a copy, $L$, of $Q$ to provide for the eventual pasting of the refining machine into the original. This will be done by recognising that the terminal states $q^i_{n_i}$ will be *merged* with their corresponding states in $Q$ as we considered in Chapter 4.

So let $K$ (the *key* states of the refinement) and $L$ be two disjoint sets, $K \cap L = \varnothing$, with $\text{Card}(K) = \text{Card}(L) = \text{Card}(Q)$ and let r: $Q \to K$ and d: $Q \to L$ be two bijections. Let also *Memory′* be a set for which there exists h: *Memory′* $\to$ *Memory* a surjective (partial) function whose domain is H.

### Definition 6.3.3.1

Then for any $q \in Q$, a stream X-machine $\mathcal{M}'(q) = (Input', Output', R_q,$ *Memory′*, $\Phi_q', F_q, q', m_q', T_q)$ is called a *refining machine in $q$* with respect to $(u, v)$ if the following are true.

1. The initial state is $q' = r(q)$. The set of terminal states is a subset of $L$ defined by:

$$T_q = \{d(q_f): \exists \text{ an arc } \phi: q \to q_f \text{ in } \mathcal{M}\}.$$

2. There is no arc emerging from any terminal state in $\mathcal{M}'(q)$.
3. If $E_q = R_q - T_q$ then $Eq \cap K = \{r(q)\}$ and $Eq \cap L = \varnothing$. Thus the internal states of $\mathcal{M}'(q)$ – i.e. those that are neither initial nor terminal – are not among the elements of $K$ and $L$.
4. If $q = q_0$ then the initial memory $m_q'$ satisfies $h(m_q') = m_0$.
5. For any $q_f' \in R_q$, $m_i' \in H$, $mf' \in Memory'$, $s^{*'} \in seq(Input')$, $g^{*'} \in seq(Output)$ and $p': r(q) \to q_f'$ path in $\mathcal{M}'(q)$ with $|p'|(m_i', s^{*'}) = (g^{*'}, m_f')$ the following are true.
   (i) if $s^{*'} \in$ domain $u$ then $q_f' \in T_q$, $m_f' \in H$, $g^{*'} \in$ domain $v$.
   (ii) if $s^{*'} \in seq_+(Input')$ – domain $u^*$ then $q_f' \in (R_q - T_q)$ and $g^{*'} \in seq_+(Output')$ – domain $v^*$.
6. For any $s \in Input$, $m_i \in Mattain_q(\mathcal{M})$, $m_i' \in h^{-1}(m_i)$ the following requirements are equivalent.
   (i) $\exists q_f \in Q$, $m_f \in Memory$, $g \in Output$ and $\phi: q \to q_f$ an arc in $\mathcal{M}$ such that $\phi(m_i, s) = (g, m_f)$.
   (ii) $\forall s^{*'} \in u^{-1}(s) \exists q_f' \in T_q$, $m_f' \in H$, $g^{*'} \in$ domain $v$ and a path $p'$ in $\mathcal{M}'(q)$ with $|p'|(m_i', s^{*'}) = (g^{*'}, m_f')$, where $q_f$, $q_f'$, $m_f$, $m_f'$, $g$ and $g^{*'}$ above satisfy $d(q_f) = q_f'$, $h(m_f') = m_f$ and $v(g^{*'}) = g$.

Basically, requirement 5 states that only sequences of inputs that are in the domain of $u$ will reach a terminal state and the corresponding output sequence will be in the domain of $v$. Requirement 6 ensures that for any arc $\phi: q_i \to q_f$ everything that is processed by $\phi$ will be processed by a path $p': r(q_i) \to d(q_f)$ in $\mathcal{M}'(q)$ from the initial state to the appropriate terminal state with essentially the same result.

## Definition 6.3.3.2

Let $\mathcal{M}$ be a stream X-machine and $\{\mathcal{M}'(q): q \in Q\}$ a set of refining machines with respect to $(u, v)$ indexed by $Q$ for which $(E_{q1} - \{r(q_1)\}) \cap (E_{q2} - \{r(q_2)\}) = \varnothing$ for any two distinct states, $q_1$ and $q_2$ of $Q$. Then a stream X-machine $\mathcal{M}' = (Input', Output', Q', Memory', \Phi', F', q_0', m_0')$ is called a *state refinement* of $\mathcal{M}$ with respect to $(u, v)$ if the following are true:

1. The state space is $Q' = \underset{q \in Q}{\cup} E_q$, where $\forall q \in Q$, $E_q = R_q - L$.
2. The initial state $q_0' = r(q_0)$ is the initial state of $\mathcal{M}'(q_0)$.
3. The initial memory $m_0'$ is the initial memory of $\mathcal{M}'(q_0)$.
4. $\Phi' = \underset{q \in Q}{\cup} \Phi_q'$
5. The next state (partial) function $F': Q' \times \Phi' \to Q'$ is defined by:

$$F'(q', \phi') = \begin{cases} F_q(q', \phi'), \text{if } F_q(q', \phi') \in E_q \\ r(d^{-1}(F_q(q', \phi'))), \text{if } F_q(q', \phi') \in T_q. \\ \bot, \text{if } F_q(q', \phi') = \bot \end{cases}$$

where $q$ is chosen such that $q' \in E_q$.

Note that F' is well defined since $\{E_q : q \in Q\}$ is a partition of $Q'$ indexed by $Q$.

Also, $\{\mathcal{M}'(q): q \in Q\}$ will be called the *refining set of* $\mathcal{M}'$.

Basically, the state transition diagram of $\mathcal{M}'$ will result by merging each terminal state of a refining machine with the appropriate key state, i.e. for any state $q \in Q$ each terminal state $d(q)$ of $\mathcal{M}'(q)$ will be merged with $r(q)$, the initial state of $\mathcal{M}'(q)$. Thus each arc $\phi: q \to q_1$ in $\mathcal{M}$ will give rise to a set of paths $\{p': r(q) \to r(q_1)\}$ in the refined machine $\mathcal{M}'$. We illustrate the construction with two examples.

### Example 6.3.3.1

Suppose that $\mathcal{M}$ is the three-state machine from Example 6.2.1 and that *Input'*, *Output'*, $u_k$ and $v$ are those of Example 6.3.1.1. Then $\mathcal{M}'(A)$, $\mathcal{M}'(B)$, $\mathcal{M}'(C)$ shown in Figure 6.6 will be refining machines in $A, B$ and $C$, respectively, with respect to $(u_1, v)$.

We take $K = Q, L = \{A_1, B_1, C_1\}, Memory' = Memory$. r and h are the identity functions and d is defined by:

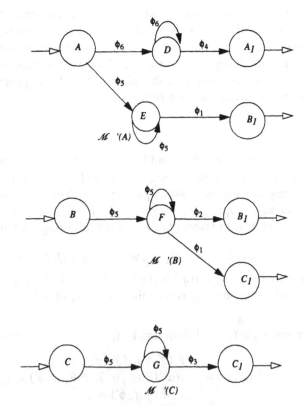

**FIG. 6.6.** Three refining machines for the machine in Figure 6.1.

$$d(A) = A_1, d(B) = B_1, d(C) = C_1$$

$$R_A = \{A, D, E, A_1, B_1\};\ T_A = \{A_1, B_1\};\ E_A = \{A, D, E\}.$$
$$R_B = \{B, F, B_1, C_1\};\ T_B = \{B_1, C_1\};\ E_B = \{B, F\}.$$
$$R_C = \{C, G, G_1\};\ T_C = \{C_1\};\ E_C = \{C, G\}.$$

The transition functions $\phi_5$ and $\phi_6$ are defined by:

$$\phi_5(a, m) = (m, b), m \in Memory$$
$$\phi_6(b, m) = (m, a), m \in Memory$$

The refined machine $\mathcal{M}'$ may be found in Figure 6.7. It is easy to see that $\mathcal{M}'$ computes $f_1'$ from Example 6.3.2.1.

### Example 6.3.3.2

We specify a simple computer program which enables users to "log in" to a computer system using their *username* and *password* and to replace their password. We require that each user can enter his or her password only once. As in Example 6.3.1.2, the keys used are character keys, enter and backspace, and each username or password will be entered as a sequence of

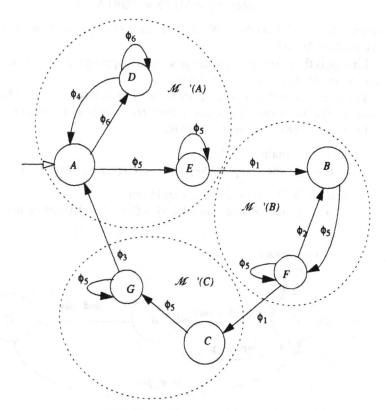

**FIG. 6.7.** The refined machine from Figure 6.1.

character keys and backspace followed by enter. For simplicity we assume that all usernames and passwords will be words of at most two characters – the general case for $n$ is similar. All usernames and passwords will be displayed along with appropriate messages.

The first stream X-machine model of the system may be found in Figure 6.8. The machine inputs will all be words of at most two characters, i.e.:

$$Input = WORDS_2$$

An output will be a pair consisting of a message given by the system (i.e. "type in your password", etc.) and the username or password displayed. Thus:

$$Output = WORDS_2 \times MSGS$$

We need five messages thus:

$$MSGS = \{msg1,..., msg5\}$$

A memory value will be a pair $(map, name)$, where $map$ will keep the map between the existing usernames and passwords for the existing accounts and $name$ will store the username entered by the current user. Thus:

$$Memory = MAPS \times WORDS_2$$

where $MAPS = WORDS_2 \rightarrow WORDS_2$ is the set of partial functions from $WORDS_2$ to $WORDS_2$.

If $map_0$ is the current username/password mapping then the initial memory value can be taken as $m_0 = (map_0, ` ')$

The five processing functions are defined as follows. We only show the effect of functions on their domain; they are undefined elsewhere.

Let $map \in MAPS$, $name$, $str \in WORDS_2$.

> if $str \in$ domain $map$ then
> **good_name**$((map, name), str) = ((msg1, str), (map, str))$

> if $str \in (WORDS_2 -$ domain $map)$ then
> **wrong_name**$((map, name), str) = ((msg2, str), (map, name))$

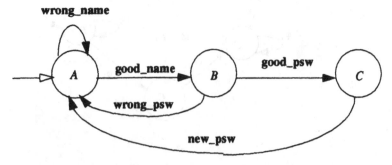

**FIG. 6.8.** A simple stream X-machine for a computer "log in" system.

if *name* ∈ domain *map* and *map(name)* = *str* then
   **good_psw**((*map, name*), *str*) = ((*msg3, str*), (*map, name*))

if ¬(*name* ∈ domain *map* and *map(name)* = *str*) then
   **wrong_psw**((*map, name*), *str*) = ((*msg4, str*), (*map, name*))

**new_psw**((*map, name*), *str*) = ((*msg5, str*), (*map', name*)) where
   *map'* = *map* ⊕ (*name* → *str*) and ⊕ denotes function overriding.

Up to this point we have not specified how the usernames and password are entered and displayed. This will be described by the refined machine along with the appropriate alphabet coverings.

The refined input and output alphabets are

$$Input' = \text{CHARS} \cup \{backspace, enter\}$$

and

$$Output' = \text{CHARS} \cup \{del\_ch, no\_display\} \cup \text{MSGS}$$

The input alphabet covering is $u_2$ with $u_n$ as defined in Example 6.3.1.2. The output covering $v$ is defined by:

$$v(msg) = (`\ ', msg), \text{where } msg \in \text{MSGS}$$

$$v(a^* :: no\_display :: msg) = v_2(a^* :: msg)$$

$$v(a^* \ del\_ch :: msg) = \begin{cases} (`a_1...a_{j-1}', msg), \text{if } v(a^* :: msg) \\ \quad = (`a_1...a_j', msg) \text{ with } j > 0 \\ \\ (`\ ', msg), \text{if } v(a^* :: msg) \\ \quad = (`\ ', msg) \end{cases}$$

where $a^* \in \text{seq}(\text{CHARS} \cup \{del\_ch, no\_display\})$

$v(a^* :: b :: msg) = `a_1...a_j \ b'$, where $v(a^* :: msg) = (`a_1...a_j', msg)$ with $j \geq 0$

where $a^* \in \text{seq}(\text{CHARS} \cup \{del\_ch, no\_display\})$, $b \in \text{CHARS}$.

The state-transition diagrams of $\mathcal{M}'(A)$, $\mathcal{M}'(B)$ and $\mathcal{M}'(C)$ are shown in Figure 6.9.

$$Memory' = Memory \times \text{WORDS}_2$$
$$m_0' = (m_0, <\ >)$$

h: *Memory* → *Memory'* is defined by:

$$h((m, <\ >)) = m, \ m \in Memory$$

We take $K = Q, L = \{A1, B1, C1\}$ and r to be defined by:

$$r(A) = A1, r(B) = B1, r(C) = C1.$$

The nine processing functions are defined as follows. To avoid unnecessary detail, we only show the effect of functions on their domain.

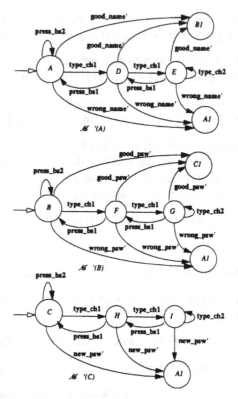

**FIG. 6.9.** Refining machines for Figure 6.8.

Let $map \in$ MAPS, $name, str \in$ WORDS$_2$, $m \in Memory$,

if $ch \in$ CHARS then
$$\textbf{type\_ch1}((m, str), ch) = (ch, (m, str'))$$

where

$$str' = \text{'}a_1...a_j \ ch\text{'}, \text{ where } str = \text{'}a_1...a_j\text{'} \text{ with } j \geq 0$$

if $ch \in$ CHARS then $\textbf{type\_ch2}((m, str), ch) = (no\_display, (m, str))$

$\textbf{press\_bs1}((m, str), backspace) = ((del\_ch, (m, str'))$
where $str' = \text{'}a_1...a_{j-1}\text{'}$, where $str = \text{'}a_1...a_j\text{'}$ with $j > 0$

$\textbf{press\_bs2}((m, str), backspace) = (no\_display, (m, str))$

if $str \in$ domain $map$ then
$\textbf{good\_name'}(((map, name), str), enter) = (msg1, ((map, str), <>))$

if $str \in$ (WORDS$_2$ – domain $map$) then
$\textbf{wrong\_name'}(((map, name), str), enter) = (msg2, ((map, name), <>))$

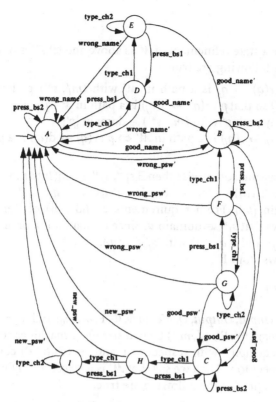

**FIG. 6.10.** The refined machine.

if $name \in$ domain $map$ and $map(name) = str$ then
$\quad$ **good_psw'**$(((map, name), str), enter) = (msg3, ((map, name), <>))$

if $\neg(name \in$ domain $map$ and $map(name) = str)$ then
$\quad$ **wrong_psw'**$(((map, name), str), enter) = (msg4, ((map, name), <>))$

**new_psw'**$(((map, name), str), enter) = (msg5, ((map', name), <>))$
$\quad$ where $map' = map \oplus (name, str)$

The state-transition diagram of the refined machine is shown in Figure 6.10.

## 6.3.4 Equivalence of Functional and State Covering

The remaining part of this chapter will show that the two types of refinement presented are functionally equivalent. More precisely, we shall prove that any state refinement of a stream X-machine $\mathcal{M}$ will also be functional refinement of $\mathcal{M}$. Conversely, the behaviour of any functional refinement of $\mathcal{M}$ can be obtained by means of state refinement. In order to prove the first implication we state a preparatory result and introduce the concept of *structural refinement*.

### Lemma 6.3.4.1

Let $\mathcal{M}'$ be a state refinement of $\mathcal{M}$ as above and let $s^{*'} \in$ domain $u$, $m_i' \in H$. Then the following are true.

1. If $p': r(q) \to q_f'$ is a path in $\mathcal{M}'$ with $(m_i', s^{*'}) \in$ domain $|p'|$ then $\exists$ $q_f \in Q$ so that $p': r(q) \to d(q_f)$ is a path in $\mathcal{M}'(q)$.
2. For any path $p'$ with $(m_i', s^{*'}) \in$ domain $|p'|$

$p': r(q) \to r(q_f)$ is a path in $\mathcal{M}' \Leftrightarrow p': r(q) \to d(q_f)$ is a path in $\mathcal{M}'(q)$

*Proof:*
1. If we assume otherwise then $\exists s_1^{*'}, s_2^{*'} \in$ seq(*Input'*) with $s_1^{*'} :: s_2^{*'} = s^{*'}$ and $p_1': r(q) \to q_1'$ a path in $\mathcal{M}'(q)$ with $q_1' \in T_q$ and $(m_i', s_1^{*'}) \in$ domain $|p_1'|$. From requirements 2 and 5(ii) of Definition 6.3.3.1 it follows that $s_1^{*'} \in$ domain $u$. Since domain $u$ is a prefix $s_1^{*'} = s^{*'}$ hence $p_1' = p'$ and $\exists q_f \in Q$ with $q_f' = d(q_f)$.
2. Follows from 1.

### Definition 6.3.4.1

Let $\mathcal{M} = (Input, Output, Q, Memory, \Phi, F, q_0, m_0)$ and $\mathcal{M}' = (Input', Output', Q', Memory', \Phi', F', q_0', m_0')$ be two stream X-machines so that seq(*Input'*) covers seq(*Input*) with respect to $u$ and seq(*Output'*) covers seq(*Output*) with respect to $v$. Then we say that $\mathcal{M}'$ is a *structural refinement* of $\mathcal{M}$ with respect to $(u, v)$ if the following are true.

1. There exists an injective map $r: Q \to Q'$ from the state space of $\mathcal{M}$ to the state space of $\mathcal{M}'$ whose image is $K$ for which $r(q_0) = q_0'$.
2. There exists a (partial) surjective function $h: Memory' \to Memory$ whose domain is $H$ for which $h(m_0') = m_0$.
3. For any $q_i' \in K$, $q_f' \in Q'$, $m_i' \in H$, $m_f' \in Memory'$, $s^{*'} \in$ seq(*Input'*), $g^{*'} \in$ seq(*Output'*) and $p': q_i' \to q_f'$ a path in $\mathcal{M}'$ with $|p'|(m_i', s^{*'}) = (g^{*'}, m_f')$ the following are true.
   (i) if $s^{*'} \in$ domain $u$ then $q_f' \in K$, $m_f' \in H$, $g^{*'} \in$ domain $v$
   (ii) if $s^{*'} \in$ seq$_+$(*Input'*) − domain $u^*$ then $g^{*'} \in$ seq$_+$(*Output'*) − domain $v^*$.
4. For any $q_i \in Q$, $s \in Input$, $m_i \in Mattain_{q_i}(\mathcal{M})$, $m_i' \in h^{-1}(m_i)$ the following requirements are equivalent.
   (i) $\exists q_f \in Q$, $m_f \in Memory$, $g \in Output$ and $\phi: q_i \to q_f$ an arc in $\mathcal{M}$ such that $\phi(m_i, s) = (g, m_f)$.
   (ii) $\forall s^{*'} \in u^{-1}(s) \exists q_f' \in K$, $m_f' \in H$, $g^{*'} \in$ domain $v$ and $p': r(q_i) \to q_f'$ a path in $\mathcal{M}'$ with $|p'|(m_i', s^{*'}) = (g^{*'}, m_f')$, where $q_f, q_f', m_f, m_f', g$ and $g^{*'}$ above satisfy $r(q_f) = q_f'$, $h(m_f') = m_f$ and $v(g^{*'}) = g$.

### Lemma 6.3.4.2

If $\mathcal{M}'$ is a structural refinement of $\mathcal{M}$ with respect to $(u, v)$ then $\mathcal{M}'$ is a functional refinement of $\mathcal{M}$ with respect to $(u, v)$.

*Proof:*

We prove the two requirements of Lemma 6.3.2.1.

1. Let $p'$ be a path in $\mathcal{M}'$ that starts in $q_0'$ with $\pi_1(|p'|(m_0', s^{*'})) = g^{*'}$.

If $s^{*'} \in (\text{domain } u)^n$, by induction on n it follows that $g^{*'} \in (\text{domain } v)^n$.

If $s^{*'} \in \text{seq}_+(Input') - \text{domain } u^*$ then from requirement 3(ii) of Definition 6.3.4.1 it follows that $g^{*'} \in \text{seq}_+(Output') - \text{domain } v^*$.

2.

"i) $\Rightarrow$ ii)"

Let $s^* = s_1 :: .... :: s_n \in \text{seq}_+(Input), g^* = g_1 :: ....:: g_n \in \text{seq}_+(Output)$ and $p$ a path in $\mathcal{M}$ that starts in $q_0$ with $\pi_1(|p|(m_0, s^*)) = g^*$. Then $\exists\ m_1,..., m_n \in$ *Memory*, $\phi_1: q_0 \to q_1,..., \phi_n: q_{n-1} \to q_n$, n arcs in $\mathcal{M}$ with $\phi_1(m_0, s_1) = (g_1, m_1),..., \phi_n(m_{n-1}, s_n) = (g_n, m_n)$. Then $\forall\ s_1^{*'} \in u^{-1}(s_1),..., s_n^{*'} \in u^{-1}(s_n)$, $m_1' \in h^{-1}(m_1),..., m_{n-1}' \in h^{-1}(m_{n-1})$

$\exists\ m_{1f}' \in h^{-1}(m_1),..., m_{nf}' \in h^{-1}(m_n), g_1^{*'} \in v^{-1}(g_1),..., g_n^{*'} \in v^{-1}(g_n)$ and $p_1': q_0' \to r(q_1),..., p_n': r(q_{n-1}) \to r(q_n)$ n paths in $\mathcal{M}'$ with $|p_1'|(m_0', s_1^{*'}) = (g_1^{*'}, m_{1f}'),..., |p_n'|(m_{n-1}', s_n^{*'}) = (g_n^{*'}, m_{nf}')$. Thus $\forall\ s_1^{*'} \in u^{-1}(s_1),..., s_n^{*'} \in u^{-1}(s_n)\ \exists$ a path $p'$ in $\mathcal{M}'$ that starts in $q_0'$ with $\pi_1(|p'|(m_0, s_1^{*'} :: ....:: s_n^{*'})) = g_1^{*'} :: ....:: g_n^{*'}$.

"ii) $\Rightarrow$ i)"

Let $s^* = s_1 :: .... :: s_n \in \text{seq}_+(Input)$ and $s^{*'} = s_1^{*'} :: ....:: s_n^{*'}$ with $\forall\ j = 1...n$, $s_j^{*'} \in u^{-1}(s_j)$ and let $p'$ be a path in $\mathcal{M}'$ that starts in $q_0'$ with $\pi_1(|p'|(m_0', s^{*'})) = g^{*'}$, where $g^{*'} \in \text{domain } v^*$. Then $\exists\ m_1',..., m_n' \in$ *Memory'*, $g_1^{*'},..., g_n^{*'} \in \text{seq}(Output')$ and $p_1': q_0' \to q_1',..., p_n': q_{n-1}' \to q_n'$ n paths in $\mathcal{M}'$ with $|p_1'|(m_0', s_1^{*'}) = (g_1^{*'}, m_1'),..., |p_n'|(m_{n-1}', s_n^{*'}) = (g_n^{*'}, m_n')$, where $g^{*'} = g_1^{*'} :: ....:: g_n^{*'}$. From requirement 3(i) of Definition 6.3.4.1 it follows that $\forall\ j = 1...n, q_j' \in K, m_j' \in H$, and $g_j^{*'} \in \text{domain } v$. Since $\forall\ j = 1...n$, $s_j^{*'} \in u^{-1}(s_j)$ are arbitrary from requirement 4 of the same definition it follows that $\exists\ \phi_1: q_0 \to q_1,..., \phi_n: q_{n-1} \to q_n$ n arcs in $\mathcal{M}$ with $\phi_1(m_0, s_1) = (g_1, m_1),..., \phi_n(m_{n-1}, s_n) = (g_n, m_n)$, where $\forall\ j = 1...n, q_j' = r(q_j), m_j = h(m_j')$ and $v(g_i^{*'}) = g_i$. Thus there exists a path $p$ in $\mathcal{M}$ that starts in $q_0$ with $\pi_1(|p|(m_0, s_1 :: ....:: s_n)) = g_1 :: ....:: g_n$.

## Lemma 6.3.4.3

If $\mathcal{M}'$ is a state refinement of $\mathcal{M}$ with respect to $(u, v)$ then $\mathcal{M}'$ is a structural refinement of $\mathcal{M}$ with respect to $(u, v)$.

*Proof:*

Requirements 3(i) and 4 of Definition 6.3.4.1 follow from requirements 5(i) and 6 respectively of Definition 6.3.3.1 and Lemma 6.3.4.1. The proof of requirement 3(ii) is given next.

Let $q_i \in Q$, $s^{*\prime} \in seq_+(Input')$ – domain $u^*$, $m_i' \in H$ and $p': r(q_i) \to q_f'$ a path in $\mathcal{M}'$ with $|p'|(m_i', s^{*\prime}) = (g^{*\prime}, m_f')$. Then either $p': r(q_i) \to q_f'$ is a path in $\mathcal{M}'(q)$ and hence $g^{*\prime} \in seq_+(Output')$ – domain $v^*$ or there exist $s_1^{*\prime},\ldots,$ $s_n^{*\prime} \in$ domain $u$, $s_{n+1}^{*\prime} \in seq_+(Input')$ – domain $u^*$, $q_1,\ldots, q_n \in Q$, $m_1',\ldots, m_n'$ $\in H$, $p_1': r(q_i) \to r(q_1)$ a path in $\mathcal{M}'(q_i)$ with $|p_1'|(m_i', s_1^{*\prime}) = (g_1^{*\prime}, m_1'),\ldots,$ $p_n': r(q_{n-1}) \to r(q_n)$ a path in $\mathcal{M}'(q_{n-1})$ with $|p_n'|(m_{n-1}', s_n^{*\prime}) = (g_n^{*\prime}, m_n')$ and $p_{n+1}': r(q_n) \to q_f'$ a path in $\mathcal{M}'(q_n)$ with $|p_{n+1}'|(m_n', s_{n+1}^{*\prime}) = (g_{n+1}^{*\prime}, m_f')$. From requirements 5(i) and 5(ii) of Definition 6.3.3.1 it follows that $g_1^{*\prime},\ldots, g_n^{*\prime}$ $\in$ domain $v$, $g_{n+1}^{*\prime} \in seq_+(Output')$ – domain $v^*$. Hence $g^{*\prime} = g_1^{*\prime} ::\ldots:: g_{n+1}^{*\prime}$ $\in seq(Output')$ – domain $v^*$.

### Corollary 6.3.4.1

If $\mathcal{M}'$ is a state refinement of $\mathcal{M}$ with respect to $(u, v)$ then $\mathcal{M}'$ is a functional refinement of $\mathcal{M}$ with respect to $(u, v)$.

Conversely, if $\mathcal{M}$ computes $f$ and $f'$ is a refinement of $f$ then there is a simple refinement $\mathcal{M}'$ of $\mathcal{M}$ that computes $f'$. This result is proven next.

### Theorem 6.3.4.1

Let $\mathcal{M}$ be a stream X-machine, $f$ the function it computes and let $f'$ be a refinement of $f$ with respect to $(u, v)$. Then there exists $\mathcal{M}'$ a state refinement of $\mathcal{M}$ with respect to $(u, v)$ so that $\mathcal{M}'$ computes $f'$.

#### Proof:
Let $\mathcal{M} = (Input, Output, Q, Memory, \Phi, F, q_0, m_0)$.

We take $K = Q$, r the identity, $Memory' = Memory \times seq(Input') \times seq(Input')$ and we define h: $Memory' \to Memory$ by:

$$h(m, x^{*\prime}, <\ >) = m, \text{ where } m \in Memory, x^{*\prime} \in \text{domain } u^*$$

Then for any $q \in Q$ we construct an X-machine $\mathcal{M}'(q) = (Input', Output',$ $R_q, Memory', \Phi_q', F_q, q', m_q', T_q)$ as follows.

1. The initial state is $q$ and $T_q$ is as in Definition 6.3.3.1
2. $R_q = \{q\} \cup T_q$.
3. If $q = q_0$ then $m_q' = (m_0, <\ >, <\ >)$
4. $\Phi_{q'} = \{\phi_q'\} \cup \{\psi_{q\,\theta}' : d(\theta) \in T_q, q \in Q\}$.

For $m \in Mattain_q(\mathcal{M})$ let $y(m) \in seq(Input')$ such that $\exists\ p: q_0 \to q$ with $\pi_2(|p|(m_0, u^*(y(m)))) = m$

Then $\phi_q'$ is defined by:

$\forall\ m \in Mattain_q(\mathcal{M})$, $x^{*\prime} \in$ domain $u^*$, $t^{*\prime} \in seq(Input')$, $s' \in Input'$ with $t^{*\prime} :: s' \notin$ domain $u$, $\phi_q'((m, x^{*\prime}, t^{*\prime}), s') = (g', (m, x^{*\prime}, t^{*\prime} :: s'))$

where:

$$g' = \begin{cases} f_{x^{*'}::\,t^{*'}}(s'), \text{ if } \exists\, p: q_0 \to q \\ \quad \text{with } \pi_2(|p|(m_0, u^*(x^{*'}))) = m \\ \\ f_{y(m)::\,t^{*'}}(s'), \text{ otherwise} \end{cases}$$

Also for any $\theta \in Q, \psi_{q\,\theta}'$ is defined by:

$\forall\, m \in Mattain_q(\mathcal{M}), x^{*'} \in domain\, u^*, t^{*'} \in seq(Input'), s' \in Input'$ with $t^{*'}::s'$
$\in domain\, u$ and $\exists\, \phi: q \to \theta$ with $(m, u(t^{*'}::s')) \in domain\, \phi$

$$\psi_{q\,\theta}'((m, x^{*'}, t^{*'}), s') = (g', (m_f, x^{*'}, t^{*'} :: s', < >)),$$

where:

$$m_f = \pi_2(\phi(m, u^*(t^{*'} :: s')))$$

$$g' = \begin{cases} f_{x^{*'}::\,t^{*'}}(s'), \text{ if } \exists\, p: q_0 \to q \\ \quad \text{with } \pi_2(|p|(m_0, u^*(x^{*'}))) = m \\ \\ f_{y(m)::\,t^{*'}}(s'), \text{ otherwise} \end{cases}$$

If the expressions attributed to $g'$ in the above formulae are not defined then $\phi_q'$ or $\psi_{q\,\theta}'$ will be considered undefined for the corresponding values.
5. $F_q$ is defined by:
$F_q(q, \phi_q') = q$
$F_q(q, \psi_{q\,\theta}') = d(\theta)$.

Using Lemma 6.3.2.2 it is easy to show that $\mathcal{M}'(q)$ satisfies requirements 5(i) and 5(ii) of Definition 6.3.3.1. Also requirement 5 follows from Lemma 6.3.2.3, the path $p'$ that corresponds to an arc $\phi: q \to \theta$ will be a sequence of $\phi_q$s followed by a $\psi_{q\,\theta}'$.

It remains to show that $\mathcal{M}'$ constructed as in Definition 6.3.3.2 computes $f$. Let $s^{*'} \in seq(Input')$ and let $n \geq 1$ the largest natural number so that $s^{*'}$ can be written as $s^{*'} = s_1^{*'} ::....:: s_n^{*'}$ with $s_1^{*'},..., s_{n-1}^{*'} \in domain\, u$ and $s_n^{*'} \in seq(Input') - domain\, u^*$ (if $s^{*'} \in domain\, u^*$ then we take $s_n^{*'} = < >$). Then by induction on the length of $s^{*'}$ it follows that:

1. If $p': q_0 \to q$ is a path in $\mathcal{M}'$ with $\pi_2(|p'|((m_0, < >, < >), s^{*'}) = (m, x^{*'}, t^{*'})$ then $x^{*'} = s_1^{*'} ::....:: s_{n-1}^{*'}$ and $t^{*'} = s_n^{*'}$.

Also by induction on the length of $s^{*'}$, using Lemma 6.3.2.3, it follows that:

2. $f(s^{*'}) = g^{*'} \Leftrightarrow \exists\, q \in Q, m \in Memory$ and a path $p': q_0 \to q$ in $\mathcal{M}'$ with $|p'|((m_0, < >, < >), s^{*'}) = ((m, s_1^{*'} ::....:: s_{n-1}^{*'}, s_n^{*'}), g^{*'})$

Hence $\mathcal{M}'$ computes $f$.

## Corollary 6.3.4.2 (The fundamental theorem of refinement)

Let $\mathcal{M}$ be a stream X-machine, $f$ the (partial) function it computes and let $f'$ be a (partial) stream function. Then $f'$ is a refinement of $f$ with respect to $(u, v)$ if and only if there exists $\mathcal{M}'$ a state refinement of $\mathcal{M}$ with respect to $(u, v)$ that computes $f'$.

# 7

# Complete Functional Testing

*Summary. State machine morphisms, state machine minimality, state equivalence, state machine testing theory, test set constructions, transition cover, characterisation set, complexity, stream X-machine testing, design for test conditions, fundamental test function, fundamental theorem of testing, expected outputs, test set complexity.*

This chapter introduces the theoretical basis of the stream X-machine based testing (SXMT) method. This generates test sets for a system specified as a stream X-machine whose application ensures that the system behaviour is identical to that of the specification *provided* that the system is made of fault-free components and some explicit "design for testing" requirements are met. The method was applied to examples in Chapters 3 and 5.

## 7.1  SOME STATE MACHINE THEORY

Some knowledge of the theory of finite state machines will be needed in our theoretical discussion and this section will briefly presents several key concepts and results. We will refer to deterministic *finite state machines without outputs* (*automata*) as defined in the first chapter of the book, denoted by tuples of the form $\mathcal{A} = (Input, Q, F, q_0)$, where *Input* is the input alphabet, $Q$ the state set, $q_0$ the initial state and $F$ the next-state (partial) function. As in the previous chapter, we shall assume that all the machine's states are terminal states, i.e. $T = Q$. The concepts and results given here are also valid for a (possibly infinite) state machine. Most of the results are well known – see, for example, Eilenberg [28] – and we will not prove them here.

## Morphisms

A *morphism* is a particular type of state mapping between two state machines. We will need to consider the mathematical relationships between two machines, one representing the specification and the other the implementation, since we want to establish, as far as possible, that their behaviours are the same. A morphism is a means of mapping states from one machine to states of the other in a way that respects the machine structure of both.

### Definition 7.1.1

Let $\mathcal{A} = (Input, Q, F, q_0)$ and $\mathcal{A}' = (Input, Q', F', q_0')$ be two state machines over the same input alphabet. Then $g: \mathcal{A} \to \mathcal{A}'$ is called a *morphism* if $g: Q \to Q'$ is a function that satisfies the following.

1. $g(q_0) = q_0'$
2. $\forall\, q \in Q$, $input \in Input$, $g(F(q, input)) = F'(g(q), input)$

Thus the two initial states must be related and a transition in the first machine must relate to the transition of the related states in the second.

The second requirement is equivalent to the following.

2′. $\forall\, q \in Q$, $input \in Input$, $(\exists\ input\!: q \to \theta$ an arc in $\mathcal{A}) \Leftrightarrow (\exists\ input\!: g(q) \to g(\theta)$ an arc in $\mathcal{A}')$.

If $g: Q \to Q'$ is a surjective morphism then $\mathcal{A}'$ is obtained from $\mathcal{A}$ by merging all states whose image through $g$ is the same. If $g$ is bijective then $\mathcal{A}$ and $\mathcal{A}'$ are identical up to a renaming of the state space. In this case $g$ is called a *state machine isomorphism*.

### Definition 7.1.2

A bijective state machine morphism is called an *isomorphism*.

### Lemma 7.1.1

If $g: \mathcal{A} \to \mathcal{A}'$ is a morphism then $\mathcal{A}$ and $\mathcal{A}'$ accept the same language.

The *language* accepted by an automaton is the set of input sequences corresponding to paths in the machine.

## State Machine Minimality

This section defines the minimal machine of an automaton and shows that this is unique up to a relabelling of the state space. Minimal machines are machines with as few states as possible for a given behaviour.

## Definition 7.1.3

Let $\mathcal{A} = (Input, Q, F, q_0)$ be a state machine. Then a state $q \in Q$ is called *accessible* if $\exists$ $input^*$: $q_0 \to q$ a path from the initial state $q_0$ to $q$. $\mathcal{A}$ is called an *accessible automaton* if all its states are accessible. Thus, in an accessible automaton we can always find a path from the initial state to a given state.

Given a state machine $\mathcal{A}$, all the non-accessible states can be removed without affecting the language accepted by $\mathcal{A}$. The resulting machine is called the *accessible part* of $\mathcal{A}$ and will be denoted by $Acc(\mathcal{A})$.

## Definition 7.1.4

Let $\mathcal{A}$ be a state machine and let $V \subseteq seq(Input)$. Then we define an equivalence relation $\sim_V$ on $Q$ by:

$$q \sim_V q' \Leftrightarrow$$

$\forall$ $input^* \in V$, $(\exists$ $input^*$, a path in $\mathcal{A}$ that starts in $q \Leftrightarrow \exists$ $input^*$, a path in $\mathcal{A}$ that starts in $q'$)

What this means is that for every path labelled by an element of $V$ from $q$ there is a path labelled by that element from $q'$ and conversely.

If $q \sim_V q'$ then we say that $q$ and $q'$ are *V-equivalent*. Otherwise we will say that $V$ *distinguishes* between $q$ and $q'$. If $V = seq(Input)$ then we say that $q$ and $q'$ are *equivalent*.

For two state machines $\mathcal{A} = (Input, Q, F, q_0)$ and $A' = (Input, Q', F', q_0')$ over the same input alphabet, we say that $\mathcal{A}$ and $\mathcal{A}'$ are *equivalent* if their initial states $q_0$ and $q_0'$ are equivalent. Since $\mathcal{A}$ and $\mathcal{A}'$ have only terminal states, $\mathcal{A}$ and $\mathcal{A}'$ are equivalent if and only if they accept the same language.

## Definition 7.1.5

A state machine $\mathcal{A}$ is called *reduced* if $\forall$ $q, q' \in Q$ if $q$ and $q'$ are equivalent then $q = q'$. Given a state machine $\mathcal{A}$, the machine constructed by merging the states of $\mathcal{A}$ that are equivalent will be called the *reduced machine* of $\mathcal{A}$ and will be denoted by $Red(\mathcal{A})$.

As shown previously, the merger of states in a state machine can be described in terms of a state machine morphism. Thus there exists a surjective state machine morphism from $\mathcal{A}$ to $Red(\mathcal{A})$.

## Definition 7.1.6

A deterministic state machine $\mathcal{A}$ is called *minimal* if it is accessible and reduced.

## Theorem 7.1.1

Given a state machine $\mathcal{A}$, there is a minimal state machine that accepts the same language as $\mathcal{A}$ and this is unique up to a state machine morphism. We will call this the *minimal machine of* $\mathcal{A}$, denoted $Min(\mathcal{A})$.

The minimal machine of an automaton $\mathcal{A}$ can be obtained by reducing $Acc(\mathcal{A})$ or by taking the accessible part of $Red(\mathcal{A})$ since the above result will ensure that the following diagram commutes (that is, either way round gives the same result).

Also, since $Min(\mathcal{A}) = Red(Acc(\mathcal{A}))$ there exists a surjective morphism from $Acc(\mathcal{A})$ to $Min(\mathcal{A})$ that merges the equivalent states of $Acc(\mathcal{A})$.

In Figure 7.1, $\mathcal{A}_2 = Acc(\mathcal{A}_1)$ and $\mathcal{A}_3 = Red(\mathcal{A}_2)$ thus $\mathcal{A}_3 = Min(\mathcal{A}_1)$. Also, it is easy to see that $g\colon \mathcal{A}_2 \to \mathcal{A}_1$ defined by:

$$g(A_2) = A_1, g(B_2) = B_1, g(C_2) = C_1, g(D_2) = D_1$$

is an injective state machine morphism and that $h\colon \mathcal{A}_2 \to \mathcal{A}_3$ defined by:

$$h(A_2) = A_3, h(B_2) = B_3, h(C_2) = C_3, h(D_2) = B_3$$

is a surjective state machine morphism.

## State Equivalence

The following results will be used later in Chapter 8.

## Lemma 7.1.2

Let $\mathcal{A} = (Input, Q, F, q_0)$ and $\mathcal{A}' = (Input, Q', F', q_0')$ be two state machines *over the same input alphabet* and $e\colon Q \leftrightarrow Q'$ a relation. Then $\mathcal{A}$ and $\mathcal{A}'$ are equivalent if the following are true.

1. $q_0 \ e \ q_0'$
2. if $q \ e \ q'$ then $\forall \ input \in Input$, $(\exists \ input_1\colon q \to \theta$ an arc in $\mathcal{A}) \Leftrightarrow (\exists \ input_1\colon q' \to \theta'$ an arc in $A')$, where $\theta \ e \ \theta'$.

*Proof:*
By induction the length of $input^* \in seq(Input)$ it follows that $\forall \ input^* \in seq(Input) \cdot (\exists \ input^*\colon q_0 \to \theta$ a path in $A \ ) \Leftrightarrow (\exists \ input^*\colon q_0' \to \theta'$ a path in $\mathcal{A}')$, where $\theta \ e \ \theta'$.

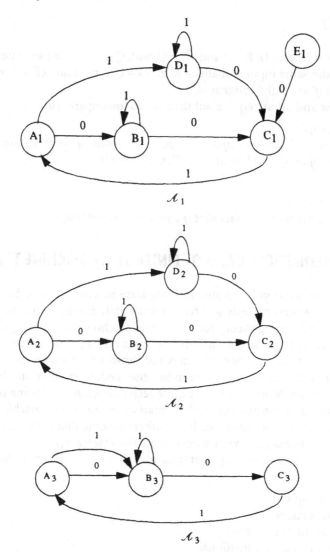

**FIG. 7.1.** State machines and reduced machines.

**Definition 7.1.7**

Let $\mathcal{A}$ = (*Input*, $Q$, $F$, $q_0$) and $A'$ = (*Input*, $Q'$, $F'$, $q_0'$) be two state machines over the same input alphabet and let $q \in Q$ and $q' \in Q'$. Then $q$ and $q'$ are said to be *right-congruent* if there exists *input** $\in$ seq(*Input*) so that *input**: $q_0 \to q$ is a path in $A$ and *input**: $q_0' \to q'$ is a path in $\mathcal{A}'$.

*Lemma 7.1.3*

Let $\mathcal{A} = (Input, Q, F, q_0)$ and $\mathcal{A}' = (Input, Q', F', q_0')$ be two state machines over the same input alphabet and $e: Q \leftrightarrow Q'$ a relation defined by $q \ e \ q' \Leftrightarrow$ $q$ and $q'$ are right-congruent.

If $\mathcal{A}$ and $\mathcal{A}'$ are equivalent then the following are true.

1. $q_0 \ e \ q_0'$
2. if $q \ e \ q'$ then $\forall \ input \in Input \cdot (\exists \ input: q \rightarrow \theta$ an arc in $\mathcal{A}) \Leftrightarrow$ $(\exists \ input: q' \rightarrow \theta'$ an arc in $\mathcal{A}')$, where $\theta \ e \ \theta'$.

*Proof:*
1. Obvious.
2. Follows from the fact that $q$ and $q'$ are equivalent.

## 7.2  THEORETICAL BASIS OF FINITE STATE MACHINE TESTING

The next section is devoted to finite state machine testing. Several methods of generating tests sets from a finite state machine specification exist. A general testing theory for finite state machines was developed by Chow [76]. It assumes that the specification and the implementation can both be expressed as finite state machines and shows how a test set that finds all the faults of the implementation can be generated. There are a number of other approaches. Most of them are quite restrictive, however. Some require that the specification and the implementation are finite state machines with the same number of states (see [93]); others assume that the specification is a finite state machine with special properties (see [94]).

In particular, testing strategies may attempt to identify the following types of faults:

- missing states;
- extra states;
- missing transitions;
- mis-directed transitions;
- transitions with faulty functions (inputs/outputs);
- extra transitions.

The *transition tour* method, [96], relies on the specification machine being minimal, strongly connected and complete. The method involves a traversal of all transitions without trying to target specific states. Efficient algorithms for determining minimal length sequences have been described [96].

The *unique input–output (UIO) sequence* method, [96], involves deriving a sequence for each state which reflects the behaviour of that state. A number of improvements and variants of this method have been found. This method identifies that all the required states are present in the implementation.

The *W method* [76], is designed for the case where there may be more states in the implementation than in the specification. This is a potential advantage for this method over the others. However a number of variations and hybrid techniques are being developed. Some of these methods produce rather shorter sequences than the W method. This is an advantage if time for testing is short or more is known about the properties of the implementation (for example, it has the same number of states as the specification).

We will focus on the adaptation of the W method because of its capability of detecting more faults in an implementation than the others. Although we do give estimates, later, of the cost of the testing method we develop we do not focus on the question of the optimisation of the test sequences or the test set. Some of the work in [77] and [97] may generalise to the stream X-machine case.

The basis of Chow's test set generation are the concepts of characterisation set, state cover and transition cover of a minimal finite state machine. These will be defined next. Note that the minimality of the automaton will ensure their existence.

### Definition 7.2.1

Let $\mathcal{A} = (Input, Q, F, q_0)$ be a minimal finite state machine. Then $S \subseteq seq(Input)$ is called a *state cover* set of $\mathcal{A}$ if $\forall q \in Q \exists input^* \in S$ so that $input^*: q_0 \to q$ is a path in $\mathcal{A}$ from the initial state $q_0$ to $q$.

So a state cover is a set of input sequences that enables us to access any state in the machine from the initial state.

### Definition 7.2.2

Let $\mathcal{A} = (Input, Q, F, q_0)$ be a minimal finite state machine. Then $T \subseteq seq(Input)$ is called a *transition cover* of $A$ if $\forall q \in Q \exists input^* \in T$ so that $input^*: q_0 \to q$ is a path in $A$ from the initial state $q_0$ to $q$ and $\forall input \in Input, input^* :: input \in T$.

In other words, for any state $q$ there are sequences in $T$ that take $\mathcal{A}$ to $q$ from $q_0$ and then attempt to exercise all possible arcs from $q$ irrespective of whether such arcs exist or not. It is easy to see that if $S$ is a state cover of $\mathcal{A}$ then $T = S \cup [S \bullet Input]$ is a transition cover of $\mathcal{A}$. Conversely, for any transition cover $T$ there exists a state cover $S$ with $S \cup [S \bullet Input] \subseteq T$.

### Definition 7.2.3

Let $\mathcal{A} = (Input, Q, F, q_0)$ be a minimal finite state machine. Then $W \subseteq seq(Input)$ is called a *characterisation set* of $\mathcal{A}$ if $W$ distinguishes between any two distinct states of $\mathcal{A}$.

Note that Chow's theory was developed in the context of finite state machines with outputs, i.e. an edge:

$$q \xrightarrow{\text{input/output}} q'$$

is labelled by a pair *input/output* with *input* ∈ *Input* and *output* ∈ *Output*; *output* is the output symbol and *Output* is called the output alphabet. In this case a path will be a sequence of input/output pairs and the definitions of state equivalence and distinguishability will refer to such input/output sequences rather than merely to sequences of inputs. However, Chow's theory remains valid for automata without outputs and this is the case we shall consider in our theoretical discussion.

For two automata $\mathcal{A}$ and $\mathcal{A}'$ over the same input alphabet, a set of input sequences will be called a *test set* of $\mathcal{A}$ and $\mathcal{A}'$ if its successful application to the two automata will ensure their equivalence.

### Definition 7.2.4

Let $\mathcal{A} = (Input, Q, F, q_0)$ and $\mathcal{A}' = (Input, Q', F', q_0')$ be two finite state machines over the input alphabet *Input*. Then a set $X \subseteq \text{seq}(Input)$ is called a *test set* of $\mathcal{A}$ and $\mathcal{A}'$ if the following is true:

if $q_0$ and $q_0'$ are X-equivalent as states in $\mathcal{A}$ and $\mathcal{A}'$ respectively then $\mathcal{A}$ and $\mathcal{A}'$ are equivalent.

The idea of a test set is that it is a set of input sequences that can be used to establish whether two finite state machines are equivalent. If they are not equivalent, in other words if their behaviour is different, then we can find an input sequence in the test set that will show this difference in behaviour. The key objective, then, is to find ways of constructing test sets. Clearly, seq(*Input*) is a test set but not a very useful one since it is infinite. We want to find *finite* test sets.

The following theorem is the basis of Chow's finite state machine testing. It describes a procedure for constructing a finite test set.

### Theorem 7.2.1 ([76])

Let $\mathcal{A}$ and $\mathcal{A}'$ be two minimal finite state machines over the input alphabet *Input*, $n$ the number of states of $\mathcal{A}$ and $n'$ the number of states of $\mathcal{A}'$. Let $T$ and $W$, respectively, be a transition cover and a characterisation set of $\mathcal{A}$, $Z = Input^k \bullet W \cup Input^{k-1} \bullet W \cup ... \cup W$ and let $X = T \bullet Z$. If $Card(Q') - Card(Q) \leq k$ and $\mathcal{A}$ and $\mathcal{A}'$ are X-equivalent, then $\mathcal{A}$ and $\mathcal{A}'$ are isomorphic.

The idea is that the transition cover $T$ ensures that all the states and all the transitions of $\mathcal{A}$ are also present in $\mathcal{A}'$ and $Z$ ensures that $\mathcal{A}'$ is in the same state as $\mathcal{A}$ after each transition is performed. Notice that $Z$ contains $W$ and also all sets $Input^i \bullet W, i = 1,..., k$. This ensures that $\mathcal{A}'$ does not contain extra states. If there were up to $k$ extra states, then each of them would be reached by some input sequence of up to length $k$ from the existing states.

If the system specification and implementation can *both* be modelled as finite state machines $\mathcal{A}$ and $\mathcal{A}'$ then the set $X = T \bullet Z$ of the above theorem will ensure that these are equivalent provided that the maximum number of states of the implementation can be estimated. Note that the finite state machine model of the implementation, $\mathcal{A}'$, need not be minimal since the above theorem can be applied to $\mathcal{A}$ and $Min(\mathcal{A}')$. Hence $\mathcal{A}$ and $Min(\mathcal{A}')$ are isomorphic, thus $\mathcal{A}$ and $\mathcal{A}'$ are equivalent.

### Corollary 7.2.1

Let $\mathcal{A}$ and $\mathcal{A}'$ be two finite state machines over the input alphabet *Input* with $\mathcal{A}$ minimal, Card($Q$) the number of states of $\mathcal{A}$ and Card($Q'$) the number of states of $\mathcal{A}'$. Let $T$, $W$, $Z$ and $X$ be as in Theorem 7.2.1. If Card($Q'$) − Card($Q$) $\leq k$ and $\mathcal{A}$ and $\mathcal{A}'$ are X-equivalent, then $X$ is a test set of $\mathcal{A}$ and $\mathcal{A}'$.

## The Construction of the Test Set and its Complexity

Since the concepts of characterisation set and transition cover will be used later on in our testing theory, we will describe their construction in detail. In what follows we will refer to a finite state machine $\mathcal{A}$ with $n$ states and $p$ input symbols.

## Constructing a Transition Cover

One way to construct a transition cover is to build a *testing tree*. A procedure of constructing testing trees is presented below.

1. Label the root of the tree with $q_0$, the initial state of $\mathcal{A}$. This is the first level of the tree.
2. Suppose we have already built the tree up to a level $m$. Then the $(m+1)$th level is built by examining nodes in the $m$th level from left to right. A node at the $m$th level is designated a terminal if its label is "Undefined" or is the same as a non-terminal at some level $l$, $l \leq m$. Otherwise let $q$ denote its label. If on an input $s$, the machine $\mathcal{A}$ goes from the state $q$ to the state $\theta$, we attach a branch and the successor node to the node labelled with $s$ and $\theta$, respectively. If there is no transition defined for $s$ from $q$ then we also attach a branch labelled $s$, but in this case the successor node will be labelled "Undefined".

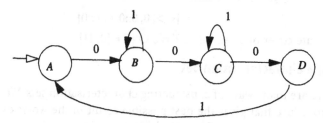

**FIG. 7.2.** A simple finite state machine.

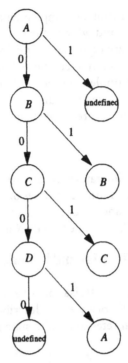

**FIG. 7.3.** The testing tree for the machine in Figure 7.2.

Obviously, the procedure above terminates since there is only a finite number of states in $\mathcal{A}$. In fact, the tree has at most $n+1$ levels, where $n$ is the number of states. Also, depending on the order in which we place the successor nodes, a different tree may result.

A transition cover $T$ results by enumerating all the partial paths in the tree and adding the empty sequence to the set obtained in this way.

It is easy to see that $T$ can be written as $T = S \cup [S \bullet Input]$, with $S$ a state cover of $\mathcal{A}$. The number of sequences of the resulting transition cover is $n. (p + 1)$. It is also clear that this is the minimum possible number of elements of any transition cover.

A testing tree of $\mathcal{A}$ from Figure 7.2 may be found in Figure 7.3. Thus a transition cover will be:

$$T = \{< >, 0, 1, 0::0, 0::1, 0::0::0, 0::0::1, 0::0::0::0, 0::0::0::1\}$$

It is easy to see that:

$$S = \{< >, 0, 0::0, 0::0::0\}$$

is a state cover of $\mathcal{A}$ and that $T = S \cup [S \bullet \{0, 1\}]$

## Building a Characterisation Set

There are many ways of constructing characterisation sets. We will present a procedure that gives the best possible result in the worst case scenario. First let us make some theoretical considerations.

Let $V, V' \subseteq$ seq(*Input*) be two sets of input sequences and $\sim_V$ and $\sim_{V'}$ respectively the equivalence relations on Q determined by them. Then we say that $\sim_V < \sim_{V'}$ if the following are true:

1. $\forall\, q, q' \in Q$ if $q \sim_{V'} q'$ then $q \sim_V q'$.
2. $\exists\, q, q' \in Q$ such that $q \sim_V q'$ and $\neg(q \sim_{V'} q')$.

On the other hand, if $\forall\, q, q' \in Q, q \sim_V q'$ if and only if $q \sim_{V'} q'$ then we say that $\sim_V = \sim_{V'}$. Also, if $V$ is seq$_i$(*Input*), the set of all sequences of $i$ inputs, then $\sim_V$ will be denoted by $\sim_i$. Then, for a minimal finite state machine $\mathcal{A}$ with $n$ states, there exists $j \leq n-1$ such that $\sim_1 < \sim_2 < \cdots \sim_j = \sim_{j+1} = \sim_{j+2} = \cdots$

This is a well-known result. A proof can be found in Eilenberg [28]. Since $\mathcal{A}$ is minimal, seq$_{n-1}$(*Input*) will distinguish any pair of states of $\mathcal{A}$. (Recall that seq$_{n-1}$(*Input*) is the set of all sequences of inputs from *Input* of length at most $n-1$.)

We can now give the following algorithm that finds a characterisation set W.

Step 1.  Initialise $V = \emptyset$ and $i = 1$.

Step 2.  (a) If $\sim_V < \sim_i$ then find $s^* \in$ seq$_i$(*Input*) that distinguishes between two states $q$ and $q'$ that are not $V$-distinguishable; the partition determined by $\sim_i$ on Q and $s^*$ can be determined from the so-called $P_k$ tables, see Gill [98]. Then $V$ will become $V \cup \{s^*\}$ and step 2 is repeated.
(b) Otherwise, go to step 3.

Step 3.  (a) If $V$ does not distinguish between any pair of states of $A$, then increment $i$.
(b) Otherwise $W = V$ is the characterisation set required.

Using a simple induction it is easy to prove that the characterisation set $W$ constructed by the algorithm will satisfy the following requirements.

1. Card($W$) $\leq n-1$;
2. $\forall\, i = 1,...,n-1 \exists$ at most $n-i$ elements of $W$ of length at least $i$.

Hence, in the worst case the above algorithm will generate a characterisation set $W = \{s_1^*,...,s_{n-1}^*\}$ with length($s_i$) $= i, i = 1,...,n-1$.

On the other hand, for any $n$ and $p$ there exists a minimal finite state machine $\mathcal{A}$ with $n$ states and $p$ inputs so that any characterisation set of $\mathcal{A}$ will contain $n-1$ sequences $s_1^*,...,s_{n-1}^*$ with $\forall\, i = 1...n-1$, length($s_i$) $\geq i$; for $p = 2$ such an automaton may be found in Figure 7.4. Thus the above algorithm will produce the best result in the worst case.

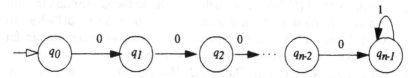

**FIG. 7.4.** The worst case scenario.

The application of the algorithm on the automaton represented in Figure 7.4 will produce the characterisation set:

$$W = \{1, 0::1, 0::0::1,..., 0^{n-2}::1\}$$

## Complexity Results

For a minimal machine with $n$ states and $p$ inputs the effort required in constructing $T$ and $W$ is roughly proportional to $n^2. p$. This can be seen as follows: $T$ is obtained by first constructing a testing tree and then enumerating the partial paths in the tree. Since for each state $q$ and each input symbol $s$ the transition from $q$ on $s$ appears exactly once in the transition tree, the complexity of the former is proportional to $n. p$. The complexity of the latter is also proportional to $n. p$ since there are $n. p + 1$ partial paths in the tree.

The transition set may be obtained from the so-called $P_k$ tables using the above algorithm. The amount of work required to construct a $P_k$ table is proportional to $n. p$, the number of entries in the table. There are at most $n-1$ such tables, thus the effort required to construct them is proportional to $n^2. p$.

## Upper Bounds for the Test Set Size

Using the above considerations regarding the sizes of a transition cover and of a characterisation set it can be deduced easily (see also [92]) that the number of test sequences required is less than $n^2. p^{k+2}/(p-1) \approx n^2. p^{k+1}$ and the total length of the test set, that is the size of the sequence obtained by putting all the test input sequences into one long sequence (a measure of the effort needed to fully test the system), is not greater than $n^2. (n+k). p^{k+2}/ (p-1) \approx n^2. (n+k). p^{k+1}$, where $k$ is the difference between the number of states of the implementation and the number of states of the specification.

Various authors (see, for example, [96]) have devised improved methods based on the use of fewer input sequences in the test set or by combining test sequences together to improve efficiency. Usually, the gain in obtaining a smaller test set is partly offset by the increased complexity of the process of generating it.

## 7.3  THEORETICAL BASIS OF STREAM X-MACHINE TESTING

This section will provide the theoretical basis for the stream X-machine testing method (SXMT). The method works on the assumption that the system specification and implementation can both be modelled as stream X-machines with the same type $\Phi$, and $\Phi$ satisfies some "design for test conditions" as presented in detail in what follows.

Thus, let $M = (Input, Output, Q, Memory, \Phi, F, q_0, m_0)$ be a stream X-machine with type $\Phi$.

## Design for Test Conditions

The method reduces the task of testing that the two machines compute the same function to that of testing that their associated automata are equivalent. If this is to work then the basic processing functions $\Phi$ will have to meet two requirements, completeness with respect to *Memory* and output-distinguishability. These ideas are defined next.

*Definition 7.3.1*

A type $\Phi$ is called *output-distinguishable* if the following is true.

$\forall \phi_1, \phi_2 \in \Phi \; \forall \; m \in Memory, s \in Input$ such that if $(m, s) \in$ domain $\phi_1$, $(m, s) \in$ domain $\phi_2$ and $\pi_1(\phi_1(m, s)) = \pi_1(\phi_2(m, s))$ then $\phi_1 = \phi_2$.

What this is saying is that any two different basic processing functions will produce different outputs on some memory-input pair.

*Definition 7.3.2*

A processing function $\phi \in \Phi$ is called *test-complete* with respect to *Memory*, (*t-complete*), if the following is true:

$\forall \; m \in Memory \; \exists \; input \in Input$ with $(m, input) \in$ domain $\phi$.

A *type* $\Phi$ is called *complete* with respect to *Memory* if $\forall \; \phi \in \Phi \; \phi$ is complete with respect to *Memory*.

In other words, any basic function will be able to process all memory values using a suitable input.

These two conditions are required of the specification machine and they will be referred to as "design for test conditions". Although these might appear as being quite restrictive, they can be easily introduced into a specification by simply extending the definitions of the $\Phi$ functions in a suitable manner, introducing extra input symbols and augmenting the output alphabet ([92]). In very simple terms, this can be done as follows:

Let $\phi \in \Phi$ be a processing function that is not complete with respect to *Memory* and let $\alpha \notin Input$ be an extra input (to be used specifically for testing process) and $g_0 \in Output$ an output chosen arbitrarily. Then the basic function $\phi_e$ defined by:

$$\phi_e(m, s) = \begin{cases} \phi(m, s), \text{if } (m, s) \in \text{domain } \phi \\ \\ (g_0, m), \text{if } s = \alpha \text{ and } m \in Memory \end{cases}$$

is complete with respect to *Memory*.

Obviously, $\phi_e$ will be a processing function of a stream X-machine whose input alphabet includes $Input \cup \{\alpha\}$ and has the same *Memory* as the original machine.

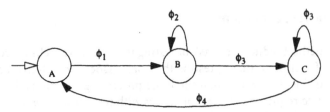

**FIG. 7.5.** A simple stream X-machine.

The above extension will be performed for *all* non-complete $\phi$s while the complete $\phi$s will remain unchanged; the resulting type will be named $\Phi_e$.

If the resulting machine is to remain deterministic, then any two $\phi$s that are used as labels for arcs emerging from the same state will use different extra inputs. Thus the maximum number of extra inputs required will be at most:

$N_{in} = \mathrm{Card}\{\phi' \in \Phi \mid \exists\, q \in Q$ such that $\phi$ and $\phi'$ are arcs emerging from $q\}$

In most cases $N_{in} << \mathrm{Card}(\Phi)$ so the number of extra inputs is usually small.

The output-distinguishability will be achieved by a further augmentation process: the output alphabet of the resulting machine will become *Output* $\times G$, where the "$G$" component of the output will be used to distinguish between any two elements of $\Phi_e$. Further details can be found in [92].

## Example 7.3.1

We illustrate the above procedure with the following example. Let $\mathcal{M}$ be the stream X-machine represented in Figure 7.5 with *Input* = $\{x, y\}$, *Output* = $\{a, b\}$, *Memory* = $\{0, 1\}$, $m_0 = 0$ and the processing functions defined by:

$$\phi_1(m, x) = (a, 0), m \in Memory$$

$$\phi_2(0, x) = (a, 0)$$

$$\phi_3(1, y) = (b, 1)$$

$$\phi_4(1, x) = (b, 0)$$

If we augment *Input* to *Input$_e$* = $\{x, y, z, w\}$ then the extended type $\Phi_e = \{\phi_1, \phi_{2e}, \phi_{3e}, \phi_{4e}\}$ is complete with respect to *Memory*, where $\phi_{2e}, \phi_{3e}, \phi_{4e}$ are defined by:

$$\phi_{2e}(0, x) = (a, 0)$$
$$\phi_{2e}(m, z) = (a, m), m \in Memory$$

$$\phi_{3e}(1, y) = (b, 1)$$
$$\phi_{3e}(m, w) = (a, m), m \in Memory$$

$$\phi_{4e}(1, x) = (b, 0)$$
$$\phi_{4e}(m, z) = (a, m), m \in Memory$$

Furthermore, if the output alphabet is augmented to $\{a, b\} \times \{c, d, e\}$ then the augmented type $\Phi' = \{\phi_1', \phi_2', \phi_3', \phi_4'\}$ will be complete with respect to *Memory* and output-distinguishable.

$$\phi_1'(m, x) = ((a, c), 0), m \in \textit{Memory}$$

$$\phi_2'(0, x) = ((a, d), 0)$$
$$\phi_2'(m, z) = ((a, d), m), m \in \textit{Memory}$$

$$\phi_3'(1, y) = ((b, d), 1)$$
$$\phi_3'(m, w) = ((a, d), m), m \in \textit{Memory}$$

$$\phi_4'(1, x) = ((b, e), 0)$$
$$\phi_4'(m, z) = ((a, e), m), m \in \textit{Memory}$$

## Fundamental Test Function

The last theoretical concept introduced is that of the fundamental test function of a stream X-machine, defined as a means of converting sequences of $\phi$s into sequences of inputs. This will be used to test paths of the machine using appropriate input sequences.

*Definition. 7.3.3*

Let $\mathcal{M} = (\textit{Input}, \textit{Output}, Q, \textit{Memory}, \Phi, F, q_0, m_0)$ be a stream X-machine with $\Phi$ t-complete with respect to *Memory* and let $q \in Q$ and $m \in \textit{Memory}$. A function $t_{q,m}: \text{seq}(\Phi) \to \text{seq}(\textit{Input})$ will be defined recursively as follows:

1. $t_{q,m} (<\,>) = <\,>$
2. For $n \geq 0$, the recursion step that defines $t_{q,m} (\phi_1::....::\phi_n::\phi_{n+1})$ as a function of $t_{q,m} (\phi_1::....::\phi_n)$ depends on the following two cases:
   (i) if $\exists$ a path $p = \phi_1::....:: \phi_n$ in $M$ starting from $q$, then:

$$t_{q,m} (\phi_1::....:: \phi_n::\phi_{n+1}) = t_{q,m} (\phi_1::....:: \phi_n) :: s_{n+1},$$

with $s_{n+1}$ chosen such that $(m_n, s_{n+1}) \in \text{domain } \phi_{n+1}$

where $m_n = \pi_2(|p|(m, t_{q,m} (\phi_1::....:: \phi_n))$ is the final memory value computed by the machine along the path $p$ on the input sequence $t_{q,m} (\phi_1::....:: \phi_n)$. Note that such $s_{n+1}$ since $\Phi$ is t-complete with respect to *Memory* there exists such $s_{n+1}$.

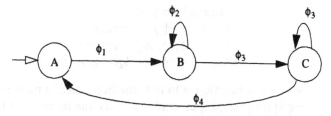

**FIG. 7.6.** A stream X-machine.

(ii) otherwise:

$$t_{q,m} (\phi_1 :: .... :: \phi_n :: \phi_{n+1}) = tq,m (\phi_1 :: .... :: \phi_n)$$

Then $t_{q,m}$ is called a *test function* of $\mathcal{M}$ with respect to $(q, m)$.

If $q = q_0$ and $m = m_0$ then $t_{q,m}$ is denoted by $t$ and is called a *fundamental test function* of $\mathcal{M}$.

If $m = m_0$ then $t_{q,m}$ is denoted by $t_q$.

In other words if $p = \phi_1 :: .... :: \phi_n$ is a path in $\mathcal{M}$ from $q$ to some state $q_n$, then $t_{q,m} (\phi_1 :: .... :: \phi_n)$ will be an input sequence which, when applied in state $q$ and with memory contents $m$, will cause the computation of the machine to follow this path, i.e. $t_{q,m} (\phi_1 :: .... :: \phi_n) = s_1 :: .... :: s_n$, where $s_1$ exercises $\phi_1, ..., s_n$ exercises $\phi_n$.

If there is no arc labelled $\phi_{n+1}$ from $q_n$, then $t_{q,m} (\phi_1 :: .... :: \phi_n :: \phi_{n+1})$ $= t_{q,m} (\phi_1 :: .... :: \phi_n) :: s_{n+1}$, where $s_{n+1}$ is an input that will exercise an arc labelled $\phi_{n+1}$ emerging from $q_n$, thus making sure that such an arc does not exist.

Also, $\forall \phi_{n+2}, ..., \phi_{n+k} \in \Phi, t_{q,m}(\phi_1 :: .... :: \phi_n :: \phi_{n+1} :: .... :: \phi_{n+k}) = t_{q,m}(\phi_1 :: .... :: \phi_n :: \phi_{n+1})$ therefore no attempt will be made to exercise the subsequent $\phi$s.

Note that a test function is not uniquely determined: many different possible test functions exist.

### Example 7.3.2

Let $\mathcal{M}$ be the stream X-machine represented in Figure 7.6 with *Input* = $\{x, y\}$, *Output* = $\{a, b\}$, *Memory* = $\{0, 1\}$, $m_0 = 0$ and the processing functions defined by:

$$\phi_1(m, y) = (a, 1), m \in Memory$$
$$\phi_2(m, x) = (a, 0), m \in Memory$$
$$\phi_3(m, y) = (b, 1), m \in Memory$$
$$\phi_4(m, x) = (b, 0), m \in Memory$$

Then we can construct a fundamental test function with the following values:

$$t (\phi_1) = y$$
$$t (\phi_1 :: \phi_2) = y :: x$$
$$t (\phi_1 :: \phi_2 :: \phi_3) = y :: x :: y$$
$$t (\phi_1 :: \phi_2 :: \phi_3 :: \phi_1) = y :: x :: y :: y$$
$$t (\phi_1 :: \phi_2 :: \phi_3 :: \phi_1 :: \phi_2) = y :: x :: y :: y$$
$$t (\phi_1 :: \phi_2 :: \phi_3 :: \phi_1 :: \phi_2 :: \phi_4) = y :: x :: y :: y$$

The scope of a test function is to test whether a certain path exists or not in $\mathcal{M}$ using appropriate input symbols, hence the name. This idea is formalized in the following lemma.

## Lemma 7.3.1

Let $\mathcal{M} = (Input, Output, Q, Memory, \Phi, F, q_0, m_0)$ and $\mathcal{M}' = (Input, Output, Q', Memory, \Phi, F', q_0', m_0)$ be two stream X-machines with the same type $\Phi$ and initial memory, $\mathcal{A}$ and $\mathcal{A}'$ their associated automata, $f$ and $f'$ the functions they compute and let $t$: $seq(\Phi) \rightarrow seq(Input)$ be a fundamental test function of $\mathcal{M}$ and $X \subseteq seq_+(\Phi)$. We assume that $\Phi$ is output-distinguishable and complete with respect to $Memory$. If $\forall$ $s^* \in t(X), f(s^*) = f'(s^*)$ then $q_0$ and $q_0'$ are X-equivalent as states in $\mathcal{A}$ and $\mathcal{A}'$ respectively.

*Proof:*

Let $\phi_1, ..., \phi_n \in \Phi$ with $f(t(\phi_1::....::\phi_n)) = f'(t(\phi_1::....::\phi_n))$. We prove that there exists a path $\phi_1::....::\phi_n$ in $\mathcal{A}$ starting from $q_0$ if and only if there exists a path $\phi_1::....::\phi_n$ in $\mathcal{A}'$ starting from $q_0'$. We have the following two cases.

1.  There exists a path $\phi_1::....::\phi_n$ in $\mathcal{A}$ starting from $q_0$. Then by induction on $i = 1...n$ using the output-distinguishability of $\Phi$ it follows that there exists a path $\phi_1::....:: \phi_i$ in $\mathcal{A}'$ starting from $q_0'$.
2.  There is no path $\phi_1::....::\phi_n$ in $\mathcal{A}$ starting from $q_0$. Then let $i \geq 0$ the maximum number for which there exists a path $\phi_1::....::\phi_i$ in $\mathcal{A}$. Then there exists a path $\phi_1::....::\phi_i$ in $\mathcal{A}'$ starting from $q_0'$. Let $q_i$ and $q_i'$, respectively, the end states of these paths. Now, if we assume that there exists an arc $\phi_{i+1}$ from $q_i'$, from the output-distinguishability of $\Phi$ it will follow that there is an arc $\phi_{i+1}$ from $q_i$, which contradicts our initial assumption. Thus there is no path $\phi_1 ::....:: \phi_n$ in $\mathcal{A}'$ starting from $q_0'$.

We can now assemble our fundamental result, which is the basis of the SXMT method.

# Fundamental Theorem of Testing

## Theorem 7.3.1

Let $\mathcal{M} = (Input, Output, Q, Memory, \Phi, F, q_0, m_0)$ and $\mathcal{M}' = (Input, Output, Q', Memory, \Phi, F', q_0', m_0)$ be two stream X-machines with the same type $\Phi$ and initial memory, $\mathcal{A}$ and $\mathcal{A}'$ their associated automata, $f$ and $f'$ the functions they compute and let $t$: $seq(\Phi) \rightarrow seq(Input)$ be a fundamental test function of $\mathcal{M}$. We assume that $\mathcal{A}$ and $\mathcal{A}'$ are minimal and that $\Phi$ is output-distinguishable and complete with respect to $Memory$. Let also $T$ and $W$, respectively, be a transition cover and a characterisation set of $\mathcal{A}$, $Z = [\Phi^k \bullet W] \cup [\Phi^{k-1} \bullet W] \cup... \cup W$, where $k$ is a positive integer, $X = T \bullet Z$ and $Y = t(X)$. If $Card(Q') - Card(Q) \leq k$ and $\forall$ $s^* \in Y, f(s^*) = f'(s^*)$ then $\mathcal{A}$ and $\mathcal{A}'$ are isomorphic.

*Proof:*

From Lemma 7.3.1 it follows that $q_0$ and $q_0'$ are X-equivalent. The rest follows from Theorem 7.2.1.

Notice that the completeness and output-distinguishability requirements can be relaxed to the attainable memory of $M$. That is, all memory values used by Definitions 7.3.1 and 7.3.2 will be in $Mattain(M)$.

### Example 7.3.3

For the machine of Example 7.3.2 we have:

$$T = \{<>, \phi_1, \phi_2, \phi_3, \phi_4, \phi_1::\phi_1, \phi_1::\phi_2, \phi_1::\phi_3, \phi_1::\phi_4,$$
$$\phi_1::\phi_3::\phi_1, \phi_1::\phi_3::\phi_2, \phi_1::\phi_3::\phi_3, \phi_1::\phi_3::\phi_4\}$$
$$W = \{\phi_1, \phi_2\}$$
$$Z = [\{\phi_1, \phi_2, \phi_3, \phi_4\}^k \bullet \{\phi_1, \phi_2\}] \cup [\{\phi_1, \phi_2, \phi_3, \phi_4\}^{k-1}$$
$$\bullet \{\phi_1, \phi_2\}] \cup ... \cup \{\phi_1, \phi_2\}$$

If we take $k = 0$ then $X = T \bullet W$ thus:

$$X = \{\phi_1, \phi_1::\phi_1, \phi_2::\phi_1, \phi_3::\phi_1, \phi_4::\phi_1, \phi_1::\phi_1::\phi_1, \phi_1::\phi_2::\phi_1,$$
$$\phi_1::\phi_3::\phi_1, \phi_1::\phi_4::\phi_1, \phi_1::\phi_3::\phi_1::\phi_1, \phi_1::\phi_3::\phi_2::\phi_1,$$
$$\phi_1::\phi_3::\phi_3::\phi_1, \phi_1::\phi_3::\phi_4::\phi_1, \phi_2, \phi_1::\phi_2, \phi_2::\phi_2, \phi_3::\phi_2, \phi_4::\phi_2,$$
$$\phi_1::\phi_1::\phi_2, \phi_1::\phi_2::\phi_2, \phi_1::\phi_3::\phi_2, \phi_1::\phi_4::\phi_2, \phi_1::\phi_3::\phi_1::\phi_2,$$
$$\phi_1::\phi_3::\phi_2::\phi_2, \phi_1::\phi_3::\phi_3::\phi_2, \phi_1::\phi_3::\phi_4::\phi_2\}$$

and:

$$Y = \{y, y::y, x, y, x, y::y, y::x::y, y::y::y, y::x, y::y::y, y::y::x,$$
$$y::y::y::y, y::y::x::y, x, y::x, x, y, x, y::y, y::x::x, y::y::x,$$
$$y::x, y::y::y, y::y::x, y::y::y::x, y::y::x::x\}$$

thus:

$$Y = \{y, y::y, x, y::x::y, y::y::y, y::x, y::y::x, y::y::y::y,$$
$$y::y::x::y, y::x::x, y::y::y::x, y::y::x::x\}$$

Note that we can simplify further by removing the sequences $y::y::y$, $y::y$ and $y$ since they all occur as an initial segment (prefix) of the sequence $y::y::y::y$.

If our aim is to ensure that the two machines compute the same function, then the minimality of $A'$ is not really necessary. This result will be given next. Also, in a similar way to the case for a finite state machine, we will define a test set of two stream X-machines as a set of input sequences of which successful application to the two machines will ensure the equivalence of their associated automata.

### Definition 7.3.4

Let $M = (Input, Output, Q, Memory, \Phi, F, q_0, m_0)$ and $M' = (Input, Output, Q', Memory, \Phi, F', q_0', m_0)$ be two stream X-machines, $A$ and $A'$ their associated automata and $f$ and $f'$ the functions they compute. Then $Y \subseteq seq(Input)$ is called a *test set* of $M$ and $M'$ if the following is true:

if $\forall s^* \in Y, f(s^*) = f'(s^*)$ then $A$ and $A'$ are equivalent.

## Corollary 7.3.1

Let $\mathcal{M} = (Input, Output, Q, Memory, \Phi, \mathbf{F}, q_0, m_0)$ and $\mathcal{M}' = (Input, Output, Q', Memory, \Phi, \mathbf{F}', q_0', m_0)$ be two stream X-machines, $\mathcal{A}$ and $\mathcal{A}'$ their associated automata, $f$ and $f'$ the functions they compute and let $t: seq(\Phi) \rightarrow seq(Input)$ be a fundamental test function of $\mathcal{M}$. We assume that $\mathcal{A}$ is minimal and that $\Phi$ is output-distinguishable and complete with respect to *Memory*. Let also $T, W, Z, X$ and $Y$ as in Theorem 7.3.1. If $Card(Q') - Card(Q) \leq k$ and then $X$ is a test set of $\mathcal{M}$ and $\mathcal{M}'$.

Obviously, if $\mathcal{A}$ and $\mathcal{A}'$ are equivalent then $f = f'$. Thus if the application of $Y$ to $\mathcal{M}$ and $\mathcal{M}'$ will produce identical results then the two machines are guaranteed to have the same input/output behaviour. Therefore, if the specification and the implementation can be both expressed as machines with the same type and the required design for testing conditions are met, then $Y$ will be a test set that detects *all* faults of the implementation.

Note that since $T$ can be written as $T = S \cup [S \bullet \Phi]$, with $S$ a state cover of $\mathcal{A}$ then the test set $Y$ can be also expressed as:

$$Y = t \,(S \bullet (\,\Phi^{k+1} \cup \Phi^k \cup ... \cup \Phi) \bullet W)$$

## Expected Outputs

For most systems, $\mathcal{M}$ will compute a total function, i.e. for any sequence of inputs $s^* \in seq(Input)$, $f(s^*)$ will be a sequence of outputs. In this case, the process of comparing the two output sequences, $f(s^*)$ and $f'(s^*)$, is straightforward. However, the method does not rely on $f$ being a total function as long as it is clear what we mean by "$f(s^*)$ is undefined", i.e. what the system is supposed to do when it receives an input sequence $s^*$ for which $f(s^*)$ is undefined. For example, this could mean that the sequence $s^*$ will cause the program specified by $\mathcal{M}$ to exit.

## Complexity and Upper Bound of the Test Set

The final question that needs to be addressed is concerned with the practicality of the method. For example, how complex is the test generation algorithm? It is clear that the complexity of the algorithm depends on the complexity of the basic functions in $\Phi$. If the complexity of each $\phi$ is at most $C$, then the complexity of the algorithm that generates the test set $Y = t\,(X)$ will be proportional to the product of $C$, the number of input symbols and the total size of $X$. Thus, the complexity will be proportional to $C. p. r^{k+1}. n^2. (n+2k)$, where $n = Card(Q)$, $k = Card(Q') - Card(Q)$, $p = Card(Input)$ and $r = card(\Phi)$.

The maximum number of test sequences required is less then $n^2. r^{k+2}/(r-1) \approx n^2. r^{k+1}$ and the total length of the test set is less then $n^2. (n+k). r^{k+2}/(r-1) \approx n^2. (n+k). r^{k+1}$. Note that these figures are the upper bounds; the actual number of inputs required may be much lower.

## Test Generation Tools

The process of constructing the complete functional test set for a stream X-machine is a lengthy and tedious process in all but the most trivial cases. It is thus important that the process should be automated. Bogdanov [99] has investigated this issue in some depth and has constructed a powerful test generation environment involving a number of tools that, together, will achieve the goal of automatic test set generation based on this theory. In this work the X-machine description can be extracted from a number of sources; one, for example, is based on the use of Statecharts [31] and STATEMATE [32] for the state diagram and the formal language Z for the transition semantics (see [33]).

# 8 Refinement Testing

*Summary. The theory of refinement testing, the refinement testing method*

In the previous chapter we gave the theoretical basis of a functional testing method for systems specified as X-machines. The method generates test sets from the specification that ensure that the system is fault-free provided that it is made of fault-free components and meets some "design for testing" requirements.

In practice, however, specifications of complex systems are seldom constructed from scratch. Instead, a process of refinement is used. This involves building several intermediary models $\mathcal{M}_1, \mathcal{M}_2, ..., \mathcal{M}_n$, where $\mathcal{M}_{i+1}$ is a refinement of some sort of $\mathcal{M}_i$ and $\mathcal{M}_n$ is the final system specification. Obviously, once the complete specification $\mathcal{M}_n$ exists, we can always test its implementation using the stream X-machine testing (SXMT) method. However, for large-scale systems this approach is not desirable since a single X-machine specification is difficult to handle. Also, the extremely large state space of such a machine will result in an unmanageable test set. Instead, a more convenient approach would be to construct the test set incrementally by generating test sets for all intermediary models. In doing this, one would hope that the test set of the $i$th model can be reused in the generation of that of the $(i+1)$th model, so that the construction of the complete test set will also be a refinement process. This chapter will address this problem in the context of the state refinement defined in Chapter 6.

## 8.1 THEORETICAL BASIS OF REFINEMENT TESTING

First, let us describe clearly the problem and the approach employed. Let $\mathcal{M}_1 = (Input, Output, Q_1, Memory, \Phi, F_1, q_{01}, m_0)$ and $\mathcal{M}_1' = (Input', Output', Q_1', Memory', \Phi', F_1', q_{01}', m_0')$ be two stream X-machine specifications

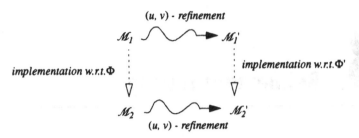

**FIG. 8.1.** A refinement and implementation relationship.

of a system so that $M_1'$ is a state refinement of $M_1$ with respect to $(u, v)$. Then our aim is to generate an input set that tests $M_1'$ against its implementation.

We assume that this implementation can be modelled as a stream X-machine $M_2' = (Input', Output', Q_2', Memory', \Phi', F_2', q_{02}', m_0')$ with the same type $\Phi'$ as $M_1'$. Furthermore, we will assume that $M_2$ is a stream X-machine implementation of the specification $M_1$ with the same type as $M_1$, and $M_2'$ can be expressed as a state refinement with respect to $(u, v)$ of $M_2$. The way in which these requirements can be enforced on the system implementation will be discussed later. The arrangement is illustrated in Figure 8.1.

Our approach will be to implement and test separately the refining machines used in the construction of $M_1'$ and to test the whole system for integration using a test set that is an augmentation of the test set of $M_1$ and $M_2$.

Before we go any further let us introduce the following concept.

## Definition 8.1.1

Let $A$ and $A'$ be two finite alphabets so that $seq(A')$ covers $seq(A)$ with respect to $u$ and let $Y \subseteq seq(A)$, $Y' \subseteq seq(A')$ be two sets. Then we say that $Y'$ *refines* $Y$ *with respect to* $u$ if the following is true

$$\forall\, a^* \in Y, \exists\, a^{*\prime} \in Y' \text{ with } u^*(a^{*\prime}) = a^*$$

Recall that $u^*$ (Definition 6.3.1.1) takes several applications of $u$ and concatenates them together in $A$, so that $a^{*\prime}$ is a concatenation of a finite sequence of elements from $Y'$.

If we denote by $u^{-1}: A \to seq(A')$ a function for which $u \circ u^{-1}$ is the identity and by $u^{-1*}: seq(A) \to seq(A')$ the sequential generalisation of $u^{-1}$, then for any $Y \subseteq seq(A)$, $Y' = u^{-1*}(Y)$ refines $Y$.

## Example 8.1.1

If for $n \geq 0$, $u_n: seq(CHARS \cup \{backspace, enter\}) \to WORDS_n$ is as in Example 6.3.1.2 then $Y'$ refines $Y$ with respect to $u_2$, and $Z'$ refines $Y$ with respect to $u_2$ where:

$Y = \{<>, \text{'1'}, \text{'11'}, \text{'10'}\text{'11'}, \text{'10'}\text{'10'}\text{'11'}\}$ and

$Y' = \{<>, 1 :: enter, 1 :: 1 :: enter, 1 :: 0 :: enter :: 1 :: 1 :: enter,$
$\qquad 1 :: 0 :: enter :: 1 :: 0 :: enter :: 1 :: 1 :: enter\}$

$Z' = \{<>, 1 :: 0 :: backspace :: enter, 1 :: 1 :: 0 :: backspace ::$
$\qquad enter, 1 :: 0 :: 0 :: backspace :: enter :: 1 :: 1 :: 0 ::$
$\qquad backspace :: enter, 1 :: 0 :: 0 :: backspace :: enter ::$
$\qquad 1 :: 0 :: 0 :: backspace :: enter :: 1 :: 1 :: 0 :: backspace$
$\qquad :: enter\}$

Let us now introduce the notation we shall be using in this section and state the assumptions we shall be making.

Let $M_1 = (Input, Output, Q_1, Memory, \Phi, F_1, q_{01}, m_0)$ and $M_2 = (Input, Output, Q_2, Memory, \Phi, F_2, q_{02}, m_0)$ be two stream X-machines with the same type, $\Phi$ and initial memory, $m_0$. Let $M_1' = (Input', Output', Q_1', Memory', \Phi', F_1', q_{01}', m_0')$ and $M_2' = (Input', Output', Q_2', Memory', \Phi', F_2', q_{02}', m_0')$ be state refinements of $M_1$ and $M_2$ respectively with respect to $(u, v)$ that also have the same type, $\Phi'$ and initial memory, $m_0'$. For simplicity we will consider that the key states of $M_1'$ and $M_2'$ respectively are $K_1 = Q_1$ and $K_2 = Q_2$, hence $q_{01}' = q_{01}$ and $q_{02}' = q_{02}$. This will not affect the generality of the results proven. We denote by $\mathcal{A}_1, \mathcal{A}_2, \mathcal{A}_1'$ and $\mathcal{A}_2'$ the associated automata of $M_1, M_2, M_1'$ and $M_2'$ respectively and $f_1, f_2, f_1', f_2'$ the functions computed by these machines.

Let $\{M_1'(q_1) : q_1 \in Q_1\}$ be the refining set of $M_1'$, with for any $q1 \in Q_1$, $M_1'(q_1) = (Input', Output', R_{q1}, Memory', \Phi', F_{q1}, q_1, m_{q1}', T_{q1})$. For any $q_1 \in Q_1$ we denote by $\mathcal{A}_1'(q1)$ the associated automaton of $M_1'(q_1)$. Similarly $\{M_2'(q_2) : q_2 \in Q_2\}$ is the refining set with for any $q_2 \in Q_2, M_2'(q_2) = (Input', Output', R_{q2}, Memory', \Phi', F_{q2}, q_2, m_{q2}', T_{q2})$ and $\mathcal{A}_2'(q_2)$ the associated automaton of $M_2'(q_2)$.

Note that the type of all refining machines was considered to be $\Phi'$. This is possible since not all processing functions have to be used as arc labels.

We shall assume that the following requirements are met.

1. $\mathcal{A}_1$ is a minimal finite state machine.
2. The types $\Phi$ and $\Phi'$ are t-complete with respect to Memory and Memory' respectively and output-distinguishable.
3. For any $q_1 \in Q_1$, $\mathcal{A}_1'(q_1)$ is an accessible finite state machine.
4. All refinement machines have been tested against their corresponding implementations using the SXMT method. Thus for any $q_2 \in Q_2$ there exists $q_1 \in Q_1$ so that $\mathcal{A}_1'(q_1)$ and $\mathcal{A}_2'(q_2)$ are equivalent.

Also, for simplicity we shall assume that $\mathcal{A}_2$ is accessible and for any $q_2 \in Q_2, \mathcal{A}_2'(q_2)$ is accessible. This will not reduce in any way the generality of our results since the accessible part of $\mathcal{A}_2'$ – and thus the input/output behaviour of $M_2'$ – will not be affected by this assumption.

## Lemma 8.1.1

Let $M_1$, $M_2$, $M_1'$, $M_2'$ be four stream X-machines as described above. Then $\mathcal{A}_1'$ and $\mathcal{A}_2'$ are equivalent if there exists $e: \mathcal{A}_2 \to \mathcal{A}_1$ a surjective finite state machine morphism such that for any $q_2 \in Q_2$, $\mathcal{A}_2'(q_2)$ and $\mathcal{A}_1'(e(q_2))$ are equivalent.

*Proof:*

We define a relation $e': Q_2' \leftrightarrow Q_1'$ by $q_2'\, e'\, q_1'$ if and only if there exist $q_2 \in Q_2, q_1 \in Q_1$ with $e(q_2) = q_1$ and $q_2'$ and $q_1'$ are right-congruent (see Definition 7.1.7) states in $\mathcal{A}_2'(q_2)$ and $\mathcal{A}_1'(q_1)$ respectively.

We prove that $e'$ satisfies the requirements of Definition 7.1.7, that is, it is a right congruence, too.

1. Obviously, $q_{02}'\, e'\, q_{01}'$.
2. Let $q_2'\, e'\, q_1'$ and let $q_2 \in Q_2, q_1 \in Q_1$ with $e(q_2) = q_1$ so that $q_2'$ and $q_1'$ are right-congruent states in $\mathcal{A}_2'(q_2)$ and $\mathcal{A}_1'(q_1)$ respectively.

Then there exists an arc $\phi': q_2' \to \theta_2'$ in $\mathcal{A}_2'(q_2)$ if and only if there exists an arc $\phi': q_1' \to \theta_1$ in $\mathcal{A}_1'(q_1)$, where $\theta_2'$ and $\theta_1'$ are right-congruent states in $\mathcal{A}_2'(q_2)$ and $\mathcal{A}_1'(q_1)$ respectively. Thus there exists an arc $\phi': q_2' \to \theta_2''$ in $\mathcal{A}_2'$ if and only if there exists an arc $\phi': q_1' \to \theta_1''$ in $\mathcal{A}_1'$.

It remains to be shown that $\theta_2''\, e'\, \theta_1''$. If $\theta_1'$ and $\theta_2'$ are both non-terminal states of $M_1'(q_1)$ and $M_2'(q_2)$ then $\theta_2'' = \theta_2'$ and $\theta_2'' = \theta_2'$ hence $\theta_2''\, e'\, \theta_2'$. Otherwise let us assume that $\theta_2'$ is a terminal state in $M_2'(q_2)$ and let $p': q_2 \to \theta_2'$ and $p': q_1 \to \theta_1'$ be paths in $\mathcal{A}_2'(q_2)$ and $\mathcal{A}_1'(q_1)$ respectively (such paths exist since $\theta_2'$ and $\theta_1'$ are right-congruent states). Let also $m \in Memory$ be a memory value of $M_2$ that is attainable in $q_2$ (such $m$ exists since $\mathcal{A}_2$ is accessible and $\Phi$ is t-complete with respect to $Memory$) and let $m' \in h^{-1}(m)$. Since $\Phi'$ is t-complete with respect to $Memory'$ there exists an input sequence $s'^*$ with $(m', s'^*) \in$ domain $|p'|$. Since $M_2'(q_2)$ is a refining machine it follows that $s'^* \in$ domain $u$ and there exists an arc $\phi_2: q_2 \to \theta_2''$ in $\mathcal{A}_2$ with $(m, u(s'^*)) \in$ domain $\phi_1$.

Since $M_1'(q_1)$ is a refining machine with respect to $u, s'^* \in$ domain $u$ and $(m', s'^*) \in$ domain $|p'|$ it follows that $\theta_1'$ is a terminal state in $M_1'(q_1)$. Also, since $e$ is a finite state machine morphism and $e(q_2) = q_1$ it is easy to see that $m$ is also a memory value of $M_1$ that is attainable in $q_1$. Thus there exists an arc $\phi_1: q_1 \to \theta_1''$ in $\mathcal{A}_1$ with $(m, u^*(s'^*)) \in$ domain $\phi_1$. Since $e(q_2) = q_1$ and $M_1$ and $M_2$ are deterministic it follows that $\phi_1 = \phi_2$. Hence $\theta_2''\, e'\, \theta_1''$.

## Lemma 8.1.2

Let $M_1$, $M_2$, $M_1'$, $M_2'$ be as above, let $Y \subseteq seq(Input)$ be a test set of $M_1$ and $M_2$ and $Y' \subseteq seq(Input')$ a set of sequences of $Input'$ that refines $Y$ with respect to $u$. If $\forall\, s'^* \in Y', f_1'(s'^*) = f_2'(s'^*)$ then there exists a surjective finite state machine morphism, $e: \mathcal{A}_2 \to \mathcal{A}_1$.

*Proof:*
If $\forall\, s'^* \in Y', f_1'(s'^*) = f_2'(s'^*) \Rightarrow \forall\, s'^* \in Y', v^*(f_1'(s'^*)) = v^*(f_2'(s'^*)) \Rightarrow$
$\forall\, s'^* \in Y', f_1(u^*(s'^*)) = f_2(u^*(s'^*)) \Rightarrow \forall\, s^* \in Y, f_1(s^*) = f_2(s^*)$. Hence $\mathcal{A}_1$ and
the minimal automaton of $\mathcal{A}_2$ are isomorphic. Since $\mathcal{A}_1$ is minimal and $\mathcal{A}_2$
is accessible there exists a surjective morphism, $e: \mathcal{A}_2 \to \mathcal{A}_1$.

### Definition 8.1.2

Let $\{\mathcal{M}_1'(q_1) : q_1 \in Q_1\}$ be the refining set of $\mathcal{M}_1'$ as above. Then $X_{q1} \subseteq \text{seq}(\Phi')$
is called a *distinguishing set* of $\mathcal{A}_1'(q_1)$ if for any $\theta_1 \in Q_1$ either $\mathcal{A}_1'(q_1)$ and
$\mathcal{A}_1'(\theta_1)$ are equivalent or $X_{q1}$ distinguishes between $q_1$ and $\theta_1$ as states in
$\mathcal{A}_1'(q_1)$ and $\mathcal{A}_1'(\theta_1)$ respectively.

### Example 8.1.2

For the refinement of Example 6.3.3.2 we can take:

$$X_A = \{\textbf{type\_ch1} :: \textbf{wrong\_name'}\}$$
$$X_B = \{\textbf{type\_ch1} :: \textbf{wrong\_psw'}\}$$
$$X_C = \{\textbf{type\_ch1} :: \textbf{type\_ch1} :: \textbf{new\_psw'}\}$$

### Definition 8.1.3

Let S be a state cover of $\mathcal{A}_1$, $k$ a positive integer and let $t : \text{seq}(\Phi) \to \text{seq}(\textit{Input})$
be a fundamental test function of $M_1$. Let also:

$$P_k = \{p \in S \bullet (\Phi^k \cup \Phi^{k-1} \cup \ldots \cup \{<\,>\}):$$
$$\exists\, p \text{ a path in } \mathcal{A}_1 \text{ that starts in } q_{01}\}$$

For any $p \in P_k$ let $q_p \in Q_1$ be the end state of $p$ and let $t(p) = s_p^*$. Since $\Phi$
is t-complete with respect to *Memory* there exists $m_p \in \textit{Memory}$ with
$\pi_2(p(m_0, s_p^*)) = m_p$. Let $s_p^{*'} \in \text{seq}(\textit{Input}')$ with $u^*(s_p^{*'}) = s_p^*$. We will denote
$s_p^{*'}$ by $u^{-1}(t(p))$.

Since $\mathcal{M}_1'$ is a state refinement of $\mathcal{M}_1$ there exists $m_p' \in h^{-1}(m_p)$ and a path
$p'$ in $\mathcal{A}_1'$ from $q_{01}$ to $q_p$ with $\pi_2(p'(m_0', s_p^{*'})) = m_p'$. Then let $t_p = t_{q_p, m_p'}$ be a
test function of $\mathcal{M}_1'(q_p)$ with respect to $(q_p, m_p')$.

Also let $X_p \subseteq \text{seq}(\Phi')$ be a distinguishing set of $A_1'(q_p)$ as defined above.
Then $U_k$, a set of sequences of *Input'*, defined by:

$$U_k = \bigcup_{p \in P_k} \{u^{-1}(t(p))\} \bullet (t_p(X_p))$$

will be called a *k-distinguishing set of the refining set*.

### Example 8.1.3

Let $\mathcal{M}$ and $\mathcal{M}'$, be the machines from Example 6.3.3.2. Then a state cover of
$\mathcal{M}$ is:

$$S = \{< >, \text{good\_name}, \text{good\_name} :: \text{good\_psw}\}$$

For $k = 2$, $P_2 = \{p_1, \dots p_{12}\}$, where:

$p_1 = < >, p_1: A \rightarrow A$
$p_2 = \text{good\_name}, p_2: A \rightarrow B$
$p_3 = \text{wrong\_name}, p_3: A \rightarrow A$
$p_4 = \text{good\_name} :: \text{good\_psw}, p_4: A \rightarrow C$
$p_5 = \text{good\_name} :: \text{wrong\_psw}, p_5: A \rightarrow A$
$p_6 = \text{wrong\_name} :: \text{good\_name}, p_6: A \rightarrow B$
$p_7 = \text{wrong\_name} :: \text{wrong\_name}, p_7: A \rightarrow A$
$p_8 = \text{good\_name} :: \text{good\_psw} :: \text{new\_psw}, p_8: A \rightarrow A$
$p_9 = \text{good\_name} :: \text{wrong\_psw} :: \text{good\_name}, p_9: A \rightarrow B$
$p_{10} = \text{good\_name} :: \text{wrong\_psw} :: \text{wrong\_name}, p_{10}: A \rightarrow A$
$p_{11} = \text{good\_name} :: \text{good\_psw} :: \text{new\_psw} :: \text{good\_name}, p_{11}: A \rightarrow B$
$p_{12} = \text{good\_name} :: \text{good\_psw} :: \text{new\_psw} :: \text{wrong\_name}, p_{12}: A \rightarrow A$

We will assume that '01' is a valid username and '1' is not a valid username, i.e. '01' $\in$ domain $\text{map}_0$ and '1' $\notin$ domain $\text{map}_0$ and that '11' is the password for '01', i.e. $\text{map}('01') = '11'$.

Then we can take $s_i^*$, $s_i^{*\prime}$, $m_i$ and $m_i'$, $i = 1\dots12$, as follows:

$s_1^* = < >$
$s_2^* = \text{'01'}$
$s_3^* = \text{'1'}$
$s_4^* = \text{'01'}\text{'11'}$
$s_5^* = \text{'01'}\text{'0'}$
$s_6^* = \text{'1'}\text{'01'}$
$s_7^* = \text{'1'}\text{'1'}$
$s_8^* = \text{'01'}\text{'11'}\text{'00'}$
$s_9^* = \text{'01'}\text{'0'}\text{'01'}$
$s_{10}^* = \text{'01'}\text{'0'}\text{'1'}$
$s_{11}^* = \text{'01'}\text{'11'}\text{'00'}\text{'01'}$
$s_{12}^* = \text{'01'}\text{'11'}\text{'00'}\text{'1'}$

$s_1^{*\prime} = < >$
$s_2^{*\prime} = 0 :: 1 :: \text{enter}$
$s_3^{*\prime} = 1 :: \text{enter}$
$s_4^{*\prime} = 0 :: 1 :: \text{enter} :: 1 :: 1 :: \text{enter}$
$s_5^{*\prime} = 0 :: 1 :: \text{enter} :: 0 :: \text{enter}$
$s_6^{*\prime} = 1 :: \text{enter} :: 0 :: 1 :: \text{enter}$
$s_7^{*\prime} = 1 :: \text{enter} :: 1 :: \text{enter}$
$s_8^{*\prime} = 0 :: 1 :: \text{enter} :: 1 :: 1 :: \text{enter} :: 0 :: 0 :: \text{enter}$
$s_9^{*\prime} = 0 :: 1 :: \text{enter} :: 0 :: \text{enter} :: 0 :: 1 :: \text{enter}$
$s_{10}^{*\prime} = 0 :: 1 :: \text{enter} :: 0 :: \text{enter} :: 1 :: \text{enter}$
$s_{11}^{*\prime} = 0 :: 1 :: \text{enter} :: 1 :: 1 :: \text{enter} :: 0 :: 0 :: \text{enter} :: 0 :: 1 :: \text{enter}$
$s_{12}^{*\prime} = 0 :: 1 :: \text{enter} :: 1 :: 1 :: \text{enter} :: 0 :: 0 :: \text{enter} :: 1 :: \text{enter}$

$$m_1 = m_3 = m_7 = (map_0, ' ')$$
$$m_2 = m_4 = m_5 = m_6 = m_9 = m_{10} = (map_0, '01')$$
$$m_8 = m_{11} = m_{12} = (new\_map, '01')$$

where $new\_map = map_0 \oplus ('01' \to '00')$

$$m_1' = m_3' = m_7' = ((map_0, ' '), <>)$$
$$m_2' = m_4' = m_5' = m_6' = m_9' = m_{10}' = ((map_0, '01'), <>)$$
$$m_8' = m_{11}' = m_{12}' = ((new\_map, '01'), <>)$$

If $X_A$, $X_B$ and $X_C$ are those from Example 8.1.2 then we can take:

$$U_2 = \{s_1{}^{*\prime} :: t_A{}^{*\prime}, s_2{}^{*\prime} :: t_B{}^{*\prime}, s_3{}^{*\prime} :: t_A{}^{*\prime}, s_4{}^{*\prime} :: t_C{}^{*\prime}, s_5{}^{*\prime} :: t_A{}^{*\prime}, s_6{}^{*\prime} :: t_B{}^{*\prime},$$
$$s_7{}^{*\prime} :: t_A{}^{*\prime}, s_8{}^{*\prime} :: t_A{}^{*\prime}, s_9{}^{*\prime} :: t_B{}^{*\prime}, s_{10}{}^{*\prime} :: t_A{}^{*\prime}, s_{11}{}^{*\prime} :: t_B{}^{*\prime},$$
$$s_{12}{}^{*\prime} :: t_A{}^{*\prime}\}$$

where $t_A{}^{*\prime} = 1 :: enter$, $t_B{}^{*\prime} = 0 :: enter$, $t_C{}^{*\prime} = 0 :: 0 :: enter$.

### Theorem 8.1.1

Let $\mathcal{M}_1$, $\mathcal{M}_2$, $\mathcal{M}_1'$, $\mathcal{M}_2'$ be as in Definition 8.1.3 above. Let $Y \subseteq seq(Input)$ be a test set of $\mathcal{M}_1$ and $\mathcal{M}_2$, $Y' \subseteq seq(Input')$ a set that refines $Y$ with respect to $u$ and $U_k$ a $k$-distinguishing set of the refining set of $\mathcal{M}_1'$, where $k = Card(Q_2)$ – $Card(Q_1)$ is the difference between the number of states of $\mathcal{M}_2$ and the number of states of $\mathcal{M}_1$ and let $Y'' = Y' \cup U_k$. If $\forall s'^* \in Y''$, $f_1'(s'^*) = f_2'(s'^*)$ then $\mathcal{A}_1'$ and $\mathcal{A}_2'$ are equivalent.

### Proof:

From the lemma it follows that there exists $e: \mathcal{A}_2 \to \mathcal{A}_1$, a surjective finite state machine morphism. Then the set $P_k$ defined as in Definition 8.1.3 is a state cover of $\mathcal{A}_2$. Indeed, since $e: \mathcal{A}_2 \to \mathcal{A}_1$ is a finite state morphism at least $Card(Q_1)$ states of $\mathcal{A}_2$ will be accessed by a path in S. Also $\forall i = 1,...(k-1)$ the set $P_{i+1}$ will access at least one of the states that has not been accessed by $P_i$.

Thus for any $q_2 \in Q_2$ there exists $p \in P_k$ so that $p: q_{02} \to q_2$ is a path in $\mathcal{M}_2$ and $p: q_{01} \to e(q_2)$ is a path in $\mathcal{M}_1$. If $s_p{}^*$, $s_p{}^{*\prime}$, $m_p$ and $m_p'$ are those from Definition 8.1.3 then there exists $p': q_{01} \to e(q_2)$ a path in $\mathcal{M}_1'$ with $\pi_2(p'(m_0', s_p{}^{*\prime})) = m_p'$. Since $\mathcal{M}_2'$ is a state refinement of $\mathcal{M}_1$ there exists $p'': q_{02} \to q_2$ a path in $\mathcal{M}_2'$ and $m_p'' \in h^{-1}(m_p)$ with $\pi_2(p''(m_0', s_p{}^{*\prime})) = m_p''$. From the output-distinguishability of $\Phi'$ it follows that $p'' = p'$ and $m_p'' = m_p'$.

Since $\Phi'$ is output-distinguishable the application of $t_{q_p}(X_p)$ in $q_2$ and $e(q_2)$ respectively with initial memory $m_p'$ will ensure that $\mathcal{A}_2'(q_2)$ and $\mathcal{A}_1'(q_1)$ are equivalent. From Lemma 8.1.1. it follows that $\mathcal{A}_1'$ and $\mathcal{A}_2'$ are equivalent.

## 8.2   THE REFINEMENT TESTING METHOD

The previous theorem can be used as the theoretical basis of a method for testing stream X-machine specifications constructed through a process of state refinement. The method will use a two-phase approach in which the refining machines are implemented and tested first and then the entire system is tested for integration.

## Phase 1. Testing the Refining Machines

These will be implemented as separate subprograms or pieces of code that can be tested in isolation from the rest of the system. Each such *subimplementation* will communicate with the rest of the system through one or more "transfer variables" whose values will correspond to the terminal states of the refining machine. Thus, the testing procedure will not only have to ensure that the input/output behaviour of the refining machine coincides with that of its implementation but also that each transfer variable identifies correctly its corresponding terminal state. Therefore we need to adapt our refining machines so that they possess the transfer variable linking mechanism. This implies that any component technology must also incorporate a suitable mechanism for specifying transfer variables. The process can be described formally by an augmented refining machine as defined next.

### Definition 8.2.1

Let $M_1'(q_1) = (Input', Output', R_{q_1}, Memory', \Phi', F_{q_1}, q_1, m_{q_1}', T_{q_1})$ be the refining machine in $q_1$, $T_{q_1} = \{t_1,..., t_m\}$ the set of terminal states and let $in_{q_1} \notin Input'$ and $Output_{Tq_1} = \{out_{t_1},..., out_{t_m}\}$ a set with $Output_{Tq_1} \cap Output' = \varnothing$. Then a stream X-machine defined by:

$$M_{1A}'(q_1) = (Input'_A, Output'_A, R_{q_1}, Memory', \Phi'_A, F_{q_1A}, q_1, m_{q_1}', T_{q_1})$$

where:

1. $Input'_A = Input' \cup \{in_{q_1}\}$.
2. $Output'_A = Output' \cup Output_{Tq_1}$.
3. $\Phi'_A = \Phi' \cup \Psi_{q_1}'$, with $\Psi_{q_1}' = \{\psi_{t_1}',..., \psi_{t_m}'\}$

such that, for any $t \in T_{q_1}$, $\psi_t'$ is defined by:

$$\psi_t'(m, in_{q_1}) = (out_t, m), m \in Memory$$

4. $F_{q_1A}: R_{q_1} \times \Phi'_A \to R_{q_1}$ is defined by:

$$F_{q_1A}(q', \phi') = \begin{cases} F_{q_1}(q', \phi'), \text{if } q' \in R_{q_1} \text{ and } \phi' \in \Phi' \\ q', \text{if } \exists\, j = 1...m \text{ with } q' = t_j \text{ and } \phi' = \psi_{t_j}' \\ \bot, \text{otherwise} \end{cases}$$

is called the *augmented refining machine* in $q_1$.

In other words, each terminal state $t$ will be identified in the augmented machine by an extra output symbol $out_t$ produced by an extra processing function $\psi_t$ that labels a loop from $t$. These loops will be triggered by an extra input $in_{q_1}$. The extra outputs will correspond to the values of transfer variables used by the implementation. The extra input $in_{q_1}$ does not necessarily exist in the implementation; it will correspond to a means of identifying the value of the transfer variables for each terminal state. The augmented refining machines of Example 6.3.3.1 may be found in Figure 8.2.

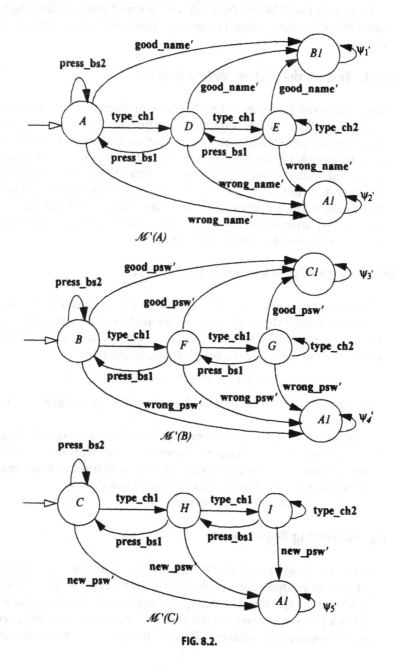

**FIG. 8.2.**

If an augmented machine $\mathcal{M}_{1A}'(q_1)$ is tested against its corresponding implementation using the SXMT method and the implementation passes the required tests then this can be modelled as a stream X-machine $\mathcal{M}_2'(q_2)$ whose associated automaton is equivalent to that of $\mathcal{M}_1'(q_1)$ and whose terminal states – that is, the transfer variables of the implementation – will match the terminal states of $M_1'(q_1)$.

Obviously, the SXMT method will require that the basic processing functions $\Phi'$ satisfy the "design for testing conditions" and are implemented correctly.

## Phase 2. Testing the System for Integration

The system will be composed of the above implementations that communicate through the transfer variables. If the first phase of our testing method has been completed then it easy to see that the entire system can be modelled by a stream X-machine $\mathcal{M}_2'$ with type $\Phi'$ that is a state refinement of a machine with the same type $\Phi$ as $\mathcal{M}_1$. Thus Theorem 8.1.1 can be used to generate a test set $Y'' = Y' \cup U_k$ whose application guarantees that the system is functionally equivalent to its specification. Recall that if W is a characterisation set of $A_1$ then $Y = t\,(S \bullet (\,\Phi^{k+1} \cup \Phi^k \cup... \cup \Phi) \bullet W)$ is a test set of $\mathcal{M}_1$ and $\mathcal{M}_2$, thus $Y' = u^{-1}*(Y)$.

## Complexity and Upper Bounds of the Test Set

If the complexity of $u^{-1}$ is $C(u^{-1})$, the complexity of each $\phi \in \Phi$ is at most $C$ and the complexity of each procedure used to determine a distinguishing set of a refining machine is at most $C_D$, then the complexity of the algorithm that generates the test set $Y''$ is proportional to:

$$C(u^{-1}).\ C.\ p.\ r^{k+1}.\ n^2.\ (n+2k) + r^k.\ n.\ C_D$$

where $n = \text{Card}(Q_1)$, $k = \text{Card}(Q_2) - \text{Card}(Q_1)$, $p = \text{Card}(Input)$ and $r = \text{card}(\Phi)$.

If all values of $u^{-1}$ are sequences of at most $l$ elements and the length of any sequence used to distinguish between any two refinement modules is at most $l$, then the upper bounds for the number of test sequences required and the total length of the test set are approximately
$l.\ n^2.\ r^{k+1}$ and $l.\ (n+k).\ r^{k+1}$ respectively.

## Design for Testing Requirements

As previously discussed, the "design for test conditions" (i.e. the t-completeness and output-distinguishability of the types $\Phi$ and $\Phi'$) can be introduced into the specification through an augmentation of the input and/or output alphabets. However, in this case, particular care is needed to ensure that the augmented machines will still be in a state refinement relation. For example, it is easy to see that $\Phi$ and $\Phi'$ of Example 6.3.3.2 are output-distinguishable but not t-complete. However, the t-completeness of $\Phi$ and $\Phi'$ can be achieved through an extension of their input alphabets:

$$In_e = In \cup \{in_1, in_2\}, \text{ where } In \cap \{in_1, in_2\} = \varnothing$$
$$In_e' = In' \cup \{in_1', in_2'\}, \text{ where } In' \cap \{in_1', in_2'\} = \varnothing$$

These extra inputs will be used to extend the processing functions in $\Phi$ and $\Phi'$ as follows. We only show the effect of the extra inputs; the processing functions remain unchanged elsewhere. Let $map \in$ MAPS, $name, str \in$ WORDS$_2$:

**good_name**$_a((map, name), in_1) = ((msg1, str), (map, name))$

**wrong_name**$_a((map, name), in_2) = ((msg2, str), (map, name))$

**good_psw**$_a((map, name), in_1) = ((msg3, str), (map, name))$

**wrong_psw**$_a((map, name), in_2) = ((msg4, str), (map, name))$

**good_name'**$_a(((map, name), str), in_1') = (msg1, ((map, name), <>))$

**wrong_name'**$_a(((map, name), str), in_{2'}) = (msg2, ((map, name), <>))$

**good_psw'**$_a(((map, name), str), in_{1'}) = (msg3, ((map, name), <>))$

**wrong_psw'**$_a(((map, name), str), in_{2'}) = (msg4, ((map, name), <>))$

It is easy to see that the augmented types are both t-complete and output-distinguishable. The only thing that remains to be done is to extend the definition of the input covering (we will call this $u_{2e}$) alphabet by:

$$u_{2e}(a^* :: in_1') = in_1$$
$$u_{2e}(a^* :: in_2') = in_2$$

$\forall\, a^* \in$ seq(CHARS $\cup \{backspace\}$) with $a^* ::$ enter $\in$ domain $u_2$.

# REFERENCES

[1] Leveson N. *Safeware*. Addison-Wesley, 1995.

[2] Pressman R. S. *Software Engineering – a Practitioner's Approach*, 3rd edn. McGraw Hill, 1994.

[3] Martin J. *Introduction to Languages and the Theory of Computation*. McGraw-Hill, 1997.

[4] Markov A. A. An example of statistical investigation in the text of *Eugene Onegin* illustrating coupling of texts in chains. *Proc. Acad. Sci., St. Petersburg*, 7, 1913.

[5] Mal'cev A. I. *Algorithms and Recursive Functions*. Wottors-Hoordhof, 1970.

[6] Cotgrove S. *Catastrophe or Cornucopia: the Environment, Politics and the Future*. Wiley, 1982.

[7] Gilb T. *Principles of Software Engineering Management*. Addison-Wesley, 1988.

[8] Myers G. *The Art of Software Testing*. Wiley, 1979.

[9] Wilks Y. and Partridge D. (eds.) *Foundations of Artificial Intelligence: a Source Book*. Cambridge University Press, 1990.

[10] Kletz T. A. *Critical Aspects of Safety and Loss Prevention*. Butterworths, 1990.

[11] Wiener L. R. *Digital Woes: Why we Should Not Depend on Software*. Addison-Wesley, 1993.

[12] Riel A. J. *Object-Oriented Design Heuristics*. Addison-Wesley, 1996.

[13] Savitch W. *Problem Solving with C++*. Addison-Wesley, 1996

[14] Arnold K. and Gosling J. *The Java Programming Language*. Addison-Wesley, 1998.

[15] Binder R. V. Testing object-oriented software: a survey. *Software Testing, Verification and Reliability*, 6(3/4), 125–152, 1996.

[16] Spivey J. M. *The Z Notation: a Reference Manual*. Prentice Hall, 1989.

[17] Jones C. B. *Systematic Software Development using VDM*. Prentice Hall, 1986.

[18] Futatsugi K., Goguen J., Jouannaud J-P. and Meseguer J. Principles of OBJ2, *Proc. 12th ACM Symp. Principles of Prog. Lang.*, 52–66, 1985.

[19] Jacob J. K. Using formal specifications in the design of a human–computer interface, *Comm. ACM*, 26(4), 259–264, 1983.

[20] Huzing C. Introduction to design choices in the semantics of statecharts, *Inf. Proc. Letters*, 37, 1991.

[21] Cutland N. J. *Computability: an Introduction to Recursive Function Theory*. Cambridge University Press, 1980.

[22] Cohen D. I. A. *Introduction to Computer Theory*. Wiley, 1991.

[23] Wulf W. M., Shaw M., Hilfinger P. N. and Flon L. *Fundamental Structures of Computer Science*. Addison-Wesley, 1981.

[24] Reisig W. *Petri Nets: an Introduction*. EATCS Monographs in Theoretical Computer Science, Springer-Verlag, 1985.

[25] Holcombe W. M. L. *Algebraic Automata Theory*. Cambridge University Press, 1982.

[26] Clements A. *The Principles of Computer Hardware*, Oxford Scientific, 1991.

[27] Wasserman A. I., Pircher P. A. and Shuwmake D. T. Building reliable interactive information systems, *IEEE Trans. Softw. Engng*. 14(10), 1512–1524, 1988.

[28] Eilenberg S. *Automata Machines and Languages*, Vol. A. Academic Press, 1974.

[29] Duan Z. and Holcombe M. Traceable x-machines as models for describing user interfaces, *Proc. 5th Int. Symp. Comp. & Inf. Sci. ISCIS*, 1, 599–608, 1990.

[30] Duan Z. and Holcombe M. The computational power of trace machines, departmental report, Department of Computer Science, University of Sheffield.

[31] Harel D. Statecharts: a visual formalism for complex systems, *Sci. Comput. Programming*, 8, 231–274, 1987.

[32] Naamad A. and Harel D. The statemate semantics of statecharts, technical report, Ilogix, 1996.

[33] Weber M. Combining statecharts and Z for the design of safety-critical systems, in Gaudel M. C. and Woodcock J. (eds) *FME '96, Industrial Benefit and Advances in Formal Methods*, 307–326, Springer-Verlag, 1996.

[34] Holcombe M. X-machines as a basis for dynamic system specification, *Software Engineering Journal*, 3(2), 69–76, 1988.

[35] Laycock G. T. *Theory and Practice of Specification Based Testing*, PhD thesis, Department of Computer Science, University of Sheffield, 1992.

[36] Ipate F. and Holcombe M. Another look at computation, *Informatica*, 20, 359–372, 1996.

[37] Holcombe M. and Duan Z. Traceable automata with ε-moves and their applications, internal report, Department of Computer Science, University of Sheffield, 1990.

[38] Milner R. *A Calculus of Communicating Systems*, Lecture Notes in Computer Science, 80, Springer-Verlag, 1980.

[39] Fairtlough M., Holcombe M., Ipate F., Jordan. J, Laycock G. and Duan Z. Using an X-machine to model a video cassette recorder, *Current Issues in Electronic Modelling*, 3, 141–151, 1995.

[40] Kapur D. and Shyamasunder R. K. Synthesizing controllers for hybrid systems, in Maler O. (ed.) *Hybrid and Real Time Systems*, Lecture Notes in Computer Science, 1201, 361–375, Springer-Verlag, 1997.

[41] Alur R., Courcoubetis C., Henzinger T. A. and Ho P-H. Hybrid automata: an algorithmic approach to the specification and verification of hybrid systems, in Grossman R. L., Nerode A., Ravn A. P. and Rischel H. (eds) *Hybrid Systems*, Lecture Notes in Computer Science, 736, 209–229, Springer-Verlag, 1993.

[42] Sinclair D. Using an object-oriented methodology to bring a hybrid system from initial concept to formal definition, in Grossman R. L., Nerode A., Ravn A. P. and Rischel H. (eds) *Hybrid Systems*, Lecture Notes in Computer Science, 736, 186–198, Springer-Verlag. 1993.

[43] Holcombe M. and Duan Z. H. From requirements to specifications for hybrid systems, *Proc. Int. Symp. Future Software Technology*, Xian, China, October, 239–246.

[44] Sommerville I. *Software Engineering*. Addison-Wesley, 1996.

[45] Billings C., Billings M. and Tower J. *Rapid Application Development with Oracle Designer 2000*. Addison-Wesley, 1997.

[46] Date C. J. *An Introduction to Database Systems*, 6th edn. Addison-Wesley, 1995.

[47] Booch G. *Object-Oriented Design with Applications*. Benjamin Cummings, 1991.

[48] Jacobson I., Christerson M., Jonsson P. and Overgaard G., *Object-Oriented Software Engineering: a Use-case Driven Approach*. Addison-Wesley/ACM Press, 1992.

[49] Liskov B. Programming with abstract data types, in Wasserman A. (ed.) *Programming Language Design*, IEEE Computer Society Press, 1980.

[50] Goldberg A. and Robson D. *Smalltalk-80: the Language and its Implementation*. Addison-Wesley, 1983.

[51] Sommerville I. and Sawyer P. *Requirements Engineering – a Good Practice Guide*. Wiley, 1997.

[52] Booch G., Rumbaugh J. and Jacobson I. *Unified Modelling Language User Guide*. Addison-Wesley, 1998.

[53] Selic B., Gullekson G. and Ward P. *Real-time Object-Oriented Modeling*. Wiley, 1994.

[54] Yap C. N. and Holcombe M. A visual Z system, *Proceedings PPIG-9*, 31–42, 1997 (ISBN 0-863-396-801).

[55] Ould, M. A. *Business Processes: Modelling and Analysis for Re-Engineering and Improvement*. Wiley, 1995.

[56] Gordon M. Proving a computer correct with the LCF_LSM hardware verification system, technical report 42, University of Cambridge Computer Laboratory, 1983.

[57] Bogdanov K., Fairtlough M., Holcombe M., Ipate F. and Jordan C. X-machine specification and refinement of digital devices, submitted.

[58] Harman N. and Tucker J. V. Algebraic models and the correctness of microprocessors, in Pierre L. and Milne G. (eds) *Correct Hardware Design and Verification Methods*, Lecture Notes in Computer Science, Springer-Verlag, 1993.

[59] Dijkstra E. Structured programming, in: Buxton J. N., Naur P., and Randell B. (eds) *Software Engineering, Concepts and Techniques*. Litton Educational, 1976.

[60] Rushby J. Formal verification of algorithms for critical systems, *IEEE Trans. Softw. Engng.* 19(1), 13–23, 1993.

[61] Howden W. E. *Functional Program Testing and Analysis*. McGraw-Hill, 1987.

[62] Laycock G. T. Formal specification and testing: a case study, *Software Testing, Verification and Reliability*, 2(1), 7–23, 1992.

[63] Hierons R. M. Testing from a Z specification, *Software Testing, Verification and Reliability,* 7(1), 19–33, 1996.

[64] Hall P. A. V. and Hierons R. Formal methods and testing, technical report, 91/16, Computing Department, Open University, 1991.

[65] Allen S. P. and Woodward M. R. Assessing the quality of algebraically specified ADTs, in Samson W. B., Marshall I. M. and Edgar-Nevill D. G. (eds) *Proc. 5th Software Quality Conference,* University of Abertay, Dundee, 1996.

[66] Natfos C. A comparison of some structural testing strategies, *IEEE Trans. Softw. Engng.* 14(6), 868–873, 1989.

[67] Fosdick L. D. and Osterweil L. J. Data flow analysis in software reliability, *ACM Computing Surveys,* 8, 305–330, 1979.

[68] Moranda P. B. Limits to program testing with random number inputs, in *Proc. COMSAC,* IEEE Press, 1978.

[69] Thévenod-Fosse P. and Waeselynck H. An investigation of statistical software testing, *Software Testing, Verification and Reliability,* 1(2), 5–25, 1991.

[70] Reid S. Module testing techniques: which are the most effective? in *Proc. EuroSTAR '97,* 1997.

[71] Littlewood B. and Strigini L. Validation of ultra-high dependability for software based systems, *Comm. ACM,* 36(11), 80, 1993.

[72] Hamlet R.G. Probable correctness theory, *Inf. Proc. Letters,* 25, 17–25, 1987.

[73] Goodenough J.B. and Gerhard S.L. Toward a theory of test data selection, *IEEE Trans. Softw. Engng,* 1(2), 156–173, 1975.

[74] Chantatub W. and Holcombe M. Software testing strategies for software requirements and design, in *Proc. EuroSTAR'94,* Brussels, 40/1- 40/28, 1994.

[75] Yap C. and Holcombe M. Using graphical icons to build Z specifications, *Northern Formal Methods Workshop,* Ilkley, Yorkshire, July (to appear in *eWics* (Electronic Workshops in Computer Science) Series, Springer-Verlag, 1997.

[76] Chow T. S. Testing software design modeled by finite state machines, *IEEE Trans. Softw. Engng,* 4(3), 178–187, 1978.

[77] Fujiwara S., von Bochmann G., Khendek F., Amalou M. and Ghedamsi A. Test selection based on finite state models, *IEEE Trans. Softw. Engng,* 17(6), 591–603, 1991.

[78] Bogdanov K. and Holcombe M. Translating statecharts and μSZ specifications into X-machines, Confidential report prepared for Daimler-Benz Research and Technology AG, 1996.

[79] Ipate F. and Holcombe M. An integration testing method that is proved to find all faults, *Int. J. Comput. Math.,* 63, (3/4), 159–178, 1997.

[80] Ipate F. and Holcombe M. X-machine based testing, departmental report, Department of Computer Science, University of Sheffield. 1994.

[81] Holcombe M. An integrated methodology for the specification, verification and testing of systems, *Software Testing, Verification and Reliability,* 3, 149–163, 1993.

[82] Ipate F. and Holcombe M. A method for refining and testing generalised machine specifications, *Int. J. Comput. Math.,* in press. (http://www.dcs.shef.ac.uk/~wmlh/)

[83] Wirth N. Program development by stepwise refinement, *Comm. ACM,* 14(4), 221–227, 1971.

[84] Parnas D. L. On the criteria to be used in decomposing systems into modules, *Comm. ACM,* 14(1), 221–227, 1972.

[85] Morgan C. *Programming from Specifications.* Prentice Hall, 1994.

[86] Hoare C. A. R. *Communicating Sequential Processes.* Prentice Hall, 1985.

[87] Microsoft. *Windows 3.11.* Microsoft Corporation.

[88] Burrows B. and Langford J. *Programming Business Applications in Visual Basic.* McGraw-Hill, 1998.

[89] Rob P. and Williams T. *Database Design and Applications Development using Access.* McGraw-Hill, 1995.

[90] Cole S. N. Deterministic pushdown store machines and real time computation, *J. ACM,* 18(2), 306–328, 1971.

[91] Ipate F. and Holcombe M. A theory of refinement and testing for X-machines, submitted.

[92] Ipate F. *Theory of X-machines with Applications in Specification and Testing*, PhD thesis, Department of Computer Science, University of Sheffield, 1995.

[93] Sidhu D. P., Motteler H. and Vallunipalli R. On testing hierarchies for protocols, *IEEE/ACM Trans. Networking*, 1, 590–599, 1993.

[94] Bhattacharrya A. *Checking Experiments in Sequential Machines*. Wiley Eastern, New Delhi, 1989.

[95] Gill A. *Introduction to the Theory of Finite State Machines*. McGraw-Hill, 1962.

[96] Ural H. Formal methods for test sequence generation, *Comput. Comm.*, 15(5), 311–325, 1992.

[97] Bogdanov K. Test set generation from statecharts and µSZ specifications, Part I, Confidential report prepared for Daimler-Benz Research and Technology AG, 104 pp, Department of Computer Science, University of Sheffield, 1997.

# Index